MW00416376

BUILDING The new ECONOMY

BUILDING THE NEW ECONOMY

Data as Capital

ALEX PENTLAND, ALEXANDER LIPTON,
AND THOMAS HARDJONO

MIT Connection Science & Engineering
connection.mit.edu

The MIT Press
Cambridge, Massachusetts
London, England

The MIT Press would like to thank the anonymous peer reviewers who provided comments on drafts of this book. The generous work of academic experts is essential for establishing the authority and quality of our publications. We acknowledge with gratitude the contributions of these otherwise uncredited readers.

This book was set in ScalaPro and ScalaSans by Westchester Publishing Services. Printed and bound in the United States of America.

Library of Congress Cataloging-in-Publication Data

Names: Pentland, Alex, 1952– author. | Lipton, Alexander, author. | Hardjono, Thomas, author.
Title: Building the new economy : data as capital / Alex Pentland, Alexander Lipton, and Thomas Hardjono.
Description: Cambridge, Massachusetts : The MIT Press, [2021] | Includes bibliographical references and index.
Identifiers: LCCN 2021000483 | ISBN 9780262543156 (paperback)
Subjects: LCSH: Digital currency. | Blockchains (Databases) | Economic history—21st century.
Classification: LCC HG1710 .B85 2021 | DDC 332.4—dc23
LC record available at https://lccn.loc.gov/2021000483

10   9   8   7   6   5   4   3   2   1

CONTENTS

BUILDING THE NEW ECONOMY: WHAT WE NEED AND HOW TO GET THERE

Alex Pentland

1.1 INTRODUCTION

With each major crisis, be it war, pandemic, or major new technology, there has been a need to reinvent the relationships between individuals, businesses, and government. In the years leading up to World War I, the rise of mass manufacturing led to such a rebalancing. This period saw the creation of regulations governing working conditions and pay, health protections for mass-produced food, and rules to prevent monopolies. After World War II, we saw the end of European colonies, greater access to higher education, and advancement of women's rights and racial equality. At about the same time, the plagues of tuberculosis and polio were defeated by early biotechnology, leading to tough new standards for medicine.

Today, we face two simultaneous disruptions: the economic and health shock created by the COVID-19 pandemic and the rise of pervasive digital data, cryptosystems, and artificial intelligence (AI). These new digital systems are being deployed to fight the current world pandemic, and technologies such as videoconferencing and artificial intelligence applications such as infection modeling have been strong allies. However, digital technologies such as social media have generated disinformation and increased confusion, and the mobile phone applications used to track infection threaten privacy rights.

These problems highlight the need to reinvent the ways data and AI are used in all of societies' civic and government systems, both to guarantee that future pandemics can be handled better and to reinvigorate the economy while spreading economic benefits throughout society. Data is now central to the economy, government, and health systems, so why are data and the AI systems that interpret the data in the hands of so few people? Communities without data about themselves and without the tools to use their data are at the mercy of those with data and AI tools.

For instance, why isn't there better infrastructure for sharing medical data? Informal networks of doctors sharing data about AIDS and infant care have dramatically improved medicine in the poorest communities. In the recent pandemic, survival rates in different hospitals differ by a factor of two, with the worst outcomes in the poorest communities. Why don't we have efficient data sharing between hospitals so that we know what treatments are being tried outside formal drug trials and how they are working? Similarly, a major impediment to drug development is data sharing, even though there are ways to do that without endangering patient confidentiality or companies' rights to proprietary data.

The same sorts of criticisms apply to how we provide social benefits, support small businesses, and levy taxes. Our systems are a siloed patchwork that prevents data sharing, are too often "one size fits none," lack transparency, and are completely unauditable.

No wonder they work so unevenly and respond to emergencies so poorly.

Data is now a full-fledged means of production, and consequently we need to think about it as a new type of capital, along with human and financial capital. Unfortunately, we do not yet have institutions and rules for ownership, exchange, and use of this new type of capital. Today, people are often afraid of the power of this new data capital, but, as economist Thomas Piketty said of financial capital, the problem is really that this capital is held in too few hands. This book is about how to make data serve all communities, both by empowering individual communities and by building a stronger, more resilient, and trustworthy fabric of social systems.

1.2   TOWARD A MORE RESILIENT SOCIETY

It is time to refresh our ideas about the ways that our society is organized in order to encompass these new digital means of production and rebalance the relationships between all the stakeholders in the economy. Central to this reinvention is building a new economy—not only restoring vibrancy and spreading financial wealth but also creating new solutions for more resilient and efficient civic and government systems, for improving digital privacy and cybersecurity, for providing more agile, inclusive, and transparent responses to society's problems, and for funding the infrastructure required by this new economy.

Within my research group, MIT Connection Science, we and our partner nations are finding that the same technologies that are causing social unrest may also enable the creation of more agile and less fragile types of systems, where power and decision-making are distributed among the stakeholders rather than concentrated in just a few hands. The key point is that distributed systems, when done right, are not only more adaptive and agile but are also more resilient to catastrophes, such as disease pandemics or political unrest, and less likely to have unintended consequences, such as climate change or social inequalities.

Resilience is the path chosen by most biological systems, and it is achieved by having many diverse system designs, each with continuous monitoring of outcomes that allows for rapid learning and adaptation across the different systems. Evolution itself is a classic example of such a learning system. To create resilient social systems, the key is not to create a new nationwide institution or law or a new international administration but rather to begin with local institutions, with the goal of building a diverse coalition of self-governed communities that learn from each other and constantly adapt.

What are some examples where these sorts of resilient innovation networks have worked? In the last few decades, informal networks of doctors sharing data about AIDS and infant care have dramatically improved medicine in those areas, reducing death rates by an order of magnitude. It wasn't the World Health Organization or the US National Institutes of Health that accomplished this miracle, although they provided critical support for experiments and for implementing improvements. The innovations came from local communities of health workers working on new ideas and learning from each other.

Similarly, today we see informal networks of scientists making great strides designing and testing new treatments for COVID-19. Again, it is not programs of the National Institutes of Health or the World Health Organization that are driving this surge of innovation. Instead, what these large organizations have contributed is the scientific infrastructure and some of the channels for information sharing that allow individual labs to have the tools and freedom needed to experiment and learn from each other.

The same spirit of resilient, bottom-up innovation is beginning to come to business and investment. A good example is the appearance of crowdsourcing for massive infrastructure projects such as hydroelectric power. The citizens and businesses who will benefit from having local hydropower buy digital tokens that give them future rights to electricity, and the pooled money provides the hundreds of millions of dollars required to build the water dam and hydropower complex. It is not governments who pay for and own this new infrastructure but rather the people who benefit directly.

Workers are also crowdsourcing innovation. Groups of "gig workers" are pooling data about their working conditions in order to obtain better pay and safer working conditions, and they are sharing these innovations with gig workers in other cities and industries. Similarly, creative workers, such as musicians and writers, are finding new ways to sell to their audience directly and avoid the media platforms that no longer provide them a living wage.

Resiliency is even coming to government to help avoid the polarization and gridlock of national and state governments. Networks of city governments have set up innovation networks, where local governments experiment with different programs and policies. By sharing data about the results of their experiments, the best ideas are able to spread quickly to other cities, all without nationwide programs or regulations.

So, just as in previous crises, sharing ideas and outcomes across networks of local communities is providing the sort of resilient innovation needed for our society to survive and come out stronger. The time has come to create systems that are more resilient by shunning optimized central control and embracing learning systems based on diverse innovation and experimentation.

1.3 A VISION OF THE NEW ECONOMY

This change from centralized systems to networks of more local systems is being driven not only by the realization that current systems are fragile and inadequately agile but also by concerns about inclusiveness, transparency, cost, and security. Today, most countries use distributed communication networks (e.g., the internet), but most transactions are still carried out using centralized and conventional enterprise management software, and humans are often part of the accounting and audit systems. These centralized elements and requirements that humans use to do routine bookkeeping are at the core of many of the problems with today's systems.

Consequently, just as happened during the development of the internet and the World Wide Web, concerns about the inadequacy of today's systems are pushing proprietary, private, legal functions to the periphery, leaving the core transaction network more distributed and entirely digital. These new distributed, all-digital systems are typically described as either distributed ledgers or blockchains. Examples of these new systems include Estonia's long-standing government infrastructure, the Swiss trust chain (which we helped develop), China's "smart city" infrastructure, and Singapore's

Project Ubin trade and logistics infrastructure. In addition, there are national digital currencies being deployed by China, Singapore, and now many other countries, as well as notorious systems such as Bitcoin. These new technologies offer new opportunities but also new challenges for policymakers and regulators.

Building a new economy will require addressing contentious social issues such as ownership of data and control of the means of production. To be successful at building the new economy, we have to present a plausible, positive vision of the future that explains how data and AI can enable better systems of capital, labor, and property.

This vision must include a renegotiation of data rights and uses in order to create user-centric data ownership and management, secure and privacy-preserving machine learning algorithms, transparent and accountable algorithms, and the introduction of machine learning fairness principles and methodologies to overcome biases and discriminatory effects. In our view, individual humans and human communities should be placed at the center of the discussion, as humans are ultimately both the actors and the subjects of the decisions made via algorithmic means. If we are able to ensure that these requirements are met, we should be able to realize the positive potential of AI-driven decision-making while minimizing the risks and possible negative unintended consequences on individuals and on society as a whole.

To develop this vision of the future, this book is organized into three sections: the human perspective, resilient systems, and finally data, AI, and the new economy. At the end of these three main sections, there is a concluding chapter on computational law, which discusses how to deploy and regulate these new societal systems.

1.4   THE HUMAN PERSPECTIVE: NEW TYPES OF ENGAGEMENT

The robot overlords are coming! Everyone is worried about how
AI will transform work and society. Central to these concerns are
the questions of who controls the data and how AI is using it.
Particularly alarming is the amount of data, and resulting power,
held by a small number of actors. During the last 200 years, questions about concentration of power have emerged each time the
economy has shifted to a new paradigm: industrial employment
replacing agricultural employment, consumer banking replacing
cash and barter, and now ultraefficient digital businesses replacing traditional physical businesses and civic systems.

As the economy was transformed by industrialization and
then by consumer banking, citizens joined together to form trade
unions and cooperative banking institutions in order to provide a
counterweight to these new, powerful forces. Eventually, laws were
passed to regulate labor and banking, and citizen organizations
were central in helping balance the economic and social power.

Part I of the book begins with chapter 2, "Building Data Cooperatives," explaining how collective organizations of citizens are emerging to move the control and use of data and AI to a broader base of
stakeholders. The chapter not only argues that such data cooperatives make the economy more responsive to citizen needs but shows
how they can increase the resiliency and economic prospects of the
community. Chapters 3 and 4 present a blueprint of the processes
and digital infrastructure needed to achieve this vision and outlines
how these processes address regulatory challenges.

Chapter 3, "Shared Data: Backbone of a New Knowledge Economy," explains how an efficient data economy can develop while

also preserving privacy, trade secrets, and general cybersecurity through the use of the sorts of data exchanges we are beginning to see emerging around the world.

Chapter 4, "Empowering Innovation through Data Cooperatives," provides concrete examples of how digital markets and cooperatives can transform the gig economy into a stable ecology that supports artistic production and other individual digital production as safe career choices. The chapter presents a blueprint for how to achieve fine-grain, inexpensive auditing of digital assets while simultaneously enabling payments for use of those assets and argues that these new capabilities can transform the way individuals choose to work and broaden the range of creative work supported by society.

Chapter 5, "From Securitization to Tokenization," the last chapter in part I, describes how large-scale infrastructure investments (e.g., hydropower, train lines, harbors) are already being deployed using broadly distributed tokenized funding mechanisms. Such infrastructure is funded by local alliances of citizen investors who also benefit directly from how the new infrastructure improves their city or province. The rise of such citizen-centric finance and management systems appears to be the beginning of a new trend to create more widely distributed infrastructure with stronger, more localized buy-in from community stakeholders.

1.5   THE HUMAN PERSPECTIVE: NEW TYPES OF ENGAGEMENT

The world seems filled with panics, crashes, and confusion. Can we make our financial systems less fragile, more transparent, and less winner-take-all? Can we make our health systems more agile and proactive? Can we spread financial and health benefits more widely? The new distributed, technology-enabled organizations that are emerging may offer a path toward a better future. Moreover, they are particularly attractive outside the developed world, in places where existing institutions are either weak or working poorly, as well as in the poorer neighborhoods of wealthy nations.

Part II begins with chapter 6, "The Tradecoin System," describing a secure, distributed approach to building currency systems based on the assets of (potentially) millions of stakeholders. The Tradecoin architecture enables large investment funds that are largely independent of centralized authorities, large nations, large banks, and the wealthy Western world. It also enables pooling of assets in new ways that can challenge current fiat currencies and multilateral institutions such as the International Monetary Fund. Versions of Tradecoin-style architecture have been incorporated into several recent digital currency proposals, ranging from China's and Singapore's digital currencies to the Libra consortium proposed by Facebook.

Chapter 7 is titled "Health IT: Algorithms, Privacy, and Data." Data is crucial for health and the life sciences, and the urgent need for solutions to the limitations of today's systems is nowhere clearer than in the handling of citizen data in the recent COVID-19 pandemic. This chapter presents a framework for deploying new, highly interoperable health IT infrastructure that deals with the various aspects of health-related data based on existing medical, health, and privacy standards in order to permit easy adoption by stakeholders.

Chapter 8, "Narrow Banks and Fiat-Backed Tokens," describes how banking can be reinvented to become much more stable and leverage Tradecoin-style digital token infrastructure to free businesses and consumers from the nightmare system of national currencies and exchange rates that we have today.

Chapter 9, "Stable Network Dynamics in a Tokenized Financial Ecosystem," the final chapter in part II, shows how an existing token-based ecosystem has become self-stabilizing despite being worldwide and generally unregulated. This analysis suggests new sorts of tools and measurements that are critical for avoiding financial catastrophes and suggests a way to prevent formation of monopolies that is applicable to all financial networks.

1.6 DATA, AI, AND THE NEW ECONOMY

What sort of infrastructure can support a world with billions of data owners, producers, and consumers? If we are to maintain innovation while achieving social goals, we will have to avoid uniform, centralized systems and instead support diverse approaches to the problems of citizens, companies, and governments. In order to work on a global scale, these diverse approaches must be interoperable so that knowledge, trade, and interaction can flow seamlessly across company and national boundaries.

The technical problems of supporting such interoperability are addressed by the four chapters in part III. Chapter 10, "Toward an Ecosystem of Trusted Data and AI," addresses the problems we are encountering as the economy and society move from a world where interactions are physical and based on paper documents toward a world that is primarily governed by digital data and AI. To manage this transition, we must create an ecosystem of trusted data and trusted AI that provides safe, secure, and human-centric services for everyone, allowing us to unlock huge societal benefits, including better health, greater financial inclusion, and a population that is more engaged with and better supported by its government.

Chapter 11, "Stablecoins," describes the evolution of our medium of exchange from the historical idea of money to the more powerful idea of digital currencies. From J. P. Morgan's Jamie Dimon to Facebook's Mark Zuckerberg, stablecoins—digital currencies with an inherently stable value—have made their way onto the agenda of today's top CEOs. We discuss how to go about creating a digital currency that has an inherently stable value and survey the different cases of stablecoin use and the underlying economic incentives for creating them. Finally, we outline the critical regulatory considerations that constrain them and summarize key factors that are driving their rapid development.

Chapter 12, "Interoperability of Distributed Systems," analyzes the notions of *interoperability*, *survivability*, and *manageability* for distributed systems, using lessons learned from the three decades of development of the internet. It then develops a design framework for an interoperable distributed architecture and identifies particular design principles that promote interoperability.

Chapter 13, "Exchange Networks for Virtual Assets," the final chapter in part III, builds on the basic function of interoperability, to allow trade and auditing of transactions. Virtual asset service providers (VASPs) face a data problem in that in order to fulfill regulatory requirements, they need access to truthful information regarding originators, beneficiaries, and other exchanges involved in a virtual asset transfer. However, getting access to data or information—regarding individuals and institutions involved in the asset transfer—means that VASPs must also address the challenges of data privacy and privacy-related regulations. This chapter lays out principles and describes a path forward to solve these problems.

1.7 CONCLUSION: LEGAL ALGORITHMS

Besides the technical challenges described in chapters 11–13, we need to address the problem that some of these new systems are likely to have disruptive and unintended negative effects on society. How can we make sure these complex virtual systems are safe and secure? How do we ensure that they achieve the sorts of social goals that we desire—fairness, inclusiveness, stability—along with high rates of innovation?

Balancing these and other elements of the new economy will be the job of law. However, the current practice of law is already unable to cope with our rapidly changing world and is becoming increasingly unable to ensure access to justice. To keep up with this rapid pace of change, the practice and application of law is becoming computerized, in ways ranging from filling out forms, to tax computation, to trial discovery.

However, the migration of our existing set of legal algorithms to computer platforms risks displacing human judgment and sensibility. Consequently, we must think carefully about how computation interacts with the processes of law and regulation. This rethinking of how to manage the computerization of law is the focus of computational law.

Part IV consists of the book's final chapter, chapter 14, "Conclusion: Legal Algorithms," which presents an introduction to the ongoing process of inventing law and computational systems that can manage diverse systems of virtual assets. This chapter describes a path to leveraging computational tools to develop more transparent, accountable, and inclusive legal, civil, and government processes. It is through this digital transformation that people everywhere will reap the benefits of true stakeholder capitalism, based on a reinvigorated social contract, together with the sort of access to justice enjoyed by very few today.

This chapter also introduces our new MIT computational law initiative, which may be seen at http://law.mit.edu and consists of an alliance of law schools and legal scholars hosted by my research group, MIT Connection Science, and is now producing the world's first computational law report.

1.8   HOW TO READ THIS BOOK

This book is intended to convey both the "big idea" and a blueprint for how to build these systems. The book does not delve into regulatory issues, although it deals with privacy, security, and transparency, because different countries will regulate these systems in different ways.

Because we present both the big idea and a blueprint, the last half of many of the chapters will be too technical for many readers' tastes. So, feel free to read the beginning of the chapter and then skip to the end. In fact, even if your goal is to understand the details, it might be a good idea to read the first part of all the chapters before you dive into the details. That way, you can better understand the context of the system design and analysis. These ideas are intended to be synergistic and to support each other, and therefore are not completely independent.

Additional material can be found at http://connection.mit.edu, http://trust.mit.edu, and http://law.mit.edu. The original academic works that support many of the chapters are the following:

- **Chapter 2: Building Data Cooperatives**
  - S. K. Chong, M. Bahrami, H. Chen, S. Balcisoy, B. Bozkaya, and A. Pentland, "Economic Outcomes Predicted by Diversity in Cities," *EPJ Data Science* 9, no. 1 (2020)
- **Chapter 6: The Tradecoin System**
  - A. Lipton, T. Hardjono, and A. Pentland, "Digital Trade Coin: Towards a More Stable Digital Currency," July 18, 2018, https://doi.org/10.1098/rsos.180155
- **Chapter 9: Stable Network Dynamics in a Tokenized Financial Ecosystem**
  - S. Somin, Y. Altshuler, G. Gordon, A. Pentland, and E. Shueli, "Network Dynamics of a Financial Ecosystem," *Scientific Reports* 10 (2020): 4587
- **Chapter 12: Interoperability of Distributed Systems**
  - T. Hardjono, A. Lipton, and A. Pentland, "Towards an Interoperability Architecture Blockchain Autonomous Systems," *IEEE Transactions on Engineering Management* 67, no. 4 (2020): 1298–1309, https://doi.org/10.1109/TEM.2019.2920154
- **Chapter 13: Exchange Networks for Virtual Assets**
  - T. Hardjono, A. Lipton, and A. Pentland, "Privacy-Preserving Claims Exchange Networks for Virtual Asset Service Providers" *Proceedings of 2nd IEEE International Conference on Blockchain and Cryptocurrency (ICBC2020)* (May 2020)

I

THE HUMAN PERSPECTIVE: NEW TYPES OF ENGAGEMENT

BUILDING DATA COOPERATIVES

Alex Pentland and Thomas Hardjono

2.1 INTRODUCTION

During the last decade, all segments of society have become increasingly alarmed by the amount of data, and resulting power, held by a
small number of actors.[1] Some famously call data "the new oil,"[2] and
they mean records of the behavior of citizens. Why, then, is control
of this powerful new resource concentrated in so few hands? During the last 150 years, questions about concentration of power have
emerged each time the economy has shifted to a new paradigm.

As the economy was transformed by industrialization and then
by consumer banking, citizens felt trapped and exploited by powerful new companies. In order to provide a counterweight to these
new powers, citizens joined together to form trade unions and
cooperative banking institutions. Eventually, the struggle reached
a point where citizens felt that powerful players such as Standard
Oil, J. P. Morgan, and a handful of others threatened freedom
itself, and the federal government instituted antitrust laws, labor
rights, and banking reforms. The citizen organizations were key
in helping to balance the economic and social power between
large and small players and between employers and workers.

Today, the same sorts of citizen organizations can help us move from the current paradigm of individuals giving up data to large organizations to a system based on collective rights and accountability, with legal standards upheld by a new class of representatives, who act as fiduciaries for their members. There are many examples of community organizations using community data to manage investments for the good of the community. For instance, since 1943, the National Rural Electric Cooperative Association has electrified communities that cover over half the land area of the United States. Similarly, there are over 1,100 community development financial institutions, mainly small banks and credit unions, investing over $220 billion in community projects, including over 300 focused primarily on economic, social, and political justice. With 100 million people being members of credit unions, the opportunity for community organizations to leverage community-owned data is huge.

Indeed, with advanced computing technologies, it is practical to automatically record and organize all the data that citizens knowingly or unknowingly give to companies and the government and store this data in community organizations' vaults. In addition, almost all these community organizations already manage their accounts through regional associations that use common software, so widespread deployment of data cooperatives could be surprisingly quick and easy.

2.2 DATA COOPERATIVES AS CITIZENS' ORGANIZATIONS

The notion of a *data cooperative* refers to the voluntary collaborative pooling by individuals of their personal data for the benefit of the members of the group or community. The motivation for individuals to get together and pool their data is driven by the need to share common insights across data that would otherwise be siloed or inaccessible. These insights provide the cooperative members as a whole with a better understanding of their current economic, health, and social conditions as compared to the other members of the cooperative in general.

It is technically straightforward to have a third party such as a cooperative hold copies of their members' data in order to help them safeguard their rights, represent them in negotiating how their data is used, alert them to how they are being surveilled, and audit the large companies and government institutions using their members' data. In fact, chapters 4 and 10 present a blueprint for the processes and software required to accomplish these tasks.

The creation of such data cooperatives also does not require new laws; many community organizations are already chartered to manage members' personal information for them. It does, however, require new regulations and oversight, similar to how the government regulates and provides oversight of financial institutions. Chapters 3 and 14 discuss in more detail how this might happen.

It is critical to note that community organizations that manage members' data must have fiduciary responsibilities to protect the sensitive information that they hold for members, as this is a central element in bringing data rights to the membership. This enables members to improve privacy and transparency regarding data use and empowers members to collectively direct the use of their data to their benefit.

Who will lead this historic and necessary transformation? The answer could well grow out of current-day credit unions, many of which are directly associated with universities, city governments, trade unions, and the like. They are already chartered to represent their members in financial transactions and hold members' data for them.

The ability to balance the world's data economy depends on creating a balance of stakeholders. Today, citizens and workers have no direct representation at the negotiating table, so they lose out. By leveraging cooperative worker and citizen organizations, which in the United States alone have over 100 million members, we can change this situation and create a sustainable digital economy that serves the many, not just the few. The power of 100 million US consumers who control their data would be a force to be reckoned with by all organizations that use citizen data and would be a very decisive way to hold these organizations accountable. The same potential for community organizations to balance today's data monoliths exists in most countries around the world.

2.3 COMMUNITIES USING THEIR DATA

What new advantages can communities have if they have the ability to analyze their data? People often think of monetizing personal data, but the reality is that while there is a great deal of value in aggregate data for specific purposes, there is no market mechanism for data exchange, so personal data does not have very much value on an individual basis. Personal data and community data will only become a serious source of revenue when privacy-respecting data exchanges become a major part of the general financial and economic landscape. This is described in more detail in chapter 3.

However, monetization is only a minor part of data's value to a community, especially in today's economic climate. A greater source of value is in improving the living conditions of community members and ensuring the success of future generations. For instance, the COVID-19 pandemic has highlighted major disparities in public health between different communities. Data about community public health is necessary to address these disparities, but today that data is unavailable to communities in all but the most general terms. Chapter 7 addresses this problem in more detail.

2.4 ECONOMIC GROWTH

Communities need data about their economic health in order to plan their future, but the data required for neighborhood-level planning is unavailable to them. Only the aggregate statistics of production and wage distribution used by economists are generally available. With the development of community-owned data cooperatives, this could change dramatically.

As an example, Chong et al.[3] recently developed a neighborhood attractiveness measure that uses the diversity of amenities within a neighborhood to predict the volume and diversity of human flows into that neighborhood, which in turn predicts economic productivity and economic growth on a neighborhood-by-neighborhood basis.

Their attractiveness measure is based on the relationship shown in figure 2.1, which illustrates the connection between the

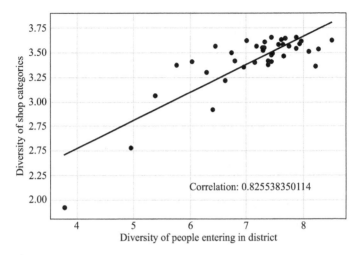

Figure 2.1
Scatter plot of the number of unique shop categories within a neighborhood versus total inflow volumes of visitors in each neighborhood in Istanbul.

number of unique shop categories in a neighborhood (defined in terms of the standardized merchant category code) and the total flows of people into each district over a period of one year. The very large correlation of 0.826 shows that measuring neighborhood attractiveness by diversity of shops and public spaces can be an excellent predictor of future foot traffic. This data is from the city of Istanbul, but similar relationships have been demonstrated in the European Union, United States, and Australia.

There is a dynamic relationship between the attractiveness of a neighborhood and its economic growth. The attractiveness of diverse amenities (e.g., parks and other public spaces) increases the inflow of people from different neighborhoods. This inflow in turn creates opportunities that boost investment and increases the availability of even more diverse amenities.

The neighborhood attractiveness measure of Chong et al.[4] allows communities to use their private data, specifically the pattern of in-store purchases, to predict what new stores and amenities will increase the economic productivity of the neighborhood. Moreover, as a neighborhood becomes more attractive through new amenities and increasingly diverse visitors, entrepreneurs respond by offering increasingly diverse amenities in order to cater to the tastes and preferences of the new people visiting the neighborhood. Consequently, the same sort of community data can be used to predict future economic growth of the community.

Figure 2.2 illustrates the measured relationship between neighborhood attractiveness and the percentage changes in economic indicators for neighborhoods in Beijing; similar results have been obtained on three different continents. In all three cases, we see that the diversity of consumption is a strong predictor of economic growth, with the correlations with economic growth in the following year being 0.71 (Istanbul), 0.54 (Beijing), and 0.52 (United States).

However, economic growth is complex and is influenced by many factors. As shown in figure 2.3, even if we also account for factors such as population density, housing price index, and the geographical centrality of the district within the city, the ability of community diversity data to predict economic growth is still quite strong, with correlations of $R = 0.41$ (Beijing), 0.72 (Istanbul), and 0.57 (United States), providing evidence on how the attractiveness of local amenities and services is a strong determinant of neighborhood growth.

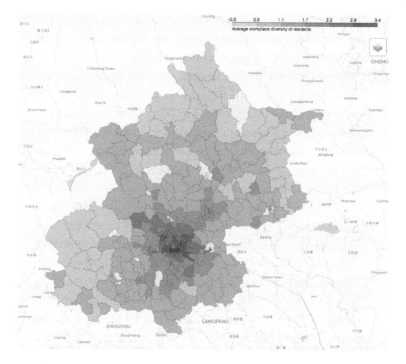

Figure 2.2

Diversity of consumption (*above*) and year-on-year economic growth (*opposite*) for neighborhoods within the city of Beijing. The diversity of consumption (or the diversity of visitors) predicts up to 50 percent of the variance in year-over-year economic growth for Beijing as well as for US and EU cities. *Source*: S. K. Chong, M. Bahrami, H. Chen, S. Balcisoy, B. Bozkaya, and A. Pentland, "Economic Outcomes Predicted by Diversity in Cities," *EPJ Data Science* 9, no. 1 (2020).

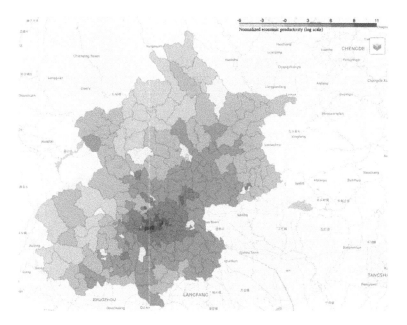

Figure 2.2 (continued)

2.5 SMALL BUSINESS PLANNING

By using community data, we can begin to build more vibrant, economically successful neighborhoods. For instance, to promote growth in a specific neighborhood, we can alter transportation networks to make the neighborhood accessible to populations that are more diverse and invest in diverse stores and amenities in order to attract diverse flows of people.

Importantly, we can use community data to evaluate how to allocate investments to maximize the expected impact on the

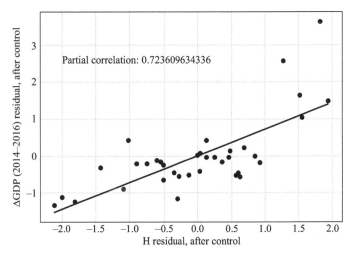

Figure 2.3
Diversity of consumption versus year-over-year growth in GDP in Istanbul after controlling for population density, housing prices, and the geographical centrality. *Source*: S. K. Chong, M. Bahrami, H. Chen, S. Balcisoy, B. Bozkaya, and A. Pentland, "Economic Outcomes Predicted by Diversity in Cities," *EPJ Data Science* 9, no. 1 (2020).

economy of the target neighborhood. Communities need not rely on annualized values of traditional economic indicators for planning purposes but would instead be able to make reliable estimates of what sorts of stores will succeed and determine whether they will contribute to the general prosperity of the neighborhood. For instance, Netto et al.[5] have shown that by combining a generic model of how people move around the city (the "gravity model") with community data describing the concentration and variety of amenities in the neighborhood, they can accurately predict the foot traffic and sales of proposed stores and public amenities.

The method they developed is far better than existing methods and is flexible and robust enough to estimate other key marketing variables, such as anticipated market share, units sold, or other forecasting goals. Consequently, community planners may use it for tax estimation purposes or to understand which types of new stores or community resources (e.g., parks) can stimulate population flow toward different neighborhoods and plan city dynamics and commercial growth, stimulating the flow of people into different areas to boost the local economy.

2.6 EMPLOYMENT

Communities also need to promote the jobs and skills that increase worker pay, create employment, and make their economies resilient to downturns. Moro et al.[6] have developed a skill connectivity measure for using community data to predict which skills will contribute most to the community's labor market resilience. This skill connectivity measure is an ecologically inspired employment matching process constructed from the similarities of every occupation's skill requirements.[7]

Looking at all the cities within the United States, Moro et al. found that this skill connectivity measure predicted the economic resilience of cities to economic downturns. The reason that skill connectivity is so important is simple: if workers can easily move from one type of job to another because the two jobs share similar skills, then they are less likely to remain unemployed for long.

As illustrated in figure 2.4, cities with greater skill connectivity experienced lower unemployment rates during the 2008 Great Recession, had increasing wages, and workers in occupations with a high degree of connectivity within a city's job network enjoyed higher wages than their peers elsewhere. Skill connectivity, together with employment diversity, contributed the most toward lowering the unemployment rate during the 2008 Great Recession.

Consequently, job training and economic development programs that promote skill overlap between the occupations within a community are likely to grow local labor markets and promote general economic resilience. Such job connectivity is also likely to

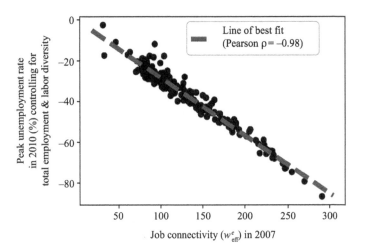

Figure 2.4
More skill connectivity between jobs increases employment resilience. *Source*: E. Moro, M. R. Frank, A. Pentland, A. Rutherford, M. Cebrian, and I. Rahwan, "Universal Resilience Patterns in Labor Markets" (forthcoming).

be important in addressing technology-driven labor challenges, such as AI and robotic automation.

2.7 BUILDING SOCIAL CAPITAL

Central to any community is the trust and social capital within the community. Today, many people have little trust in other members of their community, and this is the source of many problems, including crime, poverty, and children's adverse developmental outcomes. Many lines of research show that one of the most reliable ways to create community trust and social capital is through cooperative community projects, especially those that are community owned (see chapter 5), not just because such projects promote more communication and habits of cooperation within the community but also because they help give community members a sense of shared destiny and shared identity.

Extremely good measures of community trust and social capital can be derived from community data in a way that protects privacy by looking at the frequency and diversity of phone calls, messaging, and covisiting (going to the same meetings, stores, parks, and other places at similar times) within the community.[8] For instance, Aharony et al.[9] found that this measure could be used to very accurately predict the likelihood of giving help in time of sickness, willingness to loan money, and willingness to help with childcare.

Communities that talk together and build together are resilient and, over the long term, more successful. Knowing about the levels of trust in a community allows community leaders to prioritize projects that build increasingly inclusive trust and social capital. Access to community-level data can make this possible.

2.8 CONCLUSIONS

Today, we are in a situation where individual data assets—people's personal data—are being exploited without sufficient value being returned to them. This is analogous to the situation in the late 1800s and early 1900s that led to the creation of collective institutions such as credit unions and labor unions, so the time seems ripe for the creation of collective institutions to represent the data rights of individuals.

We have argued that data cooperatives with fiduciary obligations to members provide a promising direction for the empowerment of individuals through collective use of their own personal data. A data cooperative not only can give the individual expert community-based advice on how to manage, curate, and protect access to their personal data but can also run internal analytics that benefit the collective membership. Such collective insights provide a powerful tool for negotiating better services and discounts for the cooperative's members and for guiding investments that improve community and member economic, health, and social conditions.

NOTES

1. M. Moore and D. Tambini, *Digital Dominance: The Power of Google, Amazon, Facebook, and Apple* (Oxford: Oxford University Press, 2018).

2. World Economic Forum, *Personal Data: The Emergence of a New Asset Class*, report, 2011, http://www.weforum.org/reports/personal-data-emergence -new-asset-class.

3. S. K. Chong, M. Bahrami, H. Chen, S. Balcisoy, B. Bozkaya, and A. Pentland, "Economic Outcomes Predicted by Diversity in Cities," *EPJ Data Science* 9, no. 1 (2020), https://doi.org/10.1140/epjds/s13688-020-00234-x.

4. Chong et al., "Economic Outcomes Predicted by Diversity in Cities."

5. C. Freitas, S. Netto, M. Bahrami, V. Brei, B. Bozkaya, S. Balcisoy, and A. Pentland, "Gravitational Forecast Reconciliation" (forthcoming).

6. E. Moro, M. R. Frank, A. Pentland, A. Rutherford, M. Cebrian, and I. Rahwan, "Universal Resilience Patterns in Labor Markets," *Nature Communications* (forthcoming).

7. M. R. Frank, J. E. Bessen, E. Brynjolfsson, M. Cebrian, D. J. Deming, M. Feldman, M. Groh, et al., "Toward Understanding the Impact of Artificial Intelligence on Labor," *Proceedings of the National Academy of Sciences* 116, no. 14 (2019): 6531–6539, https://doi.org/10.1073/pnas.1900949116.

8. N. Aharony, W. Pan, C. Ip, I. Khayal, and A. Pentland, "Social FMRI: Investigating and Shaping Social Mechanisms in the Real World," *Pervasive and Mobile Computing* 7, no. 6 (2011): 643–659.

9. Aharony et al., "Social FMRI."

SHARED DATA: BACKBONE OF A NEW KNOWLEDGE ECONOMY

José Parra-Moyano, Karl Schmedders,
and Alex Pentland

3.1 INTRODUCTION

That data helps to generate value is a very robust idea.[1] We talk
about data as "the new oil," and the concept of "big data" is widely
spread. While this idea applies to many areas of modern life, it
is especially prominent in the financial sector, where data-based
insights are crucial for making the right decisions and adequately
navigating the waves of uncertainty. In the financial sector, traders analyze data to generate insights, gain knowledge, and ultimately make better investments. Researchers analyze financial
and consumer data to generate knowledge about our economy
and society. Companies analyze data to forecast the development
of their industries, to predict demand for new products, and to
be able to anticipate shocks. These applications turn data into a
production factor that, once analyzed, leads to the generation of
knowledge and value.

However, data is still not being fully understood as a production factor or being fully exploited. The central reason that data is
not yet fully understood is because it is very different from other

traditional production factors, such as capital, labor, and oil. Data is not being fully exploited because its attributes make its trade in a data market rather difficult if not outright impossible, confine it to being kept in closed silos despite its digital nature, and stop organizations from maximizing its potential value.

New technologies, such as blockchain and artificial intelligence, as well as a new conception of how data works (and, more importantly, how data can work), are changing this situation. We are embarking on a transition from *big data* to *shared data*, in which the knowledge that emerges from data is starting to securely move in our society. All this is happening thanks to the design and implementation of data exchanges. Data exchanges are platforms that gather data from many different sources and allow third parties to run algorithms on this data. As a result, these third parties can generate insights (knowledge) with new sources of data. Hence, data exchanges give rise to the concept of *shared data*, which is the natural next step of *big data*.

Data exchanges are going to profoundly transform the way in which knowledge is generated, and they are going to open the horizon for the next level of data-based value generation. Specifically, they are going to set incentives for citizens and organizations to record and share novel data—data that is going to generate value without violating the privacy of any citizen or organization. This change is going to enable organizations to generate new knowledge by analyzing these novel sources of data, and the innovative part of this transformation is that it will occur without sensitive data from any organization or individual escaping the secure boundaries of its current confinement. A new wave of value is about to come.

In this chapter, we guide the reader in understanding which characteristics make data so special as a production factor and we reflect on how data exchanges are going to change the way in which knowledge is generated. In addition, we suggest how a data exchange could greatly enhance the value of the Federal Reserve Board's Survey of Consumer Finances for businesses, policymakers, and researchers.

3.2 INTRODUCTION: DATA AS A PRODUCTION FACTOR

Data is a nonfungible production factor. This means that the concept of data is very broad: one unit of data (for example, 1 MB) can contain data about almost everything that can be recorded. Some of this data might be useful for an organization, whereas some of it might not. Let us illustrate this idea with an example. When an investment fund receives one unit of investment (e.g., one dollar), it is irrelevant for the fund which specific dollar out of the many in circulation it receives. At the end of the day, the one dollar is going to be invested and, one hopes, produce a return after some time. This makes capital a fungible production factor, since one dollar is replaceable by any other random dollar, and this replacement does not affect the fund's performance. However, if the same fund receives one unit of data (e.g., 1 MB of data) to develop a new trading algorithm, then not all the units of data will equally serve the firm. There exist health-related data, financial data, geolocation data, weather data, public data, private data, curated data, noisy data, and other types. Some of this data will serve the fund to train its algorithms, and some will not. This makes data a nonfungible production factor.

Data tends to create value when it comes in big volumes. While small amounts of data can be valuable in very particular contexts, they are useless for conducting business analytics, training an algorithm, or identifying trends. Hence, in many contexts, only the aggregation of data that results in big volumes of data has value for organizations.

Moreover, and unlike capital and labor, data is nonexclusive in its use, meaning that the same unit of data can be used, for example, by many funds at the same time.[2] This is different from what happens with capital and labor, since a dollar can only be invested in one stock at a time, just as a worker's hour of work can only take place at one firm at a time.

Data changes across time. Data can change on a daily or even hourly basis, implying that older data can become obsolete and therefore that the newer data is, the more valuable it might be. As an example, think of the price of a stock. Anticipating the value of a stock is extremely valuable, whereas knowing the price at which a trade has already happened is much less valuable.

Data about a subject belongs to the subject itself. Data about an organization belongs to the organization itself. This implies that it is illegal or inadequate to sell, share, exchange, or trade private data without the informed consent of the data owner.

In many cases, data is created not by one isolated instance but by the interaction of two or more instances. Think of a trade. The price at which a stock is traded requires a buyer and a seller. Only the interaction between the buyer and the seller generates the trade and its associated data.

3.3 THE NATURE OF DATA

Data—unlike capital and labor—is currently not openly traded in a market. Hence, organizations (e.g., firms, funds, associations, investors, banks, traders, policymakers, researchers) tend to either work only with public data or with the data that they have generated within their own organizations.[3]

The reason that no transparent data market in which individuals sell their data individually to a third party has yet emerged lies precisely in the attributes of data. First, data is nonfungible. Hence, an individual, company, or organization has no means of selling its data directly to a third party, simply because the potential buying organization would need to audit the (probably unstructured) data before purchasing it in order to assess whether the data that it is going to buy is adequate. While this is technically possible, it is a tedious process that would be associated with high costs. Second, to train algorithms, an organization is only interested in purchasing big volumes of data, since in the majority of contexts, only a high volume of data can result in insights. Third, it is illegal to offer third parties access to individual personal data that allows the identification of specific individuals without previously getting the (informed) consent of those individuals. Fourth, the data of some organizations might be very sensitive, and organizations might not want to give third parties direct access to it.

The fact that data cannot be securely and transparently traded represents market friction, because whereas capital, labor, and oil move freely in the open market to those firms at which they get the highest returns (in the form of interest in the case of capital and oil and in the form of wages in the case of labor), data does not. Only opaque deals are occurring, which is preventing all organizations from engaging in the data market. As a result, not all organizations are given access to the market, there is no standard in terms of data purchases, and hence no efficient allocation of the organizations' resources is being promoted.

3.4 DATA EXCHANGES

As a solution to the problems just mentioned, and to enable compliant, efficient, and secure sharing and selling of data, data exchanges are emerging. Data exchanges are platforms that have the permission to gather, curate, and aggregate data from many different sources (e.g., companies, universities, funds, banks, individuals) to allow third parties to gain insights (knowledge) from such data. Data exchanges are a layer between the individuals or organizations owning data and third parties. Accounting for the specific characteristics that data has as a production factor, data exchanges make the structured, secure, and legal generation of insights based on aggregated data for value generation possible. Moreover, and given the fact that data exchanges aggregate the data of many different agents and are informed about the value that data has, they can sell the data-based insights at an adequate price, and they can distribute the resulting earnings among the individuals whose data has been used to generate those insights.

Specifically, data exchanges allow third parties to run their (privacy audited) computer code on the exchanges' platforms in order to analyze the data that belongs to the individuals. By doing so, data exchanges mitigate the fact that data is nonfungible, since they can apply the code to the specific data that is relevant for each third party.

Moreover, since they aggregate data from many different agents, they provide the data volume that the algorithms need to generate value. Additionally, since data exchanges aggregate the interests of many data owners, they are in a stronger position when it comes to price assessment and negotiation. Finally, data exchanges offer insights that cannot be traced to any individual company, subject, or organization, which solves the problems of privacy and consent. The ultimate goal of data exchanges is to enable transparent, efficient, and sustained trade of insights based on aggregated data to which all organizations have equal access.

While the proposals being made regarding how to build a data exchange might differ from one another, they all share certain common characteristics. First, they directly or indirectly assume that data is nonfungible and that therefore a customized analysis of data is necessary. Second, they assume that platforms' users and firms' clients are entitled to own a digital copy of the data that they produce and that this copy can be hosted by a third party (the exchange).

A standard for this sort of exchange is the OPAL[4] initiative developed at the MIT Media Lab, Imperial College London, Orange, the World Economic Forum, and the Data-Pop Alliance. The objective of OPAL is to make broad arrays of data available for analysis in a manner that does not violate personal data privacy. OPAL achieves this by making use of three concepts. First, the algorithm goes to the environment where the data is. By doing so, the data is always kept secure in its original repository. Access to this repository is controlled by the repository's owner. Second, only aggregate answers or "safe answers" are returned. The run algorithms are made public so they can be studied and vetted by experts as "safe." Third, the data is always in an encrypted state.

This is of particular use when the data to be analyzed needs to be kept private because of its sensitivity. Private data can be kept private but at the same time be used to generate value and yield answers to the algorithms run on it.

3.4.1 Consequences of the Implementation of Data Exchanges

The economic consequence of the establishment of data exchanges would be that society would have a new, open source of data for running algorithms to generate knowledge. Organizations would be able to utilize data that they have not produced in order to generate relevant insights for themselves. This would be equivalent to data moving beyond the boundaries of the organization at which the data has been produced and becoming productive for hospitals, universities, funds, investors, traders, banks, and all organizations (in fact, for all of them at the same time). This implies that data would escape the silos in which it is currently stored and be able to generate insights that could move freely in the economy. This would solve the existing friction that we mentioned, which in turn could result in higher economic growth.

Drawing an analogy with the other factors of production, implementing a data exchange would be as positive for the economy as having a better trained and educated labor force at once or finding new oil or gold reserves (with the difference that the labor force, the oil, and the gold could only be used by one firm at a time, whereas data could be shared among many firms). This would solve the market friction problem, and data (understood now as a production factor) could work for many instances at the same time, multiplying the data-based knowledge generated by firms.

Another consequence of the establishment of data exchanges would be that the existing organizations in the financial sector, such as credit unions, banks, and funds, could transform their business strategies and monetize this data by incorporating themselves into a data exchange. And while the revenue that data owners could generate by selling their data is still unclear, it could represent a significant complement to the current revenue. These organizations could continue transmitting the generated value to lower parts of the supply chain (i.e., to the individuals who have contributed to the generation of this data).

One more consequence of the establishment of data exchanges would be that current incumbents would have to confront new competitors. Today, a small company with a bright idea, a very well-trained team (labor), and a huge investment (capital) might have difficulties competing with established giants, since its lack of data would prevent it from competing and developing useful algorithms or enough insights about its clients. With the implementation of data exchanges, smaller players could run their algorithms on the data stored in the exchanges and therefore have access to the same production factor (the data) as the incumbents.

A specific example of the impact that data exchanges can have on the generation of knowledge can be presented in the context of the Federal Reserve Board's triennial *Survey of Consumer Finances* (SCF). The SCF collects information about family incomes, net worth, balance sheet components, credit use, and other financial outcomes.[5] It is an important source of data for determining the financial well-being of households in the US economy. Moreover, researchers use the data made available by the SCF to conduct analyses and develop economic policy recommendations. This makes the data of the SCF extremely valuable. However, because of the difficulty of collecting and structuring the data (a process that involves less than 7,000 families), the data is gathered only every three years. Data from a much larger number of households, collected much more often, could potentially be very helpful for investors, private companies, policymakers, and researchers. Upgrading the SCF with data exchanges on household finance would be a way to generate broader data at a higher frequency. Since the organizations using this scarce and valuable data could be interested in paying for this upgraded data, citizens would have an incentive to frequently integrate their data on the SCF. This would result in a broader data infrastructure, which would be accessible to all organizations to generate new knowledge, and the citizens nurturing the SCF would benefit economically from this situation.

3.5 SUMMARY

Once we understand the characteristics that data has as a production factor (beyond the superficial idea that "data is the new oil"), we will be able to understand how data actually works and how we can properly interact with data exchanges. Understanding that data is a nonfungible, nonexclusive production factor is crucial for this.

Acknowledging the characteristics of data and how knowledge and value are generated by analyzing it, we—as individuals or as organizations—will be able to organize in data exchanges and interact with them to our best interest. For those who provide data to the exchange, this will become a new source of income. For those who run algorithms on the data, this will imply more knowledge and ultimately more value.

The implementation of data exchanges will open up a new stream of opportunities for individuals and organizations. The correct understanding of data as a production factor can only hasten and improve the way in which we as a society take this chance.

NOTES

1. S. Gandhi, B. Thota, R. Kuchembuck, and J. Swartz, "Demystifying Data Monetization," *MIT Sloan Management Review* (November 2018), https://sloanreview.mit.edu/article/demystifying-data-monetization/; M. Farboodi, R. Mihet, T. Philippon, and L. Veldkamp, "Big Data and Firm Dynamics," Centre for Economic Policy Research, January 2019, https://cepr.org/active/publications/discussion\papers/dp.php?dpno=13489.

2. C. I. Jones and C. Tonetti, "Nonrivalry and the Economics of Data," NBER Working Paper 26260, National Bureau of Economic Research, Cambridge, MA, September 2019, http://www.nber.org/papers/w26260.

3. J. Parra-Moyano and K. Schmedders, "The Liberalization of Data: A Welfare-Enhancing Information System," Social Science Research Network, December 2018, http://dx.doi.org/10.2139/ssrn.3302752.

4. A. Pentland, D. Shrier, T. Hardjono, and I. Wladawsky-Berger, "Towards an Internet of Trusted Data: A New Framework for Identity and Data Sharing—Input to the White House Commission on Enhancing National Cybersecurity," in *Trusted Data—a New Framework for Identity and Data Sharing*, ed. T. Hardjono, A. Pentland, and D. Shrier (Cambridge, MA: MIT Press, 2019), 15–40; T. Nishikata, T. Hardjono, and A. Pentland, "Social Capital Accounting," in *Trusted Data—a New Framework for Identity and Data Sharing*, ed. T. Hardjono, A. Pentland, and D. Shrier (Cambridge, MA: MIT Press, 2019), 227–238.

5. Board of Governors of the Federal Reserve System, *Survey of Consumer Finances*," 2020, https://www.federalreserve.gov/econres/scfindex.htm.

4

EMPOWERING INNOVATION THROUGH DATA COOPERATIVES

Thomas Hardjono and Alex Pentland

4.1 INTRODUCTION

The music industry in the United States today represents one of the most complex business ecosystems—one that is currently facing a number of challenges impacting all the entities in the music supply chain.[1] These challenges result from a number of factors, including the emergence of new delivery mechanisms (e.g., digital music streaming), the change in listening habits of the younger generation of audiences, consumers' changing notions of music ownership, the complex legal arrangements around music copyright, and other factors.

Today, artists and musicians are part of the gig economy and function much as gig workers. They are finding it increasingly difficult to make a sustainable living as artistic creators.[2] Many feel they lack visibility into the state of license issuances of their works and therefore into their projected incomes. For many songwriters and musicians, royalty payments for licenses may take several months to arrive. In many cases, the actual songwriters or artists for a given musical work are considered to be "unattributable"—which leads to payments languishing in escrow accounts around the world, unclaimed by the songwriters to whom the payments are due.[3]

The industry itself as a whole has not invested sufficiently in technological advances (e.g., digital delivery, cloud services, digital identity) and has in fact turned down various new opportunities related to digital music over the past two decades (e.g., the Napster case in the late 1990s[4]). The net result is a music ecosystem today that still uses outdated accounting setups (e.g., exchanging Excel spreadsheets), leading to gross inefficiencies, confusing royalty statements, and delayed payments, with music being tagged incorrectly, leading to mistakes in attributions.[5]

In this chapter, we look at the notion of data cooperatives in the context of artists and musicians as gig workers and how the management of music-related rights and licensing on a shared platform can reduce cost and operational complexity. We discuss the RAIDAR project[6] from MIT and the Berklee College of Music as an example of how future IT infrastructure needs to be developed based on design principles that place emphasis on the owners of music-related rights.

4.2   DATA COOPERATIVES: A BRIEF INTRODUCTION

Over the last decade, there has been a continuing decline in trust on the part of individuals with regard to the handling and fair use of personal data.[7] The public is increasingly aware of the power of big data combined with advanced analytics and artificial intelligence (AI). People are also increasingly aware of the power wielded by social media platforms in influencing their daily lives, ranging from influencing the types of advertisements they see on websites and other media to the types of goods and services they purchase online. Pew Research reported that 91 percent of Americans agree or strongly agree that consumers have lost control over how personal data is collected and used, while 80 percent who use social networking sites are concerned about third parties accessing their shared data.[8]

The World Economic Forum (WEF) reported on the state of declining trust in its 2014 report on personal data[9] and recommended ways to remedy the situation. These recommendations included increasing *transparency* by providing individuals with insight and meaningful control, improving *accountability* by orienting throughout the value chain (front end to back end), with risks being equitably distributed, and *empowering individuals* by giving them a say in how data about them is used by organizations and by giving them the capacity to use data for their own purposes.

At the same time as this decreasing trust with regard to the handling and fair use of personal data, there has been a change in the employment patterns of many people through the emergence of the *gig economy*, characterized by nontraditional, independent, short-term working relationships. In some cases, new technological platforms have paved the way and enabled the emergence of new kinds of gig employment previously unavailable (e.g., car ride-sharing services). However, the same technological advances that enabled the emergence of new forms of gig employment may also hold individual participants as captive and dependent for their livelihoods on these gig-enabling platforms.

Our notion of a digital *data cooperative* (figure 4.1) follows from the recommendation of the 2014 WEF report. We define the data

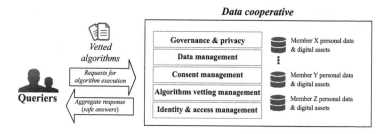

Figure 4.1
Overview of the data cooperative based on the MIT open algorithms principles.

cooperative in chapter 2 as a *member-owned* organization that has a legal *fiduciary* responsibility to its members in the access, management, and use of the members' personal data for their benefit.[10] In its simplest form, the data cooperative could be one where a group of individuals with a common purpose voluntarily pool together access to their personal data, digital assets, and other rights.

There are a range of things that members within a data cooperative can share with each other. We refer to these broadly as "personal data," which may range from data generated by electronic devices (e.g., location data) as a by-product of using the device and data generated from using a third-party service (e.g., telephone call data records) to biomedical data unique to a person (e.g., DNA sequence). Data may also include that generated as a result of a specific type of work (e.g., hospital schedule sheet for a nurse) or produced by the work itself (e.g., compositions by a songwriter, number of views on social media). The exact data being shared depends on the nature and purpose of the

cooperative and must be defined by the members of the cooperative. The cooperative may also provide digital identity management to its membership.[11]

Members of the cooperative may store their personal data and
digital assets at the data cooperative (e.g., in its cloud infrastructure). Alternatively, they can store these elsewhere (e.g., in personal
data stores) and make a copy remotely accessible to the cooperative.[12] A cooperative is a member-owned and voluntary organization, so an individual person is free at any time to leave it and
remove their personal data and other assets from it. A member
retains legal ownership rights over their data and digital assets.

4.3   A DATA COOPERATIVE FOR ARTISTS AND MUSICIANS

A comprehensive discussion of the music industry is beyond the
scope of this work and has been treated elsewhere by Hardjono
et al.[13] and Passman.[14] However, in order to facilitate the discussion, we provide a high-level summary of the roles and tasks of
the most common entities in the music licensing supply chain
(see figure 4.2). When a *composer* or songwriter creates a *musical
work*, such as a music composition or score, they obtain copyright
as soon as the musical work is realized (e.g., transcribed on a
piece of paper). In order to facilitate the licensing of the composition, the songwriter typically engages a *music publisher*, who
may additionally manage the business relationship (e.g., manage
contracts) on behalf of the songwriter. When a record label seeks
to create a sound recording of the composition performed by a
recording artist, the record label must obtain a *mechanical license*

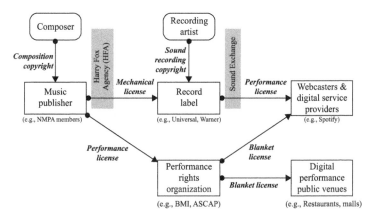

Figure 4.2
Overview of the digital music licensing supply chain.

from the music publisher (or directly from the songwriter). The term *mechanical* derives from the days when physical devices (tape rolls) or physical media (e.g., LPs or compact discs) were used as the primary means of making the sound recordings available to consumers.

Similarly, when a music streaming provider (e.g., Spotify, Pandora)—referred to more formally as a *digital service provider* (DSP)—seeks to offer streaming services to consumers, it must first obtain the appropriate *performance license* from the record label that owns the legal rights to the sound recordings. In order to collect and disburse royalties generated from digital performances (e.g., streaming), in 2003 the US Congress established a nonprofit collective rights management organization called SoundExchange. One of the key roles of SoundExchange is to set the royalty rates for digital performances. On the music publishing side, an organization called the Harry Fox Agency, which was founded in 1927, has the task of managing, collecting, and disbursing the mechanical license royalty fees on behalf of the music publishers in the United States.

One of the noted side effects of the rise of mobile devices is the change in listening habits of consumers. Increasingly, consumers desire that "music on demand" be available through their mobile devices, even when these mobile devices are disconnected from the internet. Furthermore, the mechanisms for the distribution of music have changed with the increase in service quality of internet access providers. Thus, consumers are able to obtain digital (digitized) music over the internet instead of from traditional broadcasting media, such as radio or television. Consequently, a number of DSPs—such as Spotify—have moved away from the traditional performance license models used by the record labels for physical distribution (e.g., LP or CD). The net effect has been a reduction in the revenue made by recording artists and musicians, as reflected by the sheer number of artist-driven lawsuits against Spotify. Since most artists and musicians obtain more revenue from live performances ("gigs") than from digital streaming, they have increasingly become gig workers in the true sense of the word.

The Berklee College of Music and MIT have been spearheading an effort called Open Music to explore new technological means and new incentive mechanisms to enable a new open music ecosystem to evolve. One outcome of this joint effort was the formation in 2017 of the Open Music Initiative[15] as a forum for discussion regarding the various aspects—technological, business, and employment models—of the future music industry globally.

We believe that artists and musicians as gig workers would do well to form communities based on the notion of the data cooperative, and we will discuss some aspects of such a data cooperative.

4.4 SHARED REPOSITORIES FOR MUSICAL WORKS AND ARTISTS' PERSONAL DATA

One of the significant issues in the music supply chain today is the lack of consistent, complete, and authoritative information or metadata regarding the creation of a given musical work— the individual composition or a sound recording track. In many cases, multiple entities in the music supply chain have each created their own version of the metadata for a musical work, often by manually reentering the same information or by scraping data from other sites.[16] In such cases, the effort to synchronize or correct the information becomes manually laborious and error-prone. Furthermore, confidential information regarding the legal ownership of the musical work is often commingled in the same metadata, making the entire database proprietary and thus closed. Currently, the music industry has created standards for metadata file formats (e.g., DDEX, based on XML), but the industry as a whole does not as yet have widely adopted standards that define the processes or workflows by which creation metadata is collected, displayed, and validated. This lack of standards for metadata workflows is only one of the many problems plaguing the industry as a whole, as noted, for example, by Howard[17] and Messitte.[18]

We believe the music industry needs to move to an alternative model for creation metadata following the open access paradigm found in other industries, such as in book publishing, library systems, and the automotive parts supply chain. Creation metadata needs to be separated from rights-ownership metadata as well as from licensing metadata. The creation metadata must not include the actual musical work itself (e.g., sound recording MP3 file) and must not carry the legal ownership or copyright information of the musical work.

The notion of a data cooperative is appealing here as a means of helping communities of artists and musicians manage their musical works, including the creation of authoritative metadata on a shared IT infrastructure. This allows its members to manage their metadata files and musical works (e.g., MP3 master file and song composition files) at a lower cost while retaining control over these valuable assets. This is illustrated in figure 4.3(a).

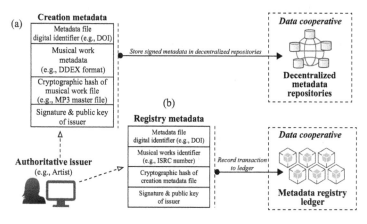

Figure 4.3
The data cooperative distributed ledger for metadata management.

4.5 SHARED LEDGER FOR MUSIC METADATA REGISTRATION

Distributed ledger technology and blockchain systems[19] have captured the attention of many artists and musicians in the past few years as a potential new paradigm that may help them obtain a more accurate indicator regarding consumers' adoption of their musical works and provide them with a more sustainable way of making a living through a more direct transaction and payment cycle.[20]

A data cooperative for artists and musicians can make distributed ledgers available to enhance and automate tasks or functions related to music rights and licensing. For example, the cooperative can establish a *metadata registry ledger* to which members can register their creation metadata. The entries in the ledger include a globally unique resolvable identifier that allows anyone to follow the linked identifier to a copy of the complete creation metadata somewhere on the internet. This is illustrated in figure 4.3(b).

There are several possible benefits to such an approach. The "publication" of the signed registry-metadata file of a musical work into the registry ledger provides legal support to the copyright claim on the part of the creator(s). The distributed ledger as a whole acts as a "notarization" service, where only the cooperative's members have write permission to add new entries to the ledger, while anyone in the public can read the metadata and validate the digital signature via the ledger transaction entry. This notarization using a distributed ledger provides relatively immutable and nonrepudiable time-stamped public evidence of the existence of the musical work.

A second benefit of the metadata registry ledger is that together with the metadata repository it becomes the authoritative source of provenance information regarding a given musical work. By being the open-readable registry for musical works metadata, the registry ledger effectively becomes the trusted source (or an "oracle of truth") for metadata that can then be referenced (linked to) by other types of ledger-based transactions, such as smart contracts that handle license issuance and rights-ownership exchanges. Even existing systems (e.g., legacy databases) can thus refer to the relevant entries (e.g., transaction ID) in the registry ledger.

4.6 SMART CONTRACTS FOR MUSIC LICENSE MANAGEMENT

Artists and musicians see distributed ledgers and smart contracts as a promising avenue for a more direct transaction engagement model. Smart contracts as stored procedures or functions (i.e., code) available on the nodes of the peer-to-peer (P2P) network offer a number of promising capabilities for increasing the efficiency of business workflows. In the context of music contract supply chain management, there are several possible applications of smart contracts implementing different business logic associated with different phases of the contract supply chain. Thus, for example, smart contracts could be used to implement the logic of the licensing of copyrighted music works (e.g., performance license and mechanical license); the tracking of payments for granted licenses; the disbursement of royalty payments to the correct rights holders; and the revocation of granted licenses or automatic expiration.

A data cooperative for artists and musicians could help their membership generally with authoring smart contracts for specific ledger systems. This allows the community to standardize on the legal terms of the license, leaving the pricing decision to each artist or musician. The sharing of common "templates" of smart contracts provides a way for artists to save on legal costs. A second possible role for a data cooperative is to operate a distributed ledger for its membership and possibly for other data cooperatives. This approach allows different data cooperatives around the world to share the costs of operating the shared ledger.

A sketch of this workflow and a copyright license management ledger is shown in figure 4.4. Here, a composer or songwriter employs a smart contract for the purpose of allowing other entities (e.g., music publishers, other artists) to obtain a license for the composer's musical work. The composer must first record the metadata to the metadata registry ledger in order to allow the smart contracts to later unambiguously refer to (point to) the musical work being licensed. This provides licensing precision in the case where several

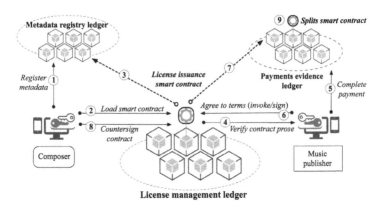

License management ledger

Figure 4.4
Overview of a cooperative copyright license management ledger and smart contract.

versions of the musical work exist (e.g., sound recordings of different lengths). This is summarized in steps 1 to 3 in figure 4.4. In the simplest implementation, the smart contract code could be one that incorporates the legal prose of the license agreement (referred to as *Ricardian* smart contracts[21]) and where the code simply applies the digital signature of the licensee.

When a licensee (e.g., music publisher) seeks to obtain a copyright license to a given composition, the licensee needs to employ the correct smart contract on the license management ledger. Depending on the specific implementation of the smart contract, the licensee may be required to make a payment in advance (e.g., using a separate payment mechanism) and provide evidence to the smart contract regarding this payment. This is summarized in steps 4 to 7 in figure 4.4. If a payment ledger is used, then there is also the opportunity for a "splits" smart contract (step 9) to be used to automatically disburse the payment portions to the correct rights holders in the case where the copyright is jointly owned by multiple people (e.g., a composition created by multiple songwriters).

4.7 THE MIT-BERKLEE RAIDAR PROJECT

One of the significant issues in the music supply chain currently is the lack of consistent, complete, and authoritative metadata regarding the creation of a given musical work. Similar to other supply chains (e.g., containerized goods in shipping), accurate information is needed about an item in order for entities across the supply chain to be able to synchronize their business processes. To this end, the MIT Connection Science group and the Berklee College of Music are leading an effort to begin developing technical solutions for standardizing the various constructs around an open access *music metadata layer*.[22] The goal of the project is to explore the various technical issues involved in creating an interconnected set of metadata repositories and to understand how this new open access music metadata layer can become the basis for future music-related transactions on a distributed ledger or blockchain system. Here we use the term *creation metadata* or simply *metadata* to denote the factual information regarding a given musical work (e.g., composition, sound recording) without including the musical work itself (e.g., sound recording files).

Currently, the music industry has created standards for metadata file formats (e.g., DDEX, based on XML), but the industry as a whole does not as yet have widely adopted standards that define the processes or workflows by which creation metadata is collected, displayed, and validated. Different parts, or "fractions," of metadata are often kept at different locations by different entities along the music supply chain.[23] Given that data accuracy is largely a solved problem in other industries (e.g., the financial industry) that employ technologies based on advanced distributed databases and tightly synchronized transaction systems (e.g., NASDAQ, NYSE, and other securities exchanges), we believe that this music metadata problem should be the first and foremost challenge the music industry needs to collectively address today. This lack of standards for metadata workflows is only one of the many problems plaguing the industry as a whole, as noted by Howard[24] and Messitte.[25]

In this section, we use the general term *musical work* to denote the individual song, composition, or track, and we consider a song composition and recorded song as two separate musical works. This holds true even for a song where the songwriter/

composer and recording artist/performer are the same person. We use the term *creation metadata* to refer to factual information regarding a given musical work. The creation metadata must not include the actual musical work itself (e.g., sound recording MP3 or WAV file) and must not carry the legal ownership or copyright information of the musical work. This is akin to the bibliographic description of a book stored by the Library of Congress and other libraries, which does not include the book itself and does not include information on the current legal owner of the copyright of the book. We use the term *rights metadata* for information pertaining to the legal ownership of rights to the musical work. In many circumstances, rights metadata may be considered confidential, and thus in those cases it should not be made available to the public. We use the term *distributed ledger* (or simply *ledger*) to denote the broader notion of blockchain systems and networks. This allows the constructs described in this chapter to be implemented using a variety of ledger implementations (e.g., Ethereum,[26] R3/Corda,[27] Hyperledger[28]).

Thus, for each atomic unit of metadata information for a given musical work (e.g., one song or track), there should be exactly one authoritative creation-metadata file for that unit. This authoritative creation-metadata file must be digitally signed and be publicly readable from multiple metadata repositories around the world. Its digital signature provides a means of detecting unauthorized modifications to the file. If a given musical work has several versions (e.g., original release, remix), then a separate creation-metadata file must be generated and signed for each.

The availability of a single authoritative creation-metadata file for each musical work allows computing processes and systems to operate based on unambiguous metadata. When a computer program (e.g., traditional software, smart contract) implements the licensing function of a musical work to a licensee, the licensee (person or business entity) can "point" the smart contract to the exact creation-metadata file of interest. If a musical work has several versions (e.g., versions of sound recordings) and the licensee seeks to obtain a license for all these versions, then the licensee can point to each of the relevant creation-metadata files corresponding to each version. Therefore, we believe this open access music metadata layer is crucial for reducing the complexity of business transactions, the error rate from misidentification of musical works, and thus the overall cost of operation for all entities in the music supply chain.

4.8 DESIGN PRINCIPLES

There are numerous design principles that should be the foundation for the technical architecture of the music metadata layer.

Data collection upstream at the point of the work's creation Artists, musicians, and relevant production-side entities (e.g., studio engineers, producers, managers) need to be empowered with correct and intuitive tools (e.g., software) to capture the creation information into a metadata file and digitally sign it (locally) as a means of asserting a claim of "authority" over the provenance of that metadata. Existing systems, such as digital audio workstations (DAWs), may be a suitable point in the supply chain for factual information regarding the creation event to be captured.

Separation of creation metadata from rights-bearing musical works
Musical works (e.g., compositions, sound recordings) must be separated from creation-metadata files for reasons of privacy and copyright enforcement. Several access control models, mechanisms, and solutions are on the market today (e.g., OAuth2.0,[29] OpenID Connect,[30] UMA[31]) to provide protected access to these valuable resources.

Separation of ownership information from factual creation metadata Ownership information should be separated from creation metadata. This is because the ownership information may be confidential and because often the ownership of a given musical work may be sold or acquired over time. Any change of ownership must not alter the creation metadata.

Open data access philosophy to creation metadata The music metadata layer should adopt an *open access philosophy*, which is already common today in other industries and sectors.

Many publications today (e.g., books, magazines, journals) have adopted the open access philosophy for the purpose of advancing knowledge for the entire human race.[32]

Private contracts and confidential information should not be placed in these public open access metadata repositories. Similarly, the actual musical works (e.g., sound recording master files) should not be placed in open access locations.

This open access philosophy for music metadata paves the way toward a more accurate attribution of musical works to artists, musicians, and other relevant creation-side persons and entities.

Additionally, an open access music metadata layer allows fans to obtain more details about the creation of the musical work (e.g., what type of keyboard the musician was using). The availability of keywords and phrases linked to metadata files allows *intelligent search* capabilities to be developed atop the music metadata layer.

Inclusion of a cryptographic hash of a musical work   Every creation metadata file must include a cryptographic hash of the digital representation of the musical work of concern (e.g., a hash of the MP3 sound recording file) as a reference to the work. This allows exact one-to-one mapping between the metadata file and the corresponding musical work.

Standard descriptor for metadata format and encoding   We anticipate that in the future there will be multiple metadata formats (e.g., DDEX-XML,[33] JSON) with various encodings (e.g., Unicode, Chinese GB) according to the community of creators. The relevant headers of every metadata file must include such information in order to aid the reader (i.e., client software) that fetches and parses these metadata files.

Digitally signed and portable metadata units   The atomic unit of metadata (e.g., song, track, or composition) must be digitally signed by an authoritative entity, such as the artist, songwriter, composer, musician, producer, or other person who has been authorized to do so. This allows the metadata unit to be self-contained and standalone, and therefore portable and replicable as a unit. Each metadata file must carry a globally unique digital identifier that allows it to be uniquely distinguished from other metadata units.

Figure 4.5(a) illustrates this notion of a signed metadata file with a unique file identifier, where the last part in figure 4.5(a) shows the signature portion (e.g., X.509[34] or XML-DSig[35]) and the signer information.

Replicated copies of metadata units The signed metadata files must be made available to the public at multiple locations throughout the internet. The digital identifier used for the metadata file must allow a user to locate one of the many copies of the metadata files on the internet. Access should be made via standardized application programming interfaces (APIs).

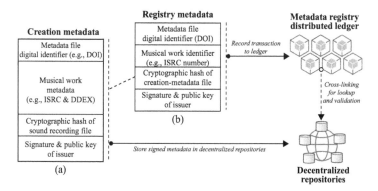

Figure 4.5

Summary of the creation metadata and registry metadata, where (a) the full *creation metadata* is placed in the decentralized replicated repositories and (b) a shorter *registry metadata* is recorded on the ledger, with a link (or hash) pointing to the full creation metadata permitting future verifications of the authenticity of the creation metadata.

Globally unique and resolvable file identifiers   Each metadata file must be assigned a unique identifier under a registered namespace that allows a user to fetch a copy from one of the many repositories around the world based on that identifier.

Digital identifier schemes such as the digital object identifier (DOI)[36] and its accompanying Handle resolver system[37] have been successfully deployed on a wide scale for over a decade. Similar in protocol behavior to the Domain Name System (DNS) infrastructure, the DOI and Handle allow efficient lookups of copies of data files (e.g., library catalog entries) stored at open repositories all over the internet.

Ledger-based notarization of signed metadata   A distributed ledger can be used as a means of *notarizing* each signed metadata unit or a shorter summary of it. For convenience, we refer to the shorter metadata as the *registry metadata*, implying that the shorter registry metadata is intended to be stored on the distributed ledger. The same file identifier (e.g., DOI) used in the creation metadata must be used in the registry metadata, signifying that both point to the same musical work. The notarization of the registry metadata provides a tamper-detectable time stamp on the musical work.

Figure 4.5(b) illustrates the notion of notarization via a *metadata registry ledger* and shows the shorter registry metadata to be recorded on the ledger. Entities that fetch a version of a metadata file must check the ledger to ensure that they have the latest version (e.g., based on the time stamp on the confirmed transaction).

Support for multiple versions of a musical work   In many circumstances, artists and musicians may create different versions of a given musical work. For example, for a given sound recording, an artist may record a short version (e.g., 2 minutes long), long version (e.g., 3 minutes long), and extended version (e.g., 6 minutes long). Since the cryptographic hash of the musical work (e.g., MP3 file) is included in the metadata file—see figure 4.5(a)— this implies that a separate metadata file must be created for each version. Furthermore, this means that each of these metadata files must have a unique identifier. This is crucial in order to allow a licensee to unambiguously point to the exact version of the sound recording for which they are seeking a license.

Support for revisions of metadata It is inevitable that errors may exist in metadata information even when the information is collected upstream at the creation end of the supply chain (e.g., in DAW software). Therefore, if a metadata file is to be corrected or revised, then the existing (old) metadata file should never be deleted or erased. When a new revision is written, the new version of the metadata file must be assigned a new file identifier and must contain a link to (e.g., hash of) the previous version. This indicates to the reader (i.e., client software) that a previous version exists. This principle is akin to source *version control* in software engineering development, which is very common today (e.g., SVN or GitHub).

Similarly, when a revised version is to be notarized via the registry ledger, the new registry metadata must include a pointer to (e.g., hash of) the previously confirmed registry metadata (e.g., transaction ID of the previously confirmed registry-metadata transaction).

Support for archival and revised metadata Revised (old) metadata files must never be erased and must be archived using the same replicated repository architecture we have discussed. Archived metadata files must remain open access in order to support tracing of the provenance and history of the metadata information.

There are at least three benefits in this approach of combining open access metadata files and the notarization using the metadata registry ledger:

- *Support of copyright claim* The "publication" of the signed registry-metadata file of a musical work onto the registry ledger provides legal support to the copyright claim on the part of the creator(s). Furthermore, the notarization using a distributed ledger (with an additional act of signing the transaction) provides relatively immutable and nonrepudiable time-stamped public evidence of the existence of the musical work.

- *Basis for music metadata oracle for other ledgers and systems* By being the open registry for musical works metadata, the registry ledger effectively becomes the *oracle* for metadata that can be referred to (linked to) by other types of ledger-based transactions, such as license request smart contracts and license-granting smart contracts. Even existing systems (e.g., legacy databases) or future systems such as those of the Mechanical Licensing Collective or the Repertoire Data Exchange can thus refer to the relevant entries (e.g., transaction ID) in the registry ledger.

- *Opportunity for tight binding between a digital identity and public key* The need to digitally sign the creation metadata and to sign the transaction submitted to the registry ledger necessitates dealing with key management of the private-public key pair of the signer. Standards for the creation of digital certificates based on the strong identification of persons have already existed in industry for over two decades.[38] New efforts to retain this binding in a decentralized fashion via a blockchain system are also under way.[39]

This in turn paves the way toward solving the current problem in the music industry of identifying rights holders (persons or legal entities) to whom royalty payments are owed.[40]

4.9 DISTRIBUTED REPOSITORIES

We envisage that the creation metadata of a given musical work should be replicated for higher availability and reliability. There are several basic requirements for the implementations of the replicated metadata repositories (figure 4.6):

- *Independence of replication technologies* Since database and replication technologies will continue to evolve over time, the creation metadata as the atomic unit must be "movable" (copyable) from one repository implementation to another.
- *Standardized service APIs for metadata repositories* The repository RESTful APIs used by a client application that reads and writes to a metadata repository must be standardized. The API definitions must be independent of the technological implementation of the repository behind the APIs. A client application calling to the APIs of a service should not need to be aware of the back-end implementation of the service.
- *Standardized import and export data format retaining signatures* When a metadata file is to be exported (read) from a metadata repository, the file must use a standardized data format. The digital signature portion of the original metadata file (as submitted initially by its creator) must remain valid when the metadata file is exported.

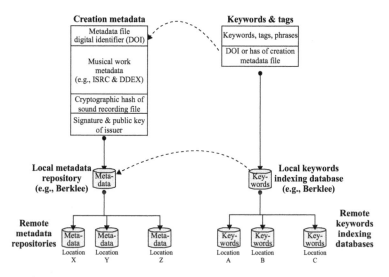

Figure 4.6
Replicated metadata repositories with linked keywords and tags indexing.

For example, consider the case where an artist employs a client application (e.g., DAW) to write a new a creation-metadata file in a given format (e.g., JSON), which is then signed by the artist using the corresponding public-key signature standard (e.g., JSON Web Signature). When the artist, via the client application, submits this file to the local metadata repository, the repository may internally disassemble the metadata file in accordance with its internal data storage architecture. However, when later a home user reads (exports) a copy of the metadata from this open access repository, the repository must be able to reassemble the original creation metadata such that its original signature can be validated by the home user.

Figure 4.7(a) illustrates a summary of the parts of the creation-metadata file:

- Part 1: *Metadata digital identifier*   The first part is the identifier of the creation-metadata file. We propose to use the digital object identifier (DOI) scheme[41] because of its long history of successful deployments around the world.

- Part 2: *Musical works metadata*   The second part pertains to the actual musical works metadata. This component may use existing music metadata formats (e.g., XML-based DDEX RIN, JSON) or other formats. The header part of this component must indicate the format and encoding of the metadata. Note that the metadata file must not contain the musical sound recording file or legal ownership information.

- Part 3: *Cryptographic hash of musical works file*   The third part of the creation-metadata file is a cryptographic hash of the musical work file. For example, this could be a hash of a sound recording master file (e.g., MP3, MPEG4) or the hash of the music notation file (e.g., PDF file, Sibelius file, Finale file).

This allows correct one-to-one mapping between the metadata file and the musical works file. This exact matching becomes relevant in business processing when there are multiple versions of a given musical work (e.g., long version, short version, or remix of a sound recording).

- Part 4: *Authoritative issuer digital signature*   The issuer of the creation metadata must digitally sign the combined parts of the metadata (i.e., parts 1 to 3).

The digital signature is performed using the existing standard techniques for public-key digital signatures and time stamps.

The signature portion is the fourth part of figure 4.7(a). It must include the standard pieces of information required for a reader to validate the file (e.g., signature algorithm ID[42]).

Henceforth, any attempt to modify any data in the assembled parts (parts 1 to 4 of figure 4.7(a)) will cause the signature verification to fail—indicating to the reader that the creation-metadata file is no longer authentic (i.e., that it has been tampered with).

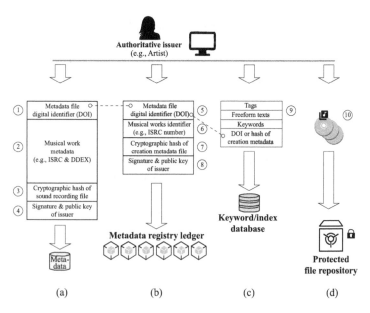

Figure 4.7

Summary of parts of (a) the creation metadata and (b) the registry metadata, where separate index/search databases (c) may be created and where the actual sound recording files are placed into protected storage (d).

4.10   METADATA REGISTRY LEDGER

The music metadata layer may benefit from the use of one or more distributed ledger networks as a means of creating a simple consensus-based, notarized *registry ledger*. Since a creation-metadata file might be large, and given that most ledger-based transaction systems are not intended to store large files, only a short summary of the metadata should be recorded on the registry-ledger system. We refer to this as the *registry-metadata* structure (see figure 4.7(b)).

The shorter registry metadata will be recorded on the registry ledger, and its resulting transaction ID on that ledger can later be used as a reference in business logic implementations and multiparty transactions on other systems and ledgers. The registry metadata must always carry the same identifier (i.e., DOI) as the creation metadata, indicating that these two data structures refer to the same musical work.

The registry ledger has two major goals:

- *Multicopy registry-metadata file and lookup*   The registry ledger provides multiple copies of the registry metadata by virtue of the P2P network of nodes. Each node independently keeps a full set of confirmed blocks of transactions (see figure 4.8), each of which carries the registry-metadata structure. The metadata identifier part (part 5 in figure 4.7(b)) includes the same file identifier (e.g., DOI) as in the creation metadata (part 1 in figure 4.7(a)). This allows any entity to use the DOI identifier found in the short registry metadata (on the public registry ledger) to fetch a copy of the full creation-metadata file from one or more repositories on the internet.

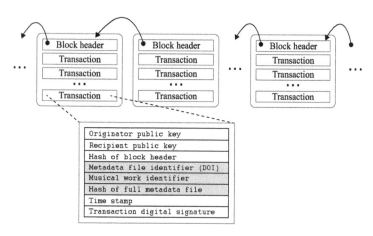

Figure 4.8
Illustration of a transaction in a block containing registry metadata (gray fields).

- *Persistent on-chain record for other infrastructure* The metadata registry ledger provides persistent evidence on which other infrastructure and systems can rely (i.e., can point to). Thus, a music licensing scheme implemented on a different ledger or blockchain system can "point to" registry metadata found on the registry ledger as part of a license issuance smart contract. Similarly, legacy systems and databases can cite the transaction ID (on the ledger) of the registry metadata in its business logic processing software.

The parts of the registry metadata are shown in figure 4.7(b) (which does not show the enveloping ledger transaction structure):

- Part 5: *Metadata digital identifier* The first part is the digital identifier of the registry-metadata file, which must be identical to the value found in the full creation metadata (part 1 of figure 4.7(a)).

- Part 6: *Musical works identifier*   The second part carries the musical works identifier that may be in use within the metadata file. Typically, this would be an identifier that is common and understood in the music industry (e.g., ISRC number for recordings or ISWC number for compositions).

- Part 7: *Cryptographic hash of full metadata file*   The third part carries the cryptographic hash of the full metadata file as a means of ensuring one-to-one correspondence between the registry metadata and the full creation-metadata file.

- Part 8: *Authoritative issuer digital signature*   The fourth part carries the digital signature of the authoritative issuer, which should be the same issuer as that of the full creation-metadata file. Although not shown, typically a time stamp is included in the digital signature data structure.

After the authoritative issuer (e.g., artist) completes the capture of the musical works metadata, he or she proceeds to create a short registry metadata, which is then enveloped within a transaction structure and transmitted to the distributed ledger. The transaction's recipient (address) is either the issuer itself (i.e., to the public key of the issuer) or is "null" (depending on the specific ledger implementation in question). This self-addressed transaction implicitly indicates that it is a notarization transaction.

4.11   DISTRIBUTED SEARCH AND LOOKUPS

Another issue closely tied to the music metadata layer relates to the ability for a user (e.g., home user, other creative artists) to search the various metadata repositories for music using keywords and phrases. We believe a separate "search infrastructure" is needed that is parallel and interconnected to the various metadata repositories.

There are a number of interesting considerations for this search infrastructure based on an interconnected set of the keyword databases shown earlier in figure 4.6 and figure 4.7(b). Some of these considerations include:

- *Separation of creation metadata from search material*   The words, tags, and phrase information—referred to here as *search material*—must be stored and managed separately from creation-metadata files. This is because while the creation metadata may remain static over time (unchanged) once it has been signed, the accumulated size of the search material—consisting of permutations and combinations of words and phrases—may grow and change over time.
- *Creator-side association of keywords and phrases*   Artists and musicians must be able to associate their own words, tags, and phrases with a given music metadata and have this search material stored locally but be read-accessible globally.
- *User-side association of keywords and phrases*   Similarly, any user or person (or AI and machine learning systems) must be able to create their own association of words, tags, and phrases for given music metadata and have this search material stored locally to them. This is analogous to the current practice of music playlists that users create on their devices and streaming accounts.

Figure 4.9 illustrates the search process. In step 1, a user employs a search application that performs searches on local keyword databases as well as others available globally. The result of this search,

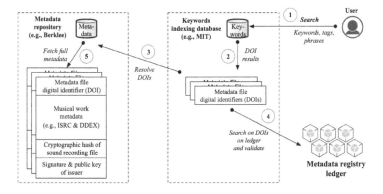

Figure 4.9
Example of search and metadata lookups.

in step 2, is a set of links or DOI values that the search application can resolve to the full metadata. When the search application presents these results, the user can choose certain DOIs (e.g., in the user's search application), which would result in the search application fetching the full creation-metadata files in step 3. In step 4, the search application has the option of verifying on the registry ledger whether newer versions of the creation-metadata file exist.

For each creation-metadata file, the user can then employ the hash of the musical work (e.g., hash of an MP3 master file) found in the creation metadata to fetch a copy of the musical work itself (e.g., the MP3 master file) from its storage location via a protected API. This last action will require that the user be authenticated and obtain authorization from the current owner of the musical work.

Currently, alternative decentralized content management systems (e.g., open index protocol[43]) are being developed to allow the decentralization of the storage of content files (e.g., using IPFS[44]) with separate locally cached search terms. The local caching of search terms (e.g., on the user's computer) avoids the centralized collection by (and hence user dependence on) large search-engine service providers. This is important because the user's choice of search terms and keywords may provide valuable insights through social analytics regarding the user's preferences among music genres as well as those of the user's friends (e.g., people with frequent interactions in the social interaction network[45]).

4.12 LAYERS OF THE FUTURE GLOBAL MUSIC ECOSYSTEM

So far, we have discussed the music metadata layer as the foundational layer for the future global music ecosystem. This layer is as central to the functioning of the digital music ecosystem as the DNS infrastructure is central to the functioning of the services on the internet today. However, in order for new services to grow organically and evolve over time, we believe that two additional layers will be needed in order for the digital music industry to truly reach its global market potential.

The three layers of future digital music are summarized in figure 4.10 and consist of the following:

- *Music metadata layer*   This is the music metadata layer that we have discussed in previous sections. It is the bottommost layer in figure 4.10.

There will be several other components of this layer that we did not discuss, such as digital identity management, cryptographic key management, protected access to musical works (e.g., sound recording files), and others. There is a key role for AI and machine learning technologies at this layer in solving the music search problem.

- *Licensing and royalty management layer*   The second layer needed is one that enables decentralized management of music rights ownership, music rights trading (i.e., buying and selling), license issuance and tracking, and the collection and distribution of royalties. This is the middle layer in figure 4.10. Here, we believe that there is a major role for smart contracts technology to be used to represent business logic as part of broader music licensing supply chain management.

It is paramount to recognize that this layer strongly depends on the bottommost music metadata layer. Digital licenses cannot be issued by smart contracts (and royalties obtained) if creation-metadata information is incomplete or if there are multiple imprecise nonauthoritative versions existing along the music supply chain, hence our design principles discussed earlier.

One important question for this layer is the confidentiality of rights-related transactions on the distributed ledgers used in this layer. Research and development continues on cryptographic schemes (e.g., zero-knowledge proof schemes) that provide some degree of privacy to entities that transact on public blockchain networks. A second key question pertains to the interoperability of distributed ledgers and blockchain systems, something that is severely lacking today.[46]

- *Music virtual assets layer*   The third layer needed is one that allows recognition of musical works and music rights as *virtual assets* in the sense of digital tokens.[47]

A new digital infrastructure is needed to allow the exchange (e.g., buying and selling) of rights in the form of digital fungible tokens (e.g., ERC-20[48]) or nonfungible tokens (e.g., ERC-721[49]). Tokens can be used to represent full or partial rights ownership of musical works and therefore can be used as the basis for distributing royalties obtained from licensees.

The eventual vision is for this layer to encompass multiple *decentralized music-rights trading networks* that operate on a global scale. Just like the internet—which is composed of multiple ISPs and networks—the interoperability across trading networks (i.e., distributed ledgers and blockchains) remains a subject for future research and development in the technology industry.

Just as the internet is not owned by any single entity, organization, or country, we believe that there will be multiple implementations and instantiations of the functions and components of the

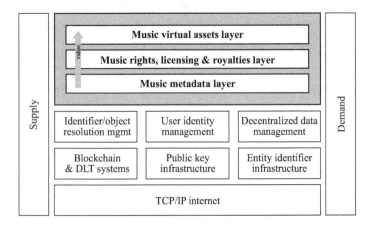

Figure 4.10
The three layers of the future digital music ecosystem.

three layers in figure 4.10. As the history of the 1980s local area network (LAN) industry has taught us,[50] it is futile and even counterproductive for any single entity to seek to own or control entire layers. Therefore, technical and operational standards are needed to ensure a high degree of interoperability of services based on common standardized APIs—and thus ensure significant competition for services in the market.

4.13   CONCLUSIONS

Today, we are in a situation where individual assets—people's personal data—are being exploited without sufficient value being returned to the individual. This is analogous to the situation in the late 1800s and early 1900s that led to the creation of collective institutions such as credit unions and labor unions, so the time seems ripe for the creation of collective institutions to represent the data rights of individuals. We have argued that data cooperatives with fiduciary obligations to members provide a promising direction for the empowerment of individuals through collective use of their own personal data. Not only can a data cooperative give the individual expert, community-based advice on how to manage, curate, and protect access to their personal data, it can run internal analytics that benefit the collective membership. Such collective insights provide a powerful tool for negotiating better services and discounts for the cooperative's members. Federally chartered credit unions are a useful model because they have already been legally empowered to act as cooperatives. We believe there are many other similar institutions that could also provide cooperative data services, and we discuss the data cooperative model in the case of empowering artists and musicians in the music industry.

In the context of a data cooperative for artists and musicians, one of the key challenges of the music supply chain today is the lack of consistent, complete, and authoritative information or metadata regarding the creation of a given musical work. We have described the notion of an open access *music metadata layer* that can become the basis for future music-related transactions on distributed ledgers or blockchain systems. The metadata layer consists of replicated and decentralized open access metadata repositories, which are a series of repositories that store creation metadata without rights-ownership information and without the copyrighted musical works (e.g., composition notes files, sound recording files). This is coupled with a registry ledger, which acts as a notarization service and allows anyone in the world to resolve the identifiers in the registry metadata to one or more copies of the complete creation metadata located on the internet. We have described a number of design principles for this music metadata layer.

We believe there is a role for a data cooperative to operate and manage the relevant IT services that implement the music metadata layer and the registry ledger for the cooperative's members. This provides artists and musicians better manageability of their assets (i.e., their creative works) and better visibility into the licensing of their works (e.g., who has licensed what works). Using smart contracts technology, licensees can obtain rights licenses (e.g., performance licenses, mechanical licenses) directly on the blockchain from artists and musicians.

Our vision is a future music industry that operates globally based on the three logical layers. Thus, in addition to the music metadata layer, we believe that a licensing and royalty management layer will be needed that can automate the business logic processing pertaining to license issuance, license tracking and accounting, rights-ownership trading (i.e., buying and selling), and royalty collection and distribution. We believe there is a promising role for smart contracts technologies to express the various types of business logic in this layer. The third and "uppermost" layer is one in which musical works and music rights can be recognized as virtual assets in the sense of digital tokens. This tokenization paves the way for the evolution toward globally interconnected networks for the exchange of virtual music assets.

NOTES

1. W. Fisher, *Promises to Keep: Technology, Law, and the Future of Entertainment* (Stanford, CA: Stanford Law and Politics, 2004).

2. G. Howard, "Imogen Heap's Mycelia: An Artists' Approach for a Fair Trade Music Business, Inspired by Blockchain," *Forbes*, July 17, 2015, https://www.forbes.com/sites/georgehoward/2015/07/17/imogen-heaps -mycelia-an-artists-approach-for-a-fair-trade-music-business-inspired-by -blockchain/?sh=6afc9ab04969; G. Howard, *Everything in Its Right Place: How Blockchain Technology Will Lead to a More Transparent Music Industry* (Beverly Farms, MA: Giant Step Books, 2017).

3. N. Messitte, "Inside the Black Box: A Deep Dive into Music's Monetization Mystery," *Forbes*, April 15, 2015, https://www.forbes.com/sites /nickmessitte/2015/04/15/inside-the-black-box-a-deep-dive-into-musics -monetization.

4. Fisher, *Promises to Keep.*

5. Howard, "Imogen Heap's Mycelia."

6. T. Hardjono, G. Howard, E. Scace, M. Chowdury, L. Novak, M. Gaudet, J. Anderson, N. d'Avis, C. Kulis, E. Sweeney, and C. Vaughan, *Towards an Open and Scalable Music Metadata Layer*, MIT Connection Science & Engineering Technical Report, November 2019, http://arxiv.org/abs/1911.08278.

7. World Economic Forum, *Personal Data: The Emergence of a New Asset Class*, report, 2011, http://www.weforum.org/reports/personal-data-emergence-new-asset-class; World Economic Forum, *Rethinking Personal Data: A New Lens for Strengthening Trust*, report, May 2014, http://reports.weforum.org/rethinking-personal-data.

8. M. Madden, "Public Perceptions of Privacy and Security in the Post-Snowden Era," Pew Research, November 2014, http://www.pewinternet.org/2014/11/12/public-privacy-perceptions/.

9. World Economic Forum, *Rethinking Personal Data*.

10. J. M. Balkin, "Information Fiduciaries and the First Amendment," *UC Davis Law Review* 49, no. 4 (April 2016): 1183–1234.

11. T. Hardjono and A. Pentland, "Core Identities," in *Trusted Data—a New Framework for Identity and Data Sharing*, ed. T. Hardjono, A. Pentland, and D. Shrier (Cambridge, MA: MIT Press, 2019), 41–81.

12. T. Hardjono and A. Pentland, "MIT Open Algorithms," in *Trusted Data—a New Framework for Identity and Data Sharing*, ed. T. Hardjono, A. Pentland, and D. Shrier (Cambridge, MA: MIT Press, 2019), 83–107.

13. Hardjono et al., "Towards an Open and Scalable Music Metadata Layer."

14. D. Passman, *All You Need to Know about the Music Business*, 10th ed. (New York: Simon & Schuster, 2019).

15. P. Panay, A. Pentland, and T. Hardjono, "Open Music: Why Success of the Music Modernization Act Depends on Open Standards," *Billboard*, October 29, 2018, https://www.billboard.com/articles/business/8482056/mma-op-ed-open-music-initiative-open-standards.

16. D. Deahl, "Metadata Is the Biggest Little Problem Plaguing the Music Industry," *The Verge*, May 2019, https://www.theverge.com/2019/5/29 /18531476/music-industry-song-royalties-metadata-credit-problems.

17. Howard, "Imogen Heap's Mycelia"; Howard, *Everything in Its Right Place*.

18. Messitte, "Inside the Black Box."

19. D. Yaga, P. Mell, N. Roby, and K. Scarfone, *Blockchain Technology Overview*, National Institute of Standards and Technology Internal Report 8202, October 2018, https://doi.org/10.6028/NIST.IR.8202.

20. Howard, *Everything in Its Right Place*.

21. I. Grigg, "Financial Cryptography in 7 Layers," in *Financial Cryptography: 4th International Conference (FC 2000)*, ed. Y. Frankel, Lecture Notes in Computer Science 1962 (Berlin: Springer-Verlag, 2000), 332–348.

22. T. Hardjono, E. Scace, and G. Howard, "Decentralized Music Metadata Registry Using Blockchain Technology" (presentation at Crypto Music 2019, Boston, May 10, 2019); Hardjono et al., "Towards an Open and Scalable Music Metadata Layer."

23. Deahl, "Metadata Is the Biggest Little Problem Plaguing the Music Industry."

24. Howard, "Imogen Heap's Mycelia"; Howard, *Everything in Its Right Place*.

25. Messitte, "Inside the Black Box."

26. V. Buterin, "Ethereum: A Next-Generation Cryptocurrency and Decentralized Application Platform," *Bitcoin Magazine*, January 2014, https:// bitcoinmagazine.com/articles/ethereum-next-generation-cryptocurrency -decentralized-application-platform-1390528211.

27. R3CEV, "R3," 2018, https://www.r3.com.

28. E. Androulaki, A. Barger, V. Bortnikov, C. Cachin, K. Christidis, A. De Caro, D. Enyeart, et al., "Hyperledger Fabric: A Distributed Operating

System for Permissioned Blockchains," in *Proceedings of the Thirteenth EuroSys Conference (Eurosys'18)*, ed. P. Felber, Y. C. Hu, and R. Oliveira (New York: ACM, 2018), 30:1–30:15.

29. D. Hardt, "The OAuth 2.0 Authorization Framework," RFC6749, IETF, October 2012, http://tools.ietf.org/rfc/rfc6749.txt.

30. N. Sakimura, J. Bradley, M. Jones, B. de Medeiros, and C. Mortimore, "OpenID Connect Core 1.0," OpenID Foundation, Technical Specification v1.0—Errata Set 1, November 2014, http://openid.net/specs/openid-connect-core-10.html.

31. T. Hardjono, E. Maler, M. Machulak, and D. Catalano, "User-Managed Access (UMA) Profile of OAuth2.0—Specification Version 1.0," Kantara Initiative, Kantara published specification, April 2015, https://docs.kantarainitiative.org/uma/rec-uma-core.html; E. Maler, M. Machulak, and J. Richer, "User-Managed Access (UMA) 2.0," Kantara Initiative, Kantara published specification, January 2017, https://docs.kantarainitiative.org/uma/ed/uma-core-2.0-10.html.

32. Wikipedia, "Open Access—Wikipedia, the Free Encyclopedia," 2019, https://en.wikipedia.org/wiki/Openaccess; P. Suber, *Open Access* (Cambridge, MA: MIT Press, 2012).

33. DDEX, "Digital Data Exchange," 2006, https://www.ddex.net.

34. M. Myers, R. Ankney, A. Malpani, S. Galperin, and C. Adams, "X.509 Internet Public Key Infrastructure Online Certificate Status Protocol—OCSP," IETF Standard RFC2560, June 1999, http://tools.ietf.org/rfc/rfc2560.txt; ITU, "ITU-T Recommendation X.509 (1997 E): Information Technology—Open Systems Interconnection—the Directory: Authentication Framework," June 1997.

35. M. Bartel, J. Boyer, B. Fox, B., LaMacchia, and E. Simon, "XML Signature Syntax and Processing Version 2.0," W3C, W3C Candidate Recommendation, July 2015, http://www.w3.org/TR/2015/NOTE-xmldsig-core2-20150723/.

36. ISO, "Digital Object Identifier System—Information and Documentation," International Organization for Standardization, ISO 26324:2012, June 2012, http://www.iso.org/iso/cataloguedetail?csnumber=43506.

37. S. Sun, L. Lannom, and B. Boesch, "Handle System Overview," RFC3650, IETF, November 2003, http://tools.ietf.org/rfc/rfc3650.txt; S. Sun, S. Reilly, and L. Lannom, "Handle System Namespace and Service Definition," RFC3651, IETF, November 2003, http://tools.ietf.org/rfc/rfc3651.txt.

38. R. Housley and T. Polk, *Planning for PKI: Best Practices for PKI Deployment* (New York: Wiley and Sons, 2001).

39. D. Reed and M. Sporny, "Decentralized Identifiers (DIDs) v0.11," W3C Draft Community Group Report, July 9, 2018, https://w3c-ccg.github.io/did-spec/.

40. Messitte, "Inside the Black Box."

41. ISO, "Digital Object Identifier System—Information and Documentation" http://www.iso.org/iso/cataloguedetail?csnumber=43506; Sun, Lannom, and Boesch, "Handle System Overview"; Sun, Reilly, and Lannom, "Handle System Namespace and Service Definition."

42. Housley and T. Polk, *Planning for PKI*.

43. Wikipedia. Open Index Protocol," . 2019, https://oip.wiki/OpenIndexProtocol.

44. Protocol Labs, "Inter Planetary File System (IPFS)," 2019, https://docs.ipfs.io.

45. A. Pentland, *Social Physics: How Social Networks Can Make Us Smarter* (New York: Penguin Books, 2015).

46. T. Hardjono, A. Lipton, and A. Pentland, "Towards an Interoperability Architecture: Blockchain Autonomous Systems," *IEEE Transactions on Engineering Management* 67, no. 4 (2020): 1298–1309, https://doi.org/10.1109/TEM.2019.2920154.

47. US Securities and Exchange Commission, *Framework for "Investment Contract" Analysis of Digital Assets.*, Report, April 2019, https://www.sec.gov /corpfin/framework-investment-contract-analysis-digital-assets; Financial Action Task Force (FATF), "International Standards on Combating Money Laundering and the Financing of Terrorism and Proliferation," FATF Revision of Recommendation 15, October 2018, http://www.fatf-gafi.org /publications/fatfrecommendations/documents/fatf-recommendations .html.

48. F. Vogelsteller and V. Buterin, "ERC-20 Token Standard (EIP 20)," Ethereum.org, Ethereum Improvement Proposals, November 2015, https://eips .ethereum.org/EIPS/eip-20.

49. W. Entriken, D. Shirley, J. Evans, and N. Sachs, "ERC-721 Non-fungible Token Standard (EIP 721)," Ethereum.org, Ethereum Improvement Proposals, January 2018, https://eips.ethereum.org/EIPS/eip-721.

50. J. Abbate, *Inventing the Internet* (Cambridge, MA: MIT Press, 1999).

FROM SECURITIZATION TO TOKENIZATION

Charles Chang

5.1 INTRODUCTION

In the late 1980s, asset securitization appeared in the banking sector in the United States and Europe as a channel for creating liquidity. Various financial assets are merged or pooled into one group, and then this group of repackaged assets is sold to investors piecemeal. Through this operation, investors receive opportunities, and originators gain more free capital. Starting with the earliest applications for home mortgages, called mortgage-backed securities, securitization has created investable assets that greatly increased portfolio choices and has played an important role in the global financial system.[1]

Today, there are a great many assets that are securitized, but securitization most often occurs with loans and assets that generate receivables, such as different types of consumer or commercial debt. Essentially, a holding vehicle is formed that "buys" the loans or other assets. The shares of this vehicle are in turn sold to participating investors. This pooling of assets provides diversification, reducing the risk of ownership, and large, global portfolios with assets sourced from around the world provide further risk reduction. Securitization further breaks the portfolio into small enough pieces for average investors to participate. Vibrant markets for these asset-backed securities (ABSs) exist in most of the most important financial markets in the world, including New York City, Singapore, Hong Kong, and London.

However, as evidenced by the 2009 global financial crisis, securitization is not without its limitations. During this time, ABSs were combined and packaged into collateralized debt obligations (CDOs). Holders of these CDOs were entitled to a stream of income derived from the repayment of the obligations underlying each ABS. However, in many cases, a single ABS may consist of thousands of debt obligations, and up to 150 ABSs may make up a single CDO. The relation between a CDO's value and the value of its underlying assets is complex and nonlinear.

Furthermore, in some economies, complexities in the ownership relationships of assets underlying ABSs make repatriation difficult. For example, a building underlying an ABS might have dozens of owners, each of whom would have to consent to the sale of the asset in the case of default. In addition, the asset selection and pooling nature of ABSs result in management fees and agency costs that are often as high as or higher than for mutual funds and other mainstream investment products. Leverage is also commonplace, as ABS managers use the assets underlying the ABS to borrow money and improve returns. As evidenced during the global financial crisis, this activity often is not transparent, leaving investors with little information as to the details of the assets they are investing in, confused by financial machinations they do not understand, and ultimately saddled with risks that are not obvious to the average investor.

Blockchain provides a tool to allay many of these concerns. First, because of the transparent, immutable, shared nature of distributed ledgers, information is fully shared and available for all to see. Assets that are written to a blockchain have clear ownership rights, and any leverage is fully revealed. Second, tokens created by the blockchain are natural units of investment into the assets on the chain and can be made easily accessible to investors around the world at very little cost. This process, known as tokenization, pools and splits the cash flows from the assets on the chain, and each token represents fractional ownership. Put simply, if there are $10 million worth of assets written to the chain and 1 million tokens issued, each one would cost $10 and would be a claim on one millionth of whatever cash flows are created by the assets. Third, because of the digitized, automated nature of blockchains, costs of operation are likewise low and hence associated fees are small. Smart contracts can be utilized to streamline and fully automate the collection and distribution of cash flows in a nonintermediated way that simultaneously reduces overall system friction and eliminates opportunities for leakages caused by unscrupulous behavior or human error.

As discussed by Chang and Wang,[2] several of the early adopting countries already have regulations and policies in place that legitimize the so-called security token asset class, including the US Securities and Exchange Commission (SEC) and authorities in Hong Kong, Singapore, and elsewhere. However, it is also important to note that tokenization is a close cousin to securitization. In many jurisdictions, it suffices simply to revise existing securitization laws and regulations to allow for tokenization. Unlike their blockchain cousins the cryptocurrencies, security tokens are not so much a totally new asset as they are the evolution of an existing asset, facilitating regulatory reform. This distinction and separation from cryptocurrencies like bitcoin has been key in the adoption of security tokens, especially in the case of certain jurisdictions (such as China) that have completely disavowed cryptocurrency only to embrace applications of security tokens.[3]

It is also important to differentiate security tokens from coins or tokens generated in initial coin offerings (ICOs).[4] In the latter, claims to assets are generated in the form of coins based on a white paper that describes the functioning of and potential uses of said coins. Because the issuer need only describe the intentions of the coin rather than demonstrate any physical assets or business model, in most cases ICOs generate tokens connected to ideas or intangible assets (such as intellectual property). In addition, white papers vary in quality and reliability, and as ICOs are built on the original intentions of complete decentralization, they are not regulated by any securities authority. As a result, ICO markets have been fraught with fraud, attracting all manner of speculation and issuers seeking to raise money selling tokens often attached to nothing, all in a space where there are seldom legal repercussions and no clear jurisdictions for prosecution. In contrast, in a security token offering (STO), the issuer must demonstrate ownership of the assets backing the token and must demonstrate viability in a formal process on par with that of the ABS or IPO.

5.2 SECURITY TOKEN APPLICATIONS

There have been a number of security token applications already. Perhaps not surprisingly, the earliest of these were linked to real estate, as was the case with ABSs. However, in most cases, tokens have been linked directly to individual pieces of property and the cash flows arising from them, rather than to mortgage obligations. Importantly, we will see that most tokenizations focus on individual assets, making ownership rights and transparency simple and easy to understand.[5] In contrast, traditional ABS pools may have hundreds of assets, each with different qualities, making it difficult for lay investors to be fully informed. While it remains unclear whether tokenizations will also take on a portfolio approach going forward, one can, of course, simply create one's own portfolio of tokens to achieve the desired level of diversification.

In January 2020, the largest real estate project yet financed by a security token offering took place in Switzerland. Executed by blockchain company BrickMark, a building in the posh Bahnhofstrasse area of Zurich was financed with a token offering of up to 120 million euros (at the time about US$150 million) (figure 5.1). This deal exhibits many of the core qualities of an STO. First, because of the efficiencies afforded by the blockchain technology, tokenizations are often on single assets rather than portfolios. They are thus free from the complex, nonlinear payout relationships that make traditional ABSs risky. Included and transparent on this chain would be information on asset ownership, leases and payment-related details, revenue-sharing confirmation and transaction tracking, and digital wallet account verification. Furthermore, the offering can be made open to institutions and individuals alike, in investment sizes that

Figure 5.1
The largest real estate tokenization to date, raising 120 million euros.

can suit even the most modest investor.[6] Built on protocols compatible with the Ethereum platform, BrickMark has positioned this to be "the start of the development of a large international real estate portfolio." The BrickMark token is also smart contract enabled and will be able to handle repatriation, distribution, and other operations in an automated way.

While real estate STOs are unique from their ABS counterparts in important ways, there are also now a number of companies performing STOs on nontraditional investments, generating liquidity in asset classes that had previously been considered untradeable. For example, companies such as LiquidArtX and ArtPi Art Exchange (figure 5.2) have expanded their businesses from simply using blockchains to verify provenance and register artwork to generating security tokens linked to pieces of art, allowing investors to take fractional ownership in pieces sometimes worth $100 million or more. Through traditional means, the huge majority of investors would have little or no access to investments of this size. Furthermore,

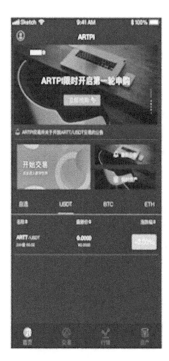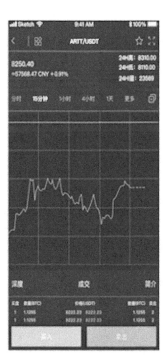

Figure 5.2
ArtPi Art Exchange (China) allows investors and collectors to trade art as if it were stock.

most investors have neither the personal knowledge nor access to expertise necessary to perform due diligence in this space. By connecting communities of experts through the blockchain and incentivizing them through tokens, these platforms provide both access to investments and the know-how needed to make investment decisions. Fraudulent behavior is all but eliminated through the rigorous artwork registration process, which requires validation through a multiparty consensus system. It is also important that living artists who register and trade their artwork through the platform are provided with tokens for each of their pieces, ensuring that they have an ownership stake even after the piece is sold. This allows the artist to continue to benefit from appreciation in their work while incentivizing them to participate in the validation process in the future.

Indeed, there is already innovation in the area of STOs of securities; that is, issuance of tokens whose value is connected to that of another security, most often unlisted stock. For example, Shares-Post (figure 5.3) is a California company whose main business is the transfer of ownership of private shares. In the United States, the number of listed firms is falling, and IPOs as a method of fundraising are waning in popularity as a result of the arduous process,

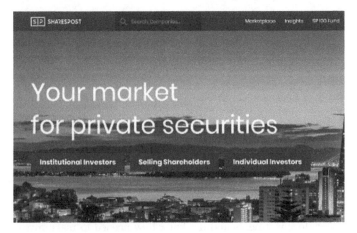

Figure 5.3
SharesPost is leading the way in the tokenization of nonlisted shares.

expense, and compliance required. Meanwhile, private funding has reached new highs, with more than 70 transactions of $100 million or more in 2017 alone. There are now nearly 400 billion-dollar "unicorn firms" (startup companies valued at over $1 billion) around the world that are unlisted, many of them in developing economies. More than 100 of these are in China, where listing rules are draconian and reform has been slow.[7] SharesPost is now introducing a new system that can provide automated liquidity for these private firms by generating security tokens written on a claim to these privately held shares. That is, the tokens derive their value from a pool of shares, most often pledged by founders, venture capitalists, and large shareholders seeking liquidity. The shares themselves cannot be easily traded, but the tokens directly linked to their value will be traded in a global settlement system they are calling GLASS (Global Liquidity and Settlement System). This system functions in full compliance with US SEC regulations and is considered an alternative trading system.

5.3 TOKENIZATION OF INFRASTRUCTURE

One area of particular importance in the application of tokenization is infrastructure finance.[8] Infrastructure projects are large, capital intensive, long-lived, and often not immediately profitable.[9] As a result, they almost always require a government subsidy or full funding and are not generally attractive to financial investors. The Taiwan High-Speed Rail, for example, was commissioned in 1997 as a benchmark case in public-private partnership. As with all infrastructure, it was long-lived (a 35-year *build-operate-transfer* (BOT) project) and capital intensive, necessitating a loan of about

US$10 billion. Beginning operation in 2007, it was clearly not a project most investment firms would have been interested in, having taken 10 years to build, compared to the 5–7-year horizons of most private equity funds. Cracking under the stress of operating shortfalls and huge debt-servicing requirements, the rail service entered default proceedings in 2008, after just one year of operation, with a 10-to-1 debt to equity ratio. Unfortunately, this example is not unique.

Infrastructure projects often generate far more value to the community than they generate in revenue for themselves. Highways, railways, and airports enable commerce, reducing logistics costs. Power plants and harbors enable business development and industrial clustering effects to bring together ecosystems of related players, to the betterment of all. Of course, there are also enormous social benefits in terms of connecting people and providing access to resources such as education and medical care. One should not be surprised to see the value of homes and businesses increase when a subway stop is added to a neighborhood or when a highway connects a village to a major metropolis. It is often our most vulnerable who require access to this core infrastructure.

The United Nations Sustainable Development Goals have outlined core areas of growth that are required for sustainable development. One of these is financial inclusion, which appears in at least seven of these goals. Tokenization provides a tool through which to achieve this inclusion while simultaneously engaging in its financing those who benefit most from infrastructure development. Tokenization allows us to take a large, capital-intensive project and split it into small pieces that are accessible to institutions and individuals alike.[10] Furthermore, by providing a channel for local constituencies from the ecosystem served by the infrastructure being built, we greatly improve the investor profile. What once would have been a heavily leveraged project driven by large financial investors interested in immediate returns is transformed into a community-financed project with investors who have a long-term view and whose personal benefits augment the returns generated by the project. Consequently, we can achieve financing that is more stable, less risky, of lower cost, and has higher stakeholder engagement.

One example is projects along China's Belt and Road Initiative (BRI). BRI spans from China, through Asia, the Middle East, and Africa, to the European Union. It connects nearly 65 percent of the world's population and engages about 40 percent of global GDP. Experts estimate it will involve US$2 trillion in infrastructure investment alone, more than any one institution or government can provide. Indeed, China's annual proportion spent on infrastructure domestically has steadily declined over the last 10 years, and there is little reason to believe it could finance the many needs of the BRI.

However, in one particular project along the Belt and Road Initiative, tokenization is playing a role. That project is a hydroelectric power plant. As a source of power, this green energy is a first-choice alternative, providing power at low marginal cost while taking advantage of the mountainous features of the country. However, as power projects go, hydro is particularly capital intensive and long-lived. Financial analysis shows that the project would return just over 4 percent, owing to the long construction period (at least five years) and large up-front cost (about 2 billion RMB). Given that foreign investment benchmarks for projects in developing countries are well in excess of 10 percent, depending on the industry, this is a project that would almost certainly not be built if it relied on financial investors. However, this project made use of the power of blockchain to simultaneously bring together core members of the community and provide opportunities for investment from those who would benefit the most from the power plant—users of electricity. That is, the commercial ecosystem that benefited from the power plant being built financed it.

Here, 1 billion RMB was raised in "ecosystem financing" in exchange for tokens worth 2 billion RMB in power going forward, providing both access to power and a hedge against growing energy costs consistent with economic growth. At a 50 percent discount, businesses, developers, and individuals were all incentivized to take part in the investment, which would clearly reconcile on their balance sheets. Assuming only 75 percent capacity, builders could also realize a 16.6 percent return on capital, as half the investment is covered by the ecosystem investment. Perhaps most importantly, a green energy project that might not otherwise have survived gets built, and the ecosystem surrounding the build is included both in the consumption of the energy and in the potential future returns of the project.

Projects like these (see figure 5.4) require the participation of government regulators (such as the power board), local businesses, competent builders and contractors, and the entire local ecosystem. However, the resulting inclusion and potential to self-finance provides long-term stability and sustainable growth that may not otherwise be attainable.[11]

Figure 5.4
Infrastructure projects can be ecosystem-financed using tokenization (not actual project pictured).

5.4 FINAL THOUGHTS

Tokenization is a natural step in the evolution of securitization enabled by blockchain technology that allows greater transparency, vastly improved transactional efficiency, and better risk management than ever before. It can provide liquidity to asset classes that had previously been untradeable and, as a result, can greatly improve financial participation and information efficiency in these markets.

Security token regulation can be seen as a natural extension of existing securities laws and policies and hence does not require us to "start from scratch." The technology is regulation-friendly and allows monitoring and risk management by regulatory authorities. In contrast, cryptocurrencies that are seeded in the spirit of full decentralization are without jurisdiction and hence lack the investor protections and monitoring necessary for mass-market growth and fraud prevention.

Applications abound, and while many of the early uses of security tokens are consistent with existing securitization practices, it is worth noting that security tokens are generally written on assets themselves and cash flows related to those assets, rather than debt obligations. Furthermore, they are being written on individual assets in fully transparent environments, so as to avoid the complexity and opaqueness that was at the root of the global financial crisis of 2008 and 2009.

Moving forward, we should expect to see ever more value-creating and creative applications of tokenization, including in assets that have heretofore been inaccessible or restricted to an exclusive set of investors. These might include natural resource investments, such as mining rights. Or perhaps movie rights and box office proceeds? How about an ownership stake in your favorite sports franchise? Through the power of blockchain and tokenization, virtually any asset can be domiciled and its cash flows or future appreciation divided in a fully automated, fully transparent and monitored, fully compliant, and virtually costless way.

NOTES

1. H. P. Minsky, "Securitization" (1987), Hyman P. Minsky Archive, https://digitalcommons.bard.edu/hm_archive/15.

2. C. Chang and X. Wang, "On Global Security Token Policies and China Policy Reform," Fudan Fanhai Fintech Research Center Working Paper Series FRC-WP20210001, 2019.

3. T. Brown, "China Bursts Bubble on Digital-Currency Speculation," Marketwatch, September 23, 2019, https://www.marketwatch.com/story/china -bursts-bubble-on-digital-currency-speculation-2019-09-23?from=timeline &isappinstalled=0.

4. L. R. Cohen, L. Samuelson, and H. Katz, "How Securitization Can Benefit from Blockchain Technology," *Journal of Structured Finance* 23, no. 2 (2017): 51–54; A. Collomb and K. Sok, "Blockchain/Distributed Ledger Technology (DLT): What Impact on the Financial Sector?," *Digiworld Economic Journal* 103 (2016): 93–111; Deloitte, JSTA, and Securitize, *Security Tokens: Improving Real Estate Investment in Japan* (Tokyo: JSTA, Deloitte Japan, and Securitize, 2019).

5. Y. Guo and C. Liang, "Blockchain Application and Outlook in the Banking Industry," *Financial Innovation* 2, no. 1 (2016): 24; J. H. Jiang, "How Much Does Trust Cost? Analysis of the Consensus Mechanism of Distributed Ledger Technology and Use-Cases in Securitization" (master's thesis, Massachusetts Institute of Technology, 2017), http://hdl .handle.net/1721.1/111454; S. Khaund, "Digital Securitization, Obfuscation, Policy and Commerce of Event Tickets," US Patent Application US20190188653A1 (2017), US Patent Office, https://patents.google.com /patent/US20190188653A1/en.

6. N. Kshetri and J. Voas, "Blockchain in Developing Countries," *IT Professional* 20, no. 2 (2018): 11–14; M. Odenbach, "Mortgage Securitization: What Are the Drivers and Constraints from an Originator's Perspective (Basel I/Basel II)?," *Housing Finance International* 17, no. 1 (2002): 52–58.

7. D. Palmer, "New Head of China's Digital Currency Says It Beats Facebook Libra on Tech Features," *CoinDesk*, September 6, 2019, https://www .coindesk.com/new-head-of-chinas-digital-currency-says-it-beats-facebook -libra-on-tech-features?from=timeline&isappinstalled=0; J. Roth, F. Schär,

and A. Schöpfer, "The Tokenization of Assets: Using Blockchains for Equity Crowdfunding," SSRN, August 27, 2019, https://doi.org/10.2139/ssrn.3443382.

8. Roth et al., "The Tokenization of Assets"; J. Smith, M. Vora, H. Benedetti, K. Yoshida, and Z. Vogel, "Tokenized Securities and Commercial Real Estate," SSRN, May 14, 2019, https://doi.org/10.2139/ssrn.3438286.

9. D. Uzsoki, *Tokenization of Infrastructure: A Blockchain-Based Solution to Financing Sustainable Infrastructure*, IISD report, January 17, 2019, https://www.iisd.org/publications/tokenization-infrastructure-blockchain-based-solution-financing-sustainable.

10. Uzsoki, *Tokenization of Infrastructure*.

11. B. Wu and T. Duan, "The Application of Blockchain Technology in Financial Markets" (paper presented at the Journal of Physics Conference Series); Q.-Y. Zhao, "Research on the Game of Securitization Based on Blockchain Technology" (paper presented at the 5th Annual International Conference on Management, Economics and Social Development (ICMESD 2019)).

II

RESILIENT SYSTEMS: MAKING SOCIETY WORK BETTER

THE TRADECOIN SYSTEM

Alexander Lipton, Thomas Hardjono,
and Alex Pentland

6.1 INTRODUCTION

Central to any economy is a medium of exchange and a store of value: money. We often think of money in the context of banks and finance, but some variation on the basic idea of money is critical to supply chains, service businesses, labor contracts, retirement planning, and more. Today, we mostly use fiat currencies issued by national governments, but there is also well-functioning "money" issued by cooperatives, national alliances, and mutual funds.

An example of a cooperative issuing "money" is the Swiss WIR, created in 1934 (during the Depression) by a cooperative of local businesses and landholders in order to spur local development, which is backed by local property and infrastructure. The International Monetary Fund's special drawing rights are backed by a basket of national currencies and issued to countries typically for national development purposes. Exchange-traded funds (ETFs) are digital certificates giving ownership rights to a basket of company stock shares or bonds.

Today, there is tremendous interest in the possibility of using cryptotechnologies and ETF-style assets to replace physical cash and national currencies. Although the notion of electronic cash (eCash) has been around for almost three decades (see, e.g., Chaum[1] and Chaum, Fiat, and Naor[2]), it was the emergence of the Bitcoin[3] system that provided the first working example of a payment system that operated based on a peer-to-peer network and could scale up operations in a decentralized fashion.

In this chapter, we outline an approach to building a consortium of sponsors, who contribute real assets; a narrow bank, handling financial transactions involving fiat currencies; and an administrator, who issues the corresponding digital token in exchange for fiat payments and makes fiat payments in exchange for digital tokens. In short, our idea is to apply distributed ledger technology to give a new lease on life to the old notion of a sound asset-backed currency and to use this currency as a transactional tool for a large pool of potential users, including small and medium-sized enterprises and individuals.

Most recently, we have seen Facebook back the Libra digital currency and the Chinese government back its own national digital currency, as well as a variety of banks beginning to use their own digital currencies in order to transfer money between partner banks. In this chapter, we will describe how to build a currency whose governance is transparent, and thus can be regulated, and encourages legitimate commerce but makes illegal activities difficult.

6.2   THE DIGITAL TRADECOIN (DTC)

In essence, we wish to replace physical cash with a supranational digital token, which is insulated from adverse actions by central banks and other parties because it is asset backed. We believe the DTC is ideally suited as a medium of exchange for groups of smaller nations or supranational organizations who wish to use it as a counterweight to large reserve currencies.

Supranational currencies have been known for two millennia. For instance, Roman, and later Byzantine and Iranian, gold coins were used along the entire Silk Road; Spanish and Austrian silver coins were a prevalent medium of exchange during the Age of Sail. Closer to our time, the British pound was used as the reserve currency for the British Empire and, to a lesser degree, the rest of the world; the US dollar and the pound were used as a reserve currency basket for the world economy in the twentieth century, to which the euro and the yen were added in the late twentieth century; and now the yuan might be used along a revived Silk Road.

Today, for the first time ever, there is the possibility of designing a digital currency that combines the best features of both physical cash and digital currencies, including finality of settlement, partial anonymity, and usability on the web. This currency is largely immune to policies of central banks that control the world's reserve currencies. Such a currency has enormous potential to improve the stability and competitiveness of trading and natural resource producing economies. In the DTC, we propose to develop a trade-oriented asset-backed digital currency aimed at facilitating international trade and making it as seamless as possible. This currency will be based on a proprietary framework combining the most recent advances in blockchain and distributed ledger technology, cryptography, and secure multiparty calculations, together with time-tested methods for preventing double spending. In view of the fact that our framework relies in part on our own research and in part on ideas readily available in the public domain, we do not anticipate specific issues related to intellectual property rights. Unlike Bitcoin, it will be fast, scalable, and environmentally friendly. It will also be transaction-friendly because of its low volatility versus fiat currencies, not to mention cryptocurrencies.

Over the past decade, potential advantages and disadvantages of distributed ledgers or blockchains have been discussed by numerous researchers. (see, e.g., Lipton[4] and references therein). While numerous potential applications of blockchains have been entertained in the literature—including title deeds, posttrade processing, trade finance, rehypothecation, and syndicated loans, to mention but a few, the main use of blockchains has so far been in the general area of payments, more specifically cryptocurrencies.

Worldwide interest in distributed ledgers was ignited by Bitcoin, which is a cryptocurrency protocol operating without a central authority. It was described first in the seminal white paper by S. Nakamoto.[5]

Since then, Bitcoin has inspired the creation of more than a thousand other cryptocurrencies, all with various degrees of novelty and utility (if any). One of the most promising is Ethereum, which is significantly more versatile than Bitcoin, not least because it supports so-called smart contracts.[6] Another interesting and popular cryptocurrency protocol is Ripple.[7] The Ripple system departs from the Nakamoto consensus approach. Because it does not rely on the thousands of anonymous (pseudonymous) mining nodes that form the peer-to-peer network underlying Bitcoin, it is not truly decentralized. Instead, the Ripple system uses a small set of nodes that act more like notaries, validating transactions at a higher throughput and much lower cost than Bitcoin. Unlike

Bitcoin, most entities in the system are known and not anonymous. By their very nature, all these currencies are native tokens residing on a blockchain. Their transition from one economic agent to the next is controlled by the set of rules that are inherent or "hardwired" in the blockchain setup and are needed to maintain the integrity of their blockchain as a whole. However, until now, attempts to build tokens backed by real-world assets—first and foremost, fiat currencies—have been unsuccessful. Yet, until this all-important problem is solved, it is virtually impossible to make cryptocurrencies part of the mainstream financial infrastructure, because otherwise the inherent volatility of cryptocurrencies will severely curtail their usability.

Although the potential application of distributed ledgers mentioned earlier, such as posttrade processing and trade finance, is particularly important, they are technical in nature and lack the revolutionary spirit. However, a distributed ledger can potentially play a truly transformative role and bring a dramatic departure from the past by making central bank digital currency (CBDC) and stable cryptocurrencies a reality.

Here, we propose a stable, asset-backed cryptocurrency, which we refer to as DTC. It can be viewed as a natural extension of a fiat-backed cryptocurrency called the utility settlement coin (USC) (see Lipton, Pentland, and Hardjono[8]). Setting aside operational aspects of gathering and managing collateral assets, we need to design a ledger associated with value transfers. Since, by design, Nakamoto's approach is neither scalable nor efficient, we need to use a different design. Our analysis indicates that combining blockchain with an earlier approach for issuing electronic cash (eCash), developed by Chaum,[9] seems to be promising. Recall that

Chaum introduced a blind signature procedure for converting bank deposits into anonymous cash. On the one hand, Chaum's protocol is much cheaper, faster, and more efficient than Bitcoin. It also offers an avenue toward true anonymity and unlinkability (as in paper cash), as compared to the weak pseudoanonymity of Bitcoin. If true anonymity is not desired, there are variations on the Chaum approach on offer; for instance, anonymity for the purchaser but not for the seller and so forth. However, on the other hand, the basic Chaum model and many of its variants rely on the integrity of the issuing bank. To alleviate this issue, we propose the use of blockchain technology itself to track the relevant transaction parameters, reducing the opportunity for parties to be dishonest. Payments between users are still direct, as in Chaum's proposal.

In the DTC, we propose a solution to the stable cryptocurrency problem, which boils down to assembling a pool of *assets*, contributed by *sponsors*; appointing an *administrator*, who will manage the pool; and digitizing the ownership rights on this pool. In addition, we build a special-purpose *narrow bank*, which facilitates activities of the administrator. By construction, neither the pool itself nor the supporting bank can fail because of market and liquidity risks. Their operations are streamlined as much as possible to limit operational risks. It is worth noting that operational risks are always present; this statement is true not only for the setup we are proposing but also for ordinary cash and bank deposits, not to mention cryptocurrencies, which are notorious for their operational risk exposure. The narrow bank receives fiat currency submitted by the users and passes it to the administrator and ultimately to sponsors, while the administrator issues digital tokens in return. These tokens will circulate within the group of users in a

fast and efficient manner by utilizing a distributed ledger mechanism, thus creating native tokens proportionally convertible into
the underlying assets at will. Their value is maintained in a relatively narrow band around the value of the underlying asset pool,
with the lower bound enforced by arbitrage and the upper bound
enforced by the administrator, assisted by sponsors.

The key insight of the chapter is that the properly designed
DTC can serve as an international reserve currency, remaining
stable in the long run and serving as a much-needed counterbalance to fiat currencies issued by individual nations, which can be
easily affected by their respective central banks.

The chapter is organized as follows. Background on asset-backed
currencies is discussed in section 6.3. The design of Bitcoin and
Ripple, including their similarities and differences, is outlined in
section 6.4. CBDC and the closely related USC, respectively, are discussed in section 6.5. DTC is discussed in section 6.6. Section 6.7
briefly discusses the Tradecoin system architecture, and section 6.8
explores the Chaumian eCash model using the assistance of ledgers. Section 6.9 looks at the notion of an environmentally friendly
DTC coins. Conclusions are drawn in section 6.10.

6.3   INTRODUCTION TO ASSET-BACKED CURRENCIES

The idea of anchoring the value of paper currency in baskets of
real assets is old (see, e.g., Haas et al.[10]). Gold and silver as well
as bimetallic standards have been used for centuries to achieve
this goal. Two approaches are common: a redeemable currency
backed by a basket of commodities or a tabular standard currency
indexed to a basket of commodities.

Lowe[11] was the first to explain how to use a tabular standard of value to control price inflation; a similar plan based on a basket of 50 commodities was developed by Scrope.[12] Jevons[13] pushed these ideas (much) further and proposed an indexation scheme based on a basket of 100 commodities, while Marshall[14] proposed a similar tabular standard.

Inspired by developments during the Great Depression, F. Graham[15] developed an automatic countercyclical policy based on 100 percent backing of bank deposits by commodities and goods, while B. Graham[16] proposed backing the US dollar with a basket of 60 percent commodities and 40 percent gold. Hayek[17] advocated establishing a universal basket of commodities, which every country would use to back its currency. At roughly the same time, Keynes[18] designed an international gold-linked multilateral transaction currency, which he called the bancor. Unfortunately, his ideas were discarded by the architects of the Bretton Woods system.

Since World War II, interest in commodity-based currencies has been lukewarm. Still, Kaldor[19] proposed a new commodity reserve currency, which he also called bancor. More recently, Zhou[20] proposed a new international reserve currency anchored to a stable commodity basket benchmark.

The choice of the actual asset basket backing DTC is not an easy one. It is dictated partly by the composition of the sponsors' pool and partly by what assets they actually possess and are willing to contribute. For instance, depending on their resources and abilities, sponsors can contribute oil, gold, base metals, and agricultural commodities. Given that storage of significant amounts of these resources is difficult and costly, it is natural to use collateral, which is in storage already, thus making stored commodities economically productive.

When discussing asset-backed currencies, it is necessary to mention the WIR, which is both an abbreviation of *Wirtschafts-ring* (economic circle) and the word *we* in German. This wordplay emphasizes WIR's dual role as an economic circle and a community. According to WIR's statutes, "Its purpose is to encourage participating members to put their buying power at each other's disposal and keep it circulating within their ranks, thereby providing members with additional sales volume." WIR issues a purely digital private currency. Participants can use WIR in combination with the Swiss franc as part of dual-currency transactions. Thus, we can view WIR as an analog precursor of the DTC.

WIR serves small and medium-sized enterprises as well as private individuals. It was founded in 1934 to address currency shortages and global financial instability, receiving a banking license in 1936. In the beginning, WIR's founders followed the theory of Silvio Gesell, which requires that money be free from interest; however, the WIR Bank eventually (and unsurprisingly) renounced Gesell's ideas in 1952 and introduced monetary interest. WIR gradually grew from its original 16 members in 1934 to more than 60,000 today. Total assets are approximately 5.3 billion Swiss francs (CHF), loans 4.5 billion CHF, and deposits of 3.9 billion CHF as of the end of 2016.

A particularly important fact about the WIR franc is that it is an electronic currency reflected in clients' trade accounts and not represented by paper money. Thus, the WIR bank maintains the entire ledger. The initial purpose of the currency was to increase sales, cash flow, and profits for qualified participants. Eventually, WIR created a credit system that issues credit in WIR francs, (over)collateralized by assets, which ensures that the currency is fully asset backed.

New WIR francs are created when a loan is issued, and they are destroyed when it is repaid, but a small amount of interest stays in the system forever and contributes to bank profits. A typical transaction between two members involves payment in both Swiss francs and WIR francs, thus reducing the amount of cash needed by the buyer but without the seller discounting the price of their product or service.

6.4   EXISTING CRYPTOCURRENCIES

In this section we briefly review the Bitcoin and Ripple systems for electronic currency.

6.4.1   Bitcoin

Since it was first announced in 2008, Bitcoin[21] has captured the imagination of the public by proposing the first cryptographic electronic currency having no intrinsic value, issued without central authority, and capable of peer-to-peer digital transfers. Anyone can join the Bitcoin ecosystem, which is both a strength and a weakness.

Because it's currently the best-known form of cryptocurrency, it's worth exploring how Bitcoin works. Financial transactions are made directly between users, without the help of designated intermediaries. Transactions are publicly broadcast and recorded in a "blockchain ledger," which can be seen by all participants.

Once a transaction is broadcast, the "miners" come into play. They aggregate individual transactions into blocks (currently of about 2,000 transactions each), verify them to ensure that there is no double spending by competitively providing *proof of work* (PoW), and receive mining rewards in bitcoins. The proof of work is based on finding a cryptographic random number (called a *nonce*) that makes the hash value of the candidate block of transactions lower than a given threshold. Therefore, the "hash power" (i.e., hardware and software processing capacity) of a node makes a difference in the likelihood that the node will find the match.

It is assumed (but not proven) that there are sufficiently many honest miners that collusion among them (known as a 51 percent attack) is not possible. A transaction is considered confirmed if there are at least six new blocks built on top of the block to which it belongs. The Bitcoin ecosystem is not without very serious issues—it can handle no more than 7 transactions per second (vs. Visa, which can handle more than 20,000 transactions per second), and it consumes enormous amounts of electricity used by miners (by virtue of the underlying PoW computation). Thus, the immutability of Bitcoin's blockchain ledger and the prevention of double spending are achieved through mining based on PoW.

In view of this, bitcoins themselves are just unspent transaction outputs of a long chain of transactions, which can be traced all the way back to the time when they were minted, either to the very first "genesis" block or as part of a "coinbase" transaction included in a block by a successful miner.

Since Bitcoin's inception in 2009, its price has gone up several orders of magnitude, making it the darling of speculators across the globe. However, a word of caution is in order. Since a bitcoin has no value, it can have any price; hence one should not be surprised if its price falls dramatically. Other than for speculative purposes, a bitcoin's uses are rather limited, because its price versus the US dollar and other fiat currencies is extremely volatile, which prevents it from becoming a medium of transaction. In addition, in spite of claims to the contrary, Bitcoin transaction costs are very high and growing.

Although Bitcoin may not be the disruptive force its supporters are claiming, the distributed ledger technology underpinning it has clear potential to transform the financial ecosystem as a whole.

6.4.2 Ripple

Ripple is a money transfer protocol; ripple is the underlying native currency. It is completely different from Bitcoin. For starters, ripples are preminted, while bitcoins are mined. In fact, Ripple is not decentralized at all. The stated purpose of the protocol is to facilitate fiat currency transfers among participating banks. However, because there is a native token, Ripple can be used along the lines of Bitcoin as well. Details of how Ripple works are given in various Ripple promotional materials, including its white paper.[22]

The main ingredients of the Ripple ecosystem are servers, which maintain the ledger; clients, who can initiate transactions; proposers, which can be any server; and the unique nodes list (UNL), indicating parties that can be trusted by the participants in the protocol.

The life cycle of a single transaction consists of several steps. First, a transaction is created and signed by an account owner. Second, this transaction is submitted to the network. If it is badly formed, this transaction may be rejected immediately; otherwise, it is provisionally included in the ledger. Validating nodes propose new ledger updates. Transmitting nodes broadcast the ledger updates to the network. Consensus is achieved by voting of the validators. The result of a successful consensus round is a validated ledger. If a consensus round fails, the consensus process repeats until it succeeds. The validated ledger includes the transaction and its effects on the ledger state.

Ripple's consensus assumptions are that every nonfaulty server makes decisions in finite time; that all nonfaulty servers arrive at the same decision; and that *both* true and false decisions regarding a given transaction are possible.

The Ripple protocol consensus algorithm (RPCA) works in rounds. Initially, every server compiles a list of valid candidate transactions. Then, each server amalgamates all candidates coming from its UNL and votes on their veracity. Next, transactions passing the minimum threshold are passed to the next round. The final round requires 80 percent agreement. In general, RPCA works well; however, it can fail when validating nodes form cliques, which cannot agree with each other.

6.5 CBDC AND USC

In this section we discuss the possibility of central banks issuing digital currencies, in the form of a CBDC or USC.

6.5.1 CBDC

Could and should central banks issue central bank digital currency? Recently, a previously academic question of the feasibility and desirability of CBDC came to the fore (see, e.g., Ali et al.[23] and Scorer[24]). By issuing CBDC, states can abandon physical cash in favor of its electronic equivalent and replace a large chunk of government debt with it. The impact on society at large will be huge.[25] CBDC can obviate the need for fractional banking and dramatically improve the stability of the financial system as a whole. On the other hand, the ability of the banking sector to create money "out of thin air" by making loans will be significantly curtailed and transferred to central banks. It is clear that developments in this direction are inevitable, but their timing and magnitude are uncertain.

Interest in CBDC has been ignited by two unrelated factors—the introduction of Bitcoin and the persistence of negative interest rates in some developed countries. In Medieval Europe, negative interest existed in the form of demurrage for centuries. Recall that demurrage is a tax on monetary wealth. In principle, demurrage encourages spending money rather than hoarding it, thus accelerating economic activity. The idea of demurrage was reborn shortly after World War I, in the form of scrip money, which requires payment of periodic tax in order for it to stay in circulation. Scrip money was proposed by German-Argentinian entrepreneur and economist Silvio Gesell,[26] whose idea was restated by Irving Fisher during the Great Depression.[27] Demurrage was thought to be a suitable replacement for mild inflation. Since in the modern economy demurrage is hard to orchestrate because of the presence of paper currency, its conversion into the electronic form is necessary for making seriously negative rates a reality.[28]

Currently, there are three approaches to creating CBDC on a large scale:

- Economic agents, from enterprises to private individuals, can be given accounts with central banks. However, in this case, central banks would have to execute know your customer (KYC) and anti-money-laundering (AML) functions, tasks that they are not equipped to perform. Besides, under duress, rational economic agents might abandon their commercial bank accounts and move their funds to central bank accounts, thus massively destabilizing the entire financial system.

- Inspired by Bitcoin,[29] CBDC can be issued as a token on an unpermissioned distributed ledger, whose integrity is maintained by designated notaries receiving payments for their services (see, e.g., Danezis and Meiklejohn[30]). Given that notary efforts do not require mining and hence are significantly cheaper and faster than those of Bitcoin miners, this construct is scalable and can satisfy needs of the whole economy. Users are pseudonymous since they are represented by their public keys. Since at any moment there is an immutable record showing the balance of every public key, it is possible to deanonymize transactions by using various inversion techniques applied to their recorded transactions,[31] thus maintaining AML requirements.

- A central bank can follow the Chaumian scheme[32] and issue numbered and blind signed currency units onto a distributed ledger, whose trust is maintained either by designated notaries or by the bank itself. In this case, it would have to rely on commercial banks, directly or indirectly, for satisfying the KYC/AML requirements.

To summarize, by using modern technology, it is possible to abolish paper currency and introduce CBDC. On the positive side, CBDC can be used to alleviate some of the societal ills and eliminate costs of handling physical cash, which are of the order of 1 percent of a country's GDP. It can help the unbanked participate in the digital economy, thus positively affecting society at large. On the negative side, it can give central authorities too much power over the economy and privacy, which can potentially be misused.

While CBDC is absolutely stable with respect to the underlying fiat currency, it does not make the fiat currency stable in itself. For that, we need a carefully constructed DTC.

6.5.2   USC

CBDC is technically possible but politically complicated. Hence, several alternatives have been proposed. One promising venue is USC, which was developed by a consortium of banks and a financial technology start-up called Clearmatics.[33] Initially, USC can be an internal token for a consortium of participating banks. These coins have to be fully collateralized by electronic cash balances of these banks, which are held by the central bank itself. Eventually, these coins can be circulated among a larger group of participants. However, in this case, issuance of USCs has to be outsourced to a narrow bank, which can perform the all-important KYC and AML functions.

Recall that a narrow bank has assets, which include solely marketable low-risk securities and central bank cash in an amount exceeding its deposit base per the regulatory prescribed capital cushion (see, e.g., Pennacchi[34] among many others). As a result, such a bank is impervious to credit and liquidity shocks. However, like any other firm, it can be affected by operational failures, including fraud, computer hacking, inability to solve the KYC/AML problem, and others. These failures can be minimized, but not eliminated, by using proper modern technology. Accordingly, narrow bank deposits would be as close to the fiat currency as technically possible.[35] Ideally, one narrow bank per fiat currency is required. Further details are given in Lipton, Pentland, and Hardjono.[36]

USC is helpful from a technical perspective, but it does not solve issues of monetary policy. We wish to address this issue by building a counterweight for fiat currencies by backing the DTC with a pool of real assets.

6.5.3 Survivability of CBDC and USC

The idea that a blockchain system can withstand a concerted attack simply because it consists of physically distributed nodes is an untested and unproven proposition. The possible types of attacks to a blockchain system have been discussed elsewhere and consist of a broad spectrum. These range from classic network-level attacks (e.g., network partitions, distributed denial of service) to more sophisticated attacks targeting the particular blockchain-specific constructs (e.g., consensus implementations) or targeting specific implementations of mining nodes or notaries (e.g., code vulnerabilities, viruses). An attack on a blockchain system may not need to cripple it entirely, as degradation in its overall service quality (e.g., slower transaction throughput) may be sufficient to disincline users to use the system.

The notion of *interoperability* across blockchain systems is an important one in the light of survivability.[37] The internet was able to expand and allowed *autonomous systems* (i.e., routing domains) to interconnect with one another because of good design principles. The design philosophy of the internet is based on three fundamental goals: (1) network survivability (internet communications must continue despite loss of networks or gateways); (2) variety of service types (the internet must support multiple types of communication services); and (3) variety of networks (the internet must accommodate a variety of networks). We believe the same fundamental goals must be adopted for the current development of blockchain technology—and more specifically they must drive the technological selection for the implementations of the DTC architecture.

6.6 DTC MOTIVATIONS AND REQUIREMENTS

There are several issues, technical and economical, with regards to DTC and ledger-based implementations. We discuss these in the following section.

6.6.1 DTC Motivations

Bitcoin and Ripple protocols can be used as a prototype for a cryptocurrency based on a distributed ledger that is more suitable for financial transactions. Several issues, some technical and some economic, have to be addressed before this goal can be achieved:

- The KYC problem has to be formulated and articulated, and a suitable framework for solving it has to be designed
- An AML mechanism has to be developed
- A highly efficient method for maintaining consensus on the ledger, with industrial-strength transactions per second (TpS) capabilities, has to be built
- A transparent and economically meaningful system for issuing new DTCs and retiring the existing ones has to be implemented
- Most importantly, a satisfactory mechanism for making DTC a stable cryptocurrency has to be designed

Although public ledgers are not truly anonymous but rather are pseudonymous, it is difficult to use them in the KYC/AML compliant fashion. Accordingly, the DTC ledger has to be made semiprivate (but probably not private) in order to solve the KYC/AML problem. At the same time, the right balance has to be struck between privacy and accountability so excessive restrictions do not impede the flow of legitimate commerce.

In order to achieve the level of speed and efficiency we desire, including a TpS on the order of several thousand, the Ripple-style consensus protocol has to be used. Following Ripple's approach, we choose a group of notaries who are known in advance and properly licensed. These notaries are responsible for updating the ledger and maintaining its integrity by ensuring Byzantine fault tolerance (see, e.g., Lamport, Shostak, and Pease[38] and Castro and Liskov[39]). For their services, notaries are paid a small fee, say a percentage of the transaction amount they approve, which is naturally denominated in DTC so that their commercial interest is aligned with their function. If notaries stay inactive or systematically approve invalid transactions, they are penalized financially. In each round, validators create their own versions of the ledger and propose them to the rest of the group. Several rounds of voting take place until a supermajority candidate ledger is selected. This approach is similar in spirit to the well-known Paxos algorithm. In order to increase the TpS number, we use the idea of sharding and assign individual notaries to particular sets of addresses. In this setup, a quorum verifies its own shard, while the full ledger is assembled out of the corresponding shards.

The DTC architecture recognizes that there are two or three types of application-level transactions commonly found in many blockchain implementations. The first is the one-party recording of assets to the ledger. Logically, the DTC represents this on an *assets ledger*. The second type is the two-party transfer transaction, exemplified by the transfer of coins from one party to another. The DTC captures these logically on the *coins ledger*. The third type of transaction is the off-chain transfer of value (i.e., eCash) in a privacy-preserving manner. Here the goal is to allow a limited amount of coin-backed anonymous eCash to be transferred from one user to another, following the classic Chaum approach. Relevant parameters of the eCash flow are recorded on the DTC *tracking ledger* in order to reduce the opportunity of fraud by entities involved in the eCash flows.

This design decision of recognizing the three types of application-level transactions provides the broadest flexibility for the DTC architecture to be tailored for specific use cases and for different implementations of the three ledgers to be chosen according to the requirements of the use case.

6.6.2 Creation and Annihilation of DTC

For now, we consider this pool and its associated narrow bank as given and describe the creation and annihilation mechanisms for the DTC. New coins are injected into the distributed ledger by virtue of the following mechanism. During the initial stage, participants who wish to acquire a freshly minted DTC have to proceed as follows. First, they must have a conventional fiat account, which can be held either directly with the narrow bank or with their commercial bank. Second, they have to open an initially empty wallet ready to accept DTCs. Third, participants transfer the desired amount of fiat currency to the narrow bank. Fourth, the narrow bank transfers these funds to sponsors, who in turn release some of the DTCs created when the asset pool is built to the pool administrator. Fifth, the administrator transfers the corresponding DTCs from its public-key address to the public-key address provided by the participant. Thus, in effect, the participant becomes a shareholder in the pool administrator. Subsequently, participants can acquire DTCs from other participants in exchange for goods and services, so a newborn DTC starts its journey from one address represented by a public key to the next, until it is annihilated by a participant sending it to the administrator in exchange for cash. When a participant in the ledger wishes to receive fiat currency for their DTC, they transfer DTCs from their public key to the public key of the administrator, who in turn sells an appropriate proportion of the assets and deposits proceeds with the associated narrow bank, which in turn credits fiat currency either to the account on its own ledger or to a designated account in a different bank. The corresponding DTCs are destroyed by sending them to the "terminal" public key without a private key.

As a result, the administrator is in possession of real assets, sponsors receive fiat currency, and the general public receives DTCs, which can always be converted into fiat at the current market price.

6.6.3   Mechanisms of Stabilization of DTC

Finally, the value of the DTC is kept relatively stable by virtue of the independent actions of participants and the administrator. If the value of a DTC goes below the value of the fraction of the asset pool it represents, which we call its intrinsic value, then rational economic agents will turn it back to the administrator in exchange for cash. If, on the other hand, the market value starts to deviate upward compared to the intrinsic value, then, after a certain threshold is breached, the sponsors will contribute more assets to the pool, which can come from their own sources or be purchased on the open market, in exchange for DTCs, which they will sell on the open market, thus pushing the market price of DTCs down. These two complementary mechanisms can keep the market price of the DTC in a bank around the market price of the underlying basket.

More precisely, the price P_{DTC} of DTC will be close to (but not exactly at) the market price of the corresponding asset pool, P_M. Indeed, if P_{DTC} falls significantly below P_M, economic agents will give DTC back to the administrator, who will have to sell a fraction of the pool's assets for cash and pass the proceeds to these agents. If P_{DTC} increases significantly above P_M, sponsors will supply more assets to the administrator, who will issue additional DTC and pass it to sponsors, who will sell it for cash, just pushing the price down. This mechanism ensures that $|P_{DTC} - P_M|/P_M << 1$, a very desirable feature, especially compared to conventional cryptocurrencies, which habitually exhibit extreme volatility. At the same time, outright manipulation by central banks is not possible either. Note that the notion of economic agents (e.g., sponsors with assets) is distinct from system entities (e.g., notaries) in the DTC architecture.

6.7 ARCHITECTURE AND DESIGN PRINCIPLES

In order for DTC to be a stable and durable digital currency that can store value as well as provide utility, there are a number of principles driving its architecture. The DTC architecture seeks to be a "blueprint" that allows the DTC to be implementable for various use cases. Some use cases that have been identified are as a reserve digital currency shared by a number of geopolitically diverse small countries as a means of providing local financial stability and as a digital currency operating for a narrow bank that can provide relative stability during financially volatile periods. A number of system design principles are as follows:

- *Unambiguous identifiability and ownership of properties*   Assets (represented digitally), coins, and eCash must be uniquely identifiable and have unambiguous ownership at any given time. A corollary of true ownership is that these must be transferable (portable) by their owner.
- *Identifiability of entities and devices*   All entities (e.g., sponsors) must be uniquely identifiable using identifiers that are legally recognized (e.g., legal entity identifier[40]). Similarly, all devices interacting on the blockchain must be uniquely identifiable, and each device must have an owner. Additionally, the users and devices must be authenticable.

Anonymity of node devices may lead to concentrations of hash power.[41] In some permissionless blockchain networks, any entity can take the role of a mining node and be identified on the blockchain solely by their public key (i.e., "address"). Although this anonymity may be considered a virtue in some blockchain networks (e.g., Bitcoin[42]), there may be some disadvantages to this approach. One disadvantage is the potential for the amassing (centralization) of hashing power by a handful of anonymous nodes or entities, which goes against the proposition of decentralization of the blockchain paradigm. Such entities could conceivably use this concentration of hash power to skew or manipulate the network over time.

- *Visibility into shared state*   Entities in the ecosystem should have visibility into the state of the DTC system and network and have equal access to such information. More specifically, this means visibility into the assets that back the issuance of coins and visibility into the circulation of coins and eCash.

• *Mechanisms implementing monetary policies*   In order for the DTC ecosystem to operate according to the desired community behavior, there must be technical mechanisms that allow agreed policies to be carried out in the system as a whole. Such mechanisms can be controlled centrally (e.g., by a single entity), controlled in a group-oriented manner (e.g., by consensus of entities), or a combination of both (e.g., by leader election protocols).

• *Correct, accurate, and unhindered systemwide reporting*   Each system component that implements DTC must be unhindered in the reporting of its internal state. Furthermore, there must be ways to validate the reported state so misbehavior can be detected and acted on. Such misbehavior can be the result of human or system error, degradation in system components over time (hardware and software), or active or passive compromises (i.e., attacks).

• *Well-defined operations (limited programmability)*   One of the key factors in the success of the Bitcoin[43] system is the very limited number of available operations (op-codes). These operations are geared toward a very specific application of the blockchain: electronic peer-to-peer payments. This is in contrast to the Ethereum system,[44] which was touted to be a highly programmable platform for distributed applications. However, the high degree of programmability may be a double-edged sword in the sense that human error and malicious code can be deployed on the platform and harm other users or applications (e.g., DAO Hack[45]).

These system design principles borrow from a number of key design principles underlying the internet.[46] The need for unambiguous ownership of an asset is an obvious one. The DTC seeks to use standard object identification solutions (e.g., the globally unique identifier (GUID) standard) for digital assets. The legal ownership of assets is a construct that is external to the DTC system and as such must be established prior to assets being introduced by their legal owner (e.g., sponsor) into a given DTC deployment.

The principle of visibility is driven by the need for entities in a DTC implementation to have equal access to data, and it is implemented through the assets ledger and coins ledger. The consortium administration must have full visibility into all operational aspects of a given DTC implementation. Certain DTC implementations may restrict visibility of parts of the systems (e.g., assets ledger) to entities that have "skin in the game" (e.g., sponsors who have actual assets on the DTC assets ledger).

A key aspect of the success of a DTC implementation is the ability of the consortium to carry out monetary policies and other governance rules in the system as a whole. Technical mechanisms can be implemented as "hooks" or control points through which policy decisions are executed. For example, a DTC implementation may require that each sponsor have assets (in the assets ledger) above a given threshold (i.e., reserve ratio) at all times. The actual value of the threshold should be dynamically adjustable according to the consortium-agreed policies and be carried out by the consortium administration as the appointed authority. In this case, the consortium administration can transmit a special "policy implementation" transaction (to the assets ledger and coins ledger) setting the new threshold value. Notaries observe such policy decisions by declining an asset-to-coin conversion transaction from a sponsor if it causes the sponsor's asset reserves to dip below the new threshold value.

Key to the operation of a DTC implementation is the ability of entities to identify and authenticate each other. We believe this is closely related to the principle of systemwide reporting. Some DTC implementations may choose to deploy advanced crypto-graphic techniques that provide anonymity and untraceability of entities. However, such features must still satisfy the principle of unambiguous identifiability and mutual authentication.

6.7.1 Sponsors, Consortium, and Users

There are a number of active (human-driven) entities in the DTC ecosystem (figure 6.1):

- *Sponsor* A sponsor is an entity who supplies assets to the DTC ecosystem in return for coins. The community of sponsors forms a consortium tasked with the various management aspects of coins and eCash in the ecosystem.
- *Consortium* A community of sponsors forms a consortium operating under an agreed governance model that specifies the

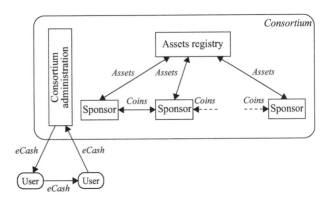

Figure 6.1
Tradecoin entities.

legal, business, and technical operational rules of members of the consortium. In essence, the consortium is a network of sponsors who are participating in the DTC ecosystem.

Additionally, a *consortium administration* carries out the monetary policies of the membership of the consortium. The consortium administration is legally empowered by the consortium membership to implement (centralized) control over certain system functions.

▪ *Users* A user is an entity that obtains eCash from the consortium for the purpose of making payments for goods and services from other users.

6.7.2 Logical Functions

The DTC architecture logically separates functions into those pertaining to assets, coins, and eCash (figure 6.2). Here, to allow us to focus on logical functions that meet the system design principles stated earlier, we use the term *ledger* generically without calling out specific realizations.

Specific technical implementations of the ledger may include a distributed database system, a peer-to-peer network of nodes, a fully distributed blockchain system, or even an append-only single database system.

▪ *Assets management* Visibility into the assets that sponsors contribute in exchange for coins represents a foundational requirement in DTC. DTC employs an *assets registry* and an *assets ledger*. The registry records verified real-world assets associated with a sponsor, who forwards that asset to the consortium.

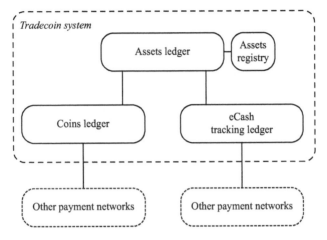

Figure 6.2
The assets ledger, coins ledger, and eCash tracking ledger.

The assets ledger captures the binding between real-world assets (put forward by a sponsor) and the amount of coins equivalent to (proportional to) those assets. The assets ledger also records the proportion of coins that are in the consortium's reserves and those that are in a sponsor's reserve. These coin equivalents are considered noncirculation.

- *Coin circulation* Allowing sponsors to exchange (i.e., sell or lend) their asset-backed coins with each other represents a cornerstone of DTC. The *coins ledger* records the coin movements and transactions in the DTC ecosystem (figure 6.4). The coins ledger is used by sponsors and the consortium administration. Sponsors exchange or "trade" coins with each other on this ledger.

- *eCash circulation* Providing stable digital currency to users also represents a cornerstone of DTC. The eCash *tracking ledger* records the movement of eCash (i.e., cryptographic keys and parameters) between users.

Each of the three ledgers in DTC are independent but are connected in the sense that a transaction in one ledger may refer to (point to) recorded transactions in other ledgers. This independence of ledgers is important not only from the perspective of technological choice (i.e., adoption of new ledger technologies) but also crucial to the operational resilience of the system as a whole.

An example of the connection of the ledgers is the "pushing" (or pulling) of coins into (or out of) circulation by a sponsor following the policies of a given DTC implementation. When a sponsor seeks to have its assets (on the assets ledger) converted to coins and for the resulting coins to be accessible by the sponsor on the coins ledger, the sponsor must transmit a push transaction. This results in a transaction occurring on the assets ledger and a corresponding transaction occurring on the coins ledger. These two transactions—albeit on different ledgers—are related in that one refers to (i.e., carries a hash of) another. In the push case, the transaction on the coins ledger points to a completed transaction on the assets ledger.

6.7.3   Converting Assets to Coins

The purpose of the assets ledger together with the assets registry is to satisfy the design principles with regard to the conversion of real-world assets into their coin equivalent (see figure 6.3).

A key requirement here is the validation of the legal ownership of assets as claimed by a given sponsor. The sponsor must provide legal evidence in such a way that a digital representation of the evidence can be captured and presented within the assets ledger.

Examples of such evidence include a paper certificate and its digital representation that has been digitally signed by the issuer using legally acceptable digital-signature technology (e.g., the Digital Signature Act of 2000). For example, a digital version of a gold certificate (e.g., unallocated gold) could be signed by an authority and presented by a sponsor as evidence. It is the responsibility of the consortium administration to validate the evidence.

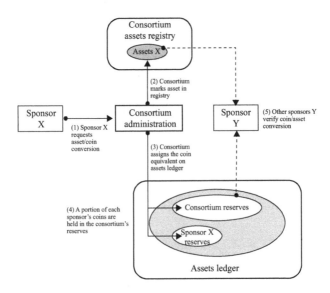

Figure 6.3
Converting assets to coins.

6.7.4 Pushing and Pulling Coins

The medium for sponsors to exchange coins with each other is the *coins ledger*. The notion here is that coins are bought, lent, and returned among sponsors on the ledger, providing transparency and visibility into the trading behavior of all sponsors in the DTC network.

Prior to having access to coins on this ledger, a sponsor must explicitly request that the consortium "push" the sponsor's coins from the assets ledger (from the sponsor's reserves) into circulation on the coins ledger (see figure 6.4). The consortium administration

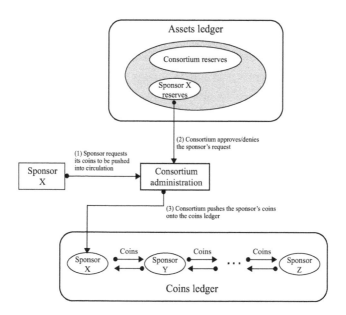

Figure 6.4

"Pushing" coins into circulation.

must respond to this request in an explicit manner (request granted, denied, or postponed) on the assets ledger. A request that is granted is followed by the consortium administration transferring coins from its account on the coins ledger to the sponsor's account on the same ledger.

This explicit request-response paradigm is a manifestation of the mechanism to implement monetary policies. It is a "hook" into the system in which the consortium administration—as the representative of the community of sponsors—enforces policies agreed to by the community. A simple example of a monetary policy decision is the *reserve ratio* that must be met by each sponsor on the assets ledger. A sponsor that exhausts its reserves on the assets ledger, thereby violating the policy of sponsors maintaining a minimum reserve, should not be granted a request to push further coins into circulation onto the coins ledger.

A symmetric operation to pushing coins to the coins ledger is that of "pulling" coins from circulation (see figure 6.5). This may occur when a sponsor wishes to enlarge its reserves on the assets ledger by moving coins from the coins ledger to the assets ledger.

6.8   LEDGER-ASSISTED ELECTRONIC CASH

We believe that there are scenarios for Chaumian electronic cash (eCash)[47] in the context of day-to-day consumer usage. In this section, we explore how eCash schemes could be integrated into the DTC model. In general, a *user* (i.e., consumer) is distinguished from a sponsor in that a user does not possess assets in the consortium. The user obtains eCash in exchange for fiat currencies that are acceptable by the consortium. The goal of the user is

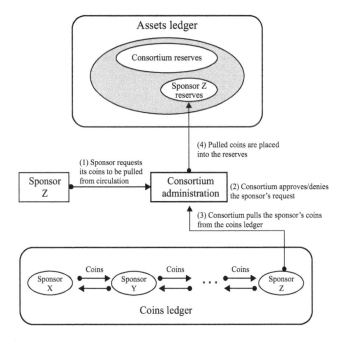

Figure 6.5
"Pulling" coins from circulation.

to utilize a convenient and low-cost (zero-cost) eCash payment method that is stable on a day-to-day basis and can store value over a reasonably long period.

In DTC, the entity that issues and redeems is the consortium itself. This ensures that the stability of eCash is directly related to the stability of coins and assets in the consortium, all three of which are under the monetary control of the consortium as a community. As the issuer of eCash to a user, the consortium enacts monetary policies that govern how much eCash a user can request specifically at any one time. More generally, the consortium can govern how much eCash is permitted to be in circulation at any given moment as a function of the total assets at the consortium.

6.8.1 Background: Key Features of eCash

The notion of *electronic cash* (e-cash) was first put forward in the landmark work by Chaum.[48] One key goal of the original e-cash proposal was that of preserving (as far as possible) the privacy features of paper cash; that is, to prevent third parties from discovering the identity of the payer and payee, the amount, and the time of payment. Therefore, many eCash schemes use cryptographic constructs (e.g., blind signatures, zero-knowledge proofs) that hide an entity's true identity. Another important goal was to prevent collusion of entities from defeating the scheme as a whole. An example would be collusion between the issuer (e.g., bank) and payee (e.g., merchant) that harms the payer. Similarly, a colluding payer and payee must not be able to cheat an honest bank.

In general, e-cash schemes seek to possess the technical features of *blindness* on the part of the bank, which prevents it from seeing what the payer is spending; *unlinkability*, which prevents the bank from correlating e-cash units belonging to the same payer; and *unforgeability*, which prevents payers and payees from creating fake e-cash.[49] Other desirable features include *exculpability* of honest entities (i.e., defend them from being framed by dishonest entities).

The basic flows of currency units in eCash systems are typically three-party. A person, Alice (payer), withdraws eCash from her account at the bank (sponsor) and delivers the eCash *directly* to a merchant, Bob (payee). The merchant must then present the eCash to the same bank in order to get his account credited with the amount. It's worth noting here that the transferal of the e-cash units from Alice to Bob is a direct one, without the mediation of a ledger or third parties.

Aside from the cryptographic complexity of many proposed e-cash schemes, there are a number of practical factors that have prevented their wide adoption over the past two decades. These include:

- *Reliance on a centralized entity* In many e-cash schemes, the bank plays the dual role of the issuing authority and the redeeming (clearing) authority for e-cash. Therefore, for daily use, such e-cash schemes offer little benefit over traditional credit cards.
- *Unmediated peer transferability* Many e-cash schemes suffer from inefficiencies with regard to the multihop transferability (portability) of e-cash units (e.g., Alice to Bob to Charlie) without the mediation of the bank.

The need for the bank entity to be online all the time has often been cited as a stumbling block. However, in the current age of internet connectivity, this may no longer be a factor.

The GNU *Taler* system[50] is one of the more recent practical iterations of Chaum's electronic cash proposal. The Taler system is notable because it provides anonymity only to the payer entity. The payee is assumed to be a merchant and thus for taxation purposes its identity must be disclosed upon redeeming the eCash to the bank.

6.8.2 eCash Support: Motivations and Goals

The following summarizes the high-level goals of the ledger-assisted eCash:

- *Support off-ledger direct payment mechanisms using eCash*
  Provide users to perform payments of eCash without an adverse impact on the Tradecoin ecosystem.
- *Retain visibility into the circulation of eCash in a privacy-preserving way*
  Retain visibility into the circulation of eCash backed by coins while preserving the privacy of the user.
  The relevant entities are prevented from colluding to defraud or damage the Tradecoin ecosystem.
- *Reduce the risk from possible collusion in eCash*
  Provide the necessary mechanisms to prevent collusion by entities in the eCash flow that adversely impact the Tradecoin ecosystem.

6.8.3 Constraints and Assumptions

We impose a number of design constraints on the use of eCash in the Tradecoin ecosystem. These are summarized as follows:

- *Consortium as the issuer of eCash*   In Tradecoin, the consortium (administration) is the issuer (source) of all eCash. That is, the consortium plays the role of the bank in the classic Chaum model.
- *Limited three-party flow*   The eCash flow follows the classic Chaum three-party flows. This consists of the consortium (as issuing bank); the payer (Alice), who withdraws eCash; and the payee (merchant), who receives payment from the payer. The loop is closed when the merchant deposits the eCash back to the consortium.

- *Limited amounts of eCash withdrawals* Users are permitted to obtain only limited amounts of eCash from the consortium. The amount and rate are subject to monetary policies. As such, this approach provides an early detection mechanism for users who are hoarding large amounts of Tradecoin eCash outside their accounts at the consortium. We believe this limitation is a reasonable constraint that reflects the current paper cash withdrawal limitations imposed in the US banking industry.

- *User anonymity to the merchant only* In the Tradecoin usage of eCash, the user is anonymous only to the merchant. The consortium knows the identities of the user and the merchant.

- *User identification at eCash withdrawal* A user that seeks to withdraw eCash from the account at the consortium must be strongly authenticated by the consortium. This constraint is also reasonable and reflects the current industry practice where a person needs to authenticate themselves at the teller/counter or at the ATM machine before withdrawing paper cash.

- *Merchant nonanonymity* Another constraint in Tradecoin is the nonanonymity of the merchant (payee). That is, the merchant entity is known and identified by the user and by the consortium. This is in line with the recent GNU Taler project.[51]

- *Nontransferability across peer users* Currently, Tradecoin precludes the notion of peer transferability (i.e., multihop transfers) between users. Thus, the payee (merchant) is not able to forward the eCash to other entities without mediation. The merchant has only one option, which is to deposit the eCash to its account at the consortium.

- *Size of eCash circulation subject to monetary policy* An overall constraint is that the total value of eCash in circulation at any given time is subject to the Tradecoin community's monetary policy.

6.8.4 The Tracking Ledger

The tracking ledger (figure 6.6) is an *append-only distributed log* mechanism. That is, the tracking ledger is read-and-append (read/write) accessible to the consortium and to parties involved in the eCash-related flows (consortium, payer, and payee). It is read-accessible (read-only) for all parties in the Tradecoin ecosystem.

When the consortium issues eCash to a payer or redeems it from a payee, it makes use of the tracking ledger to "declare" these actions. In essence, even though the identity of the user obtaining eCash is anonymized from the rest of the world, the consortium is making an assertion on the tracking ledger that it has issued some eCash units that correspond to a given set of coins.

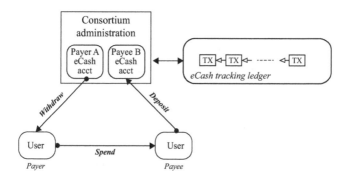

Figure 6.6

Overview of the Tradecoin eCash tracking ledger.

This act of the consortium declaring eCash issuance on the tracking ledger allows the sponsors to have visibility into the size of the eCash units being issued at any given time. It also allows the payer and payee to verify that the consortium has behaved honestly (i.e., has issued the correct number of eCash units to the payer).

6.8.5 The eCash Ledger Identities

In order to preserve the true identity of the payer, it is important that the payer not employ its ledger identity when sending payments to the payee (merchant) and that at spend flow the payer not link to transactions recorded on the ledger that may disclose its identity to the payee.

6.8.6 What Is Recorded on the Tracking Ledger

One purpose of the tracking ledger, among others, is to record the actions taken by entities (consortium, payer, and payee) in such a way that there is a mechanism for the consortium as a whole to observe the flow of eCash in the Tradecoin ecosystem. Since some of the parameters in an eCash system are confidential (e.g., blinded parameters) and are typically exchanged between parties pairwise over a secure channel (e.g., SSL or HTTP/S connection), the tracking ledger relies on the honesty of each entity to record a hash of the relevant parameters to the tracking ledger.

The generic eCash protocol flows that are most representative of the variants of the Chaum schemes consist of three groups: the *withdraw, spend,* and *deposit* protocols. The evidence to be recorded on the tracking ledger pertains to pairwise interactions between two entities involved in each of the three Chaum flows. Thus, for example, when a payer withdraws eCash from the consortium administration, both the parameters sent by the administration to the payer and the parameters received by the payer from the administration are recorded to the ledger. That is, both the sender and recipient must log what they sent and received, respectively. This is illustrated in figure 6.7.

The following provides an outline of the states relating to the ledger-assisted eCash protocol flows.

Evidence of the withdrawal When a payer withdraws eCash from his or her account at the consortium (i.e., as the eCash issuer), each eCash unit takes the form of a *serial number* (call it S_{iss}) plus the consortium's signature part over that eCash unit (call it *sigS*). Step 1(a) of figure 6.7 shows the withdrawal stage.

In addition to storing each of these eCash units (i.e., the serial number and the issuer's signature) in its internal system, the

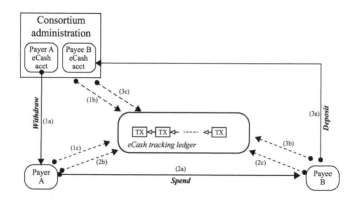

Figure 6.7
The eCash tracking ledger flows.

consortium must record a hash of the following values on the tracking ledger such that they are visible to the other Tradecoin entities:

- Identity of consortium (issuer)
- Hash of signed eCash (serial number S_{iss} and its signature $sigS$)
- eCash denomination (name of eCash scheme)
- eCash unit value
- Time stamp

This is shown in step 1(b) of figure 6.7. The payer may also record on the ledger a hash of what it received from the consortium (step 1(c) of figure 6.7).

Evidence at prespend   When the payer has obtained the eCash unit in the form of a serial number S_{iss}, the payer must transform this unit in such a way that it retains some desired properties of the unit (e.g., the payer becomes anonymous at spend time).

We denote this transformation simply as the serial number S_{payer}, where $S_{payer} = F\ (S_{iss})$ for some function F specific to the eCash scheme. These transformed serial numbers S_{payer} are the units that the payer spends or delivers to the payee.

For its exculpability, the payer must record a hash of the transformed serial numbers on the tracking ledger (step 2(b) of figure 6.7) consisting of:

- Identity of consortium (from which the payer obtains the serial numbers)
- Hash of original serial number (the hash of S_{iss})
- Hash of transformed serial number (the hash of S_{payer})
- eCash denomination (name of eCash scheme)
- eCash unit value

- Pointer to corresponding earlier withdrawal transaction on the tracking ledger
- Time stamp

Evidence at spend Typically, the act of spending the eCash units involves a challenge-response exchange between the payee and the payer (step 2(a) of figure 6.7). Here the payee sends a challenge value C_{payer} to the payer. The payer then must prove that the serial number S_{payer} is valid by responding to the challenge with the response R_{payer}.

Evidence at postspend For its own exculpability, the payee must keep a transcript of the challenge-response exchange and also record parts of it on the tracking ledger (step 2(c) of figure 6.7):

- Hash of transcript (the hash of the set of values S_{payer}, C_{payer}, and response R_{payer})
- eCash denomination (name of eCash scheme)
- The spent eCash unit value
- Pointer to corresponding prespend transaction (flow 2) on the tracking ledger
- Time stamp

Evidence at predeposit When the payee (e.g., merchant) deposits the serial number received from the payer into the payee's account at the consortium (step 3(a)), the payee must deliver the values S_{payer}, C_{payer}, and response R_{payer} to the consortium.

For its exculpability, the payee must capture or log the eCash parameters it deposited to the consortium (step 3(b) of figure 6.7):

- Hash of signed eCash (serial number S_{iss} and its signature $sigS$)
- eCash denomination (name of eCash scheme)
- eCash unit value
- Pointer to corresponding postspend transaction on the tracking ledger
- Time stamp

For its exculpability, the consortium must keep a transcript of the exchange with the payee for deposits and also record parts of the transcript on the tracking ledger.

6.9 ENVIRONMENTALLY FRIENDLY DIGITAL TRADECOIN

Climate change has a profound negative impact, visible in a plethora of very unpleasant physical consequences, such as the need to move entire cities (including capitals, such as Jakarta) to avoid perennial flooding, refitting industrial plants on a gigantic scale, and the like. It also has a profound financial component. In addition to utilities, extractive industries, construction, and others, some of the financially oriented industries, including banking, insurance, asset management, and pension funds, will suffer very substantial losses. The *Wall Street Journal* dubbed the recent bankruptcy of the major California utility PG&E "the first climate-change bankruptcy." There is no doubt in our mind that it is not going to be the last. According to the Bank of England, "Climate change poses significant risks to the economy and to the financial system, and while these risks may seem abstract and far away, they are in fact very real, fast approaching, and in need of action today."

Experience suggests that protestations alone are insufficient to convince people to make their behavior more environmentally friendly. Thus, we need to introduce a set of suitable financial tools and incentives that can gently push people in the right direction.

We can achieve that goal by introducing the environmental DTC (EDTC)—an environmentally friendly version of the DTC. We can model such a coin on a coalition loyalty program. A loyalty program can be conceptualized as an amalgamation of several single-issuer loyalty programs so that loyalty points can be accrued and redeemed at a variety of participating businesses. From their humble beginning in the 1970s, when American Airlines launched the first frequent flyer program (incidentally introducing the term itself), loyalty programs have grown exponentially.

The economic value of these programs is enormous. For instance, in January 2019, Air Canada, along with TD, CIBC, and Visa, acquired a loyalty program called Aeroplan, which has about 5 million active members, from Aimia for C$450 million in cash. They also assumed liability for the unused Aeroplan points at an estimated value of C$1.9 billion, at 2.5 cents a mile. Given these facts, the potential benefit of the EDTC-related deployment along the loyalty program lines can be substantial.

A vital part of loyalty programs, including EDTCs, is a platform for business intelligence reporting and analytics, which analyzes member information, tracks purchasing patterns, identifies profiles of loyal members, and aligns its loyalty program with members' preferences. For the EDTC to be successful, the utmost attention should be paid to privacy-preserving measures.

The EDTC ecosystem consists of several components. Its heart is an efficient, precise, and easy-to-use app that records positive actions by program participants. This app is a "money print-ing press." The next constituent part of the ecosystem consists of individual participants interested in fighting climate change and attracted by suitable financial initiatives. Their natural counter-point is corporate sponsors—companies and taxing authorities suf-ficiently concerned about climate change to be prepared to spend money to fight it. Currently, all major companies with exposure to climate change and sustainability have substantial budgets to sup-port environmentally friendly proposals. In turn, environmental DTC presents them with a source of income via attracting more customers and increasing revenues and profitability, cutting costs on sustainability infrastructure, and a tool for reducing climate change bankruptcy risk such as experienced by PG&E. The glue holding the EDTC ecosystem together consists of coalition mem-bers, who are prepared to accept EDTCs as partial payment for their goods and services. For instance, a utility provider might allow pay-ing up to 10 percent of utility bills with EDTCs. A coffee shop might charge up to 10 percent in EDTCs and use them for buying environ-mentally friendly coffee beans or paying its electricity bills. AI-based data collection systems and blockchain technology can be used to record EDTC balances of all activities of participants, sponsors, and coalition members in a robust and reliable ledger.

Since participants earn EDTCs for performing seemingly unre-lated activities, such as walking instead of using a car or consum-ing green electric power instead of using conventional sources, a fair mechanism that brings all these actions to a common denomi-nator is crucially important. There are several possibilities. For example, different activities can be valued based on their reduction in the participant's CO_2 footprint.

Implementation of a robust monetary policy, which determines the rate of disappearance of EDTCs earned by participants over time, is crucial for the stability of the ecosystem as a whole. A comparison with successful loyalty programs suggests that a form of demurrage is the most natural. In simple terms, it means that EDTCs accumulated by participants should expire and disappear after a certain period, the same mechanism that exists in various frequent flyer programs.

It is necessary to design suitable circulation rules by identifying "sources and sinks" for EDTCs. If we follow a strict loyalty point analogy, we must conclude that EDTCs are created at the "source" when individual participants perform environmentally friendly actions and are destroyed at the "sink" when they are used as partial payment for goods and services. This setting is overly restrictive because it obliterates the useful WIR analogy, by which EDTCs should not disappear at all. It appears that an intermediate solution is in order. EDTCs can be both earned by participants and borrowed by sponsors. There is an intermediate level of businesses accepting EDTCs, which also can use them with the participating coalition members as partial payment for their own needs. Finally, there are "super sponsors" who accept EDTCs but destroy rather than recirculate them. Such sponsors may include tax authorities and major multinationals spending part of their climate change budgets on promoting environmentally friendly policies.

6.10 CONCLUSIONS

We have discussed conceptual underpinnings and technical approaches to building DTCs. We have shown that DTCs have several decisive advantages compared to more established cryptocurrencies such as Bitcoin and Ripple. In addition to being a convenient transactional cryptocurrencies for the internet era, DTCs can serve as an important counterbalance to fiat currencies and, when fully developed, can play the role of a supranational currency, facilitating international commerce and allowing groups of small countries to create their own viable currencies.

NOTES

1. D. L. Chaum, "Untraceable Electronic Mail, Return Addresses, and Digital Pseudonyms," *Communications of the ACM* 24, no. 2 (February 1981): 84–88.

2. D. L. Chaum, A. Fiat, and M. Naor, "Untraceable Electronic Cash," in *Advances in Cryptology (CRYPTO 88)*, ed. S. Goldwasser, Lecture Notes in Computer Science 403 (New York: Springer-Verlag, 1990), 319–327, http://dl .acm.org/citation.cfm?id=88314.88969.

3. S. Nakamoto, "Bitcoin: A Peer-to-Peer Electronic Cash System," 2008, https://bitcoin.org/bitcoin.pdf.

4. A. Lipton, "Blockchains and Distributed Ledgers in Retrospective and Perspective," *Journal of Risk Finance* 19, no. 1 (2018): 4–25, https://doi.org /10.1108/JRF-02-2017-0035.

5. Nakamoto, "Bitcoin."

6. V. Buterin, "Ethereum: A Next-Generation Smart Contract and Decentralized Application Platform," white paper, 2014, https://github.com /ethereum/wiki/wiki/White-Paper.

7. D. Schwartz, N. Youngs, and A. Britto, "The Ripple Protocol Consensus Algorithm," Ripple Labs Inc. White Paper 5, 2014.

8. A. Lipton, A. Pentland, and T. Hardjono, "Narrow Banks and Fiat Backed Digital Coins," *Capco Institute Journal* 47 (2018): 101–116

9. Chaum, "Untraceable Electronic Mail, Return Addresses, and Digital Pseudonyms"; Chaum, Fiat, and Naor, "Untraceable Electronic Cash."

10. A. Haas, L. J. Ussher, K. Töpfer, and C. C. Jaeger, "Currencies, Commodities, and Keynes" (unpublished manuscript, March 6, 2014).

11. J. Lowe, *The Present State of England in Regard to Agriculture, Trade and Finance: With a Comparison of the Prospects of England and France* (Edinburgh: E. Bliss and E. White, 1824).

12. G. P. Scrope, *An Examination of the Bank Charter Question* (London: John Murray, 1833).

13. W. S. Jevons, *Money and the Mechanism of Exchange*, vol. 17 (New York: Kegan Paul, Trench, 1885).

14. A. Marshall, *Remedies for Fluctuations of General Prices* (London: n.p., 1887).

15. F. D. Graham, "The Primary Functions of Money and Their Consummation in Monetary Policy," *American Economic Review* 30, no. 1 (1940): 1–16.

16. B. Graham, "Stabilized Reflation," *Economic Forum* 1, no. 2 (1933): 186–193.

17. F. A. Hayek, "A Commodity Reserve Currency," *Economic Journal* 53, no. 210–211 (1943): 176–184.

18. J. M. Keynes, "The Objective of International Price Stability," *Economic Journal* 53, no. 210–211 (1943): 185–187.

19. N. Kaldor, *Causes of Growth and Stagnation in the World Economy* (Cambridge: Cambridge University Press, 2007).

20. Z. Xiaochuan, "Reform the International Monetary System," *Bank for International Settlements Quarterly Review* 41 (2009): 1–3, https://www.bis.org/review/r090402c.pdf.

21. Nakamoto, "Bitcoin."

22. Schwartz, Youngs, and Britto, "The Ripple Protocol Consensus Algorithm."

23. R. Ali, J. Barrdear, R. Clews, and J. Southgate, "The Economics of Digital Currencies," *Bank of England Quarterly Bulletin*, Q3, September 2014, 276–286, https://www.bankofengland.co.uk/quarterly-bulletin/2014/q3/the-economics-of-digital-currencies.

24. S. Scorer, "Central Bank Digital Currency: DLT or not DLT? That Is the Question," June 5, 2017, https://bankunderground.co.uk/2017/06/05/central-bank-digital-currency-dlt-or-not-dlt-that-is-the-question/.

25. K. Rogoff, *The Curse of Cash* (Princeton, NJ: Princeton University Press, 2016).

26. C. Ilgmann, "Silvio Gesell: A Strange, Unduly Neglected Monetary Theorist," *Journal of Post Keynesian Economics* 38, no. 4 (2015): 532–564.

27. I. Fisher, *Stamp Scrip* (New York: Adelphi Company, 1933).

28. A. Lipton, "The Decline of the Cash Empire," *Risk Magazine* 29, no. 11 (2016): 53, https://www.risk.net/risk-management/2475663/decline-cash-empire.

29. Nakamoto, "Bitcoin."

30. G. Danezis and S. Meiklejohn, "Centrally Banked Cryptocurrencies" (preprint, 2015), http://arxiv.org/abs/1505.06895.

31. F. Reid and M. Harrigan, "An Analysis of Anonymity in the Bitcoin System," in *Security and Privacy in Social Networks* , ed. Y. Altshuler, Y. Elovici, A. Cremers, N.. Aharony, and A. Pentland (New York: Springer, 2013), 197–223, https://doi.org/10.1007/978-1-4614-4139-7_10.

32. Chaum, "Untraceable Electronic Mail, Return Addresses, and Digital Pseudonyms"; Chaum, Fiat, and Naor, "Untraceable Electronic Cash."

33. The lead author is a member of their advisory board.

34. G. Pennacchi, "Narrow Banking," *Annual Review of Financial Economics* 4, no. 1 (2012): 141–159.

35. As always, Shakespeare put it best: "Neither a borrower nor a lender be, for loan oft loses both itself and friend, and borrowing dulls the edges of husbandry." *Hamlet,* act 1, scene 3.

36. Lipton, Pentland, and Hardjono, "Narrow Banks and Fiat Backed Digital Coins."

37. T. Hardjono, A. Lipton, and A. Pentland, "Towards an Interoperability Architecture: Blockchain Autonomous Systems," *IEEE Transactions on Engineering Management* 67, no. 4 (2020): 1298–1309, https://doi.org/10.1109/TEM.2019.2920154.

38. L. Lamport, R. Shostak, and M. Pease, "The Byzantine Generals Problem," *ACM Transactions on Programming Languages and Systems (TOPLAS)* 4, no. 3 (1982): 382–401.

39. M. Castro and B. Liskov, "Practical Byzantine Fault Tolerance," in *Proceedings of the Third Symposium on Operating Systems Design and Implementation (OSDI)* (February 1999), 173–186.

40. Global Legal Entity Identifier Foundation (GLEIF), *LEI in KYC: A New Future for Legal Entity Identification,* GLEIF Research Report, May 2018, https://www.gleif.org/en/lei-solutions/lei-in-kyc-a-new-future-for-legal-entity-identification.

41. T. Hardjono and N. Smith, "Decentralized Trusted Computing Base for Blockchain Infrastructure Security," *Frontiers Journal—Special Issue on Finance, Money and Blockchains* 2 (December 2019): 1–15, https://doi.org/10.3389/fbloc.2019.00024.

42. Nakamoto, "Bitcoin."

43. Nakamoto, "Bitcoin."

44. Buterin, "Ethereum."

45. D. Siegel, "Understanding the DAO Attack," *CoinDesk*, June 2016, https://www.coindesk.com/understanding-dao-hack-journalists.

46. Hardjono, Lipton, and Pentland, "Towards an Interoperability Architecture."

47. Chaum, "Untraceable Electronic Mail, Return Addresses, and Digital Pseudonyms."

48. Chaum, "Untraceable Electronic Mail, Return Addresses, and Digital Pseudonyms."

49. Chaum, "Untraceable Electronic Mail, Return Addresses, and Digital Pseudonyms"; Chaum, Fiat, and Naor, "Untraceable Electronic Cash"; J. Camenisch, S. Hohenberger, and A. Lysyanskaya, "Compact E-Cash," in *Advances in Cryptology—EUROCRYPT 2005*, ed. R. Cramer (Berlin: Springer, 2005), 302–321.

50. C. Grothoff, "GNU Taler—a Privacy-Preserving Online Payment System for Libre Society," July 27, 2016, https://grothoff.org/christian/fsfe2016.pdf.

51. Grothoff, "GNU Taler."

HEALTH IT: ALGORITHMS, PRIVACY, AND DATA

Thomas Hardjono, Anne Kim, and Alex Pentland

7.1 INTRODUCTION

Data is crucial for health and the life sciences, and the foundation of a new health IT infrastructure consists of developing highly interoperable platforms that deal with the various aspects of health-related data processing in a secure and confidential manner, with patient consent and data privacy. These platforms that will make up the future health IT infrastructure need to be based on interoperable standards that allow easy adoption by stakeholders in the ecosystem. Data collected by all healthcare agents needs to be treated with the highest regard for the privacy of the parties concerned.

The urgent need for solutions to the various challenges of health IT is nowhere clearer than in the issues related to the handling of citizen data during the recent COVID-19 pandemic. Several proposals were put forward based on the idea of *contact tracing* using mobile devices belonging to individuals in communities. The basic idea is that by collecting location data (e.g., GPS, Bluetooth) from the mobile devices of healthy individuals and comparing their proximity to diagnosed patients over time, individuals can obtain some rough measure as to their probability of being exposed to the virus. Such individuals could then be motivated to obtain a laboratory test to confirm any suspicions.

Like many other data-intensive projects in the area of health and the life sciences generally, several questions arise regarding the handling of citizen data—including location data of mobile devices. Thus, in the case of the various contact-tracing proposals, one of the many outstanding issues pertains to "how" and "where" the data matching is performed and whether such data processing activities may affect the privacy of citizens in various communities. A further concern would be the social reactions and implications of such revelatory information (e.g., leading to diagnosed patients being outcast). Today, consumer confidence in institutions is declining.[1] Reports regarding data loss, theft, and hacking[2] exacerbate this situation. Thus, any notion of establishing a nationwide contact-tracing program, albeit championed by leading tech companies such as Apple and Google,[3] may be met with some degree of skepticism on the part of the public. One valid concern here is that a program created during an emergency (such as the current COVID-19 pandemic) may continue to be used long after the emergency ends, thereby leading to potential surveillance abuses. Another concern would be the "ownership" of this kind of mobility data, which could be validly viewed as a new class of digital asset belonging to the individual.[4]

In this chapter, we extend our previous work (Ackerman et al.[5]) and explore the open algorithms paradigm[6] coupled with confidential computing strategies in the context of addressing the need to preserve the privacy of individuals whose data is used in computations:

- *Open algorithms for minimizing data movement and data loss*   Today, society, governments, and institutions need data in order to operate. Rather than exporting, copying, or moving citizen data as is commonly done today—leading to the proliferation of copies of data files and therefore a broader attack surface for theft—we explore the open algorithms paradigm, which shifts computations to the location of the data repository.

- *Federated consent and authorizations across institutions*   Consent issuance, propagation, and retraction remains one of the complex problems in health because of the complex nature of relationships.[7] Proposed approaches based on federated data systems—such as that outlined by the World Economic Forum (WEF)[8]—must address the question of consent and privacy in order to obtain buy-in from communities at large.

In line with the open algorithms paradigm, we explore the notion of "consent to execute" an algorithm (over data) but without consent to read or copy the data. We believe this approach may be suitable for certain types of health data (e.g., aggregate computations over cohort data). We discuss the current approaches based on the popular authorization tokens.

- *Protecting data in collaborative computations*   In some cases, different data is held by entities who are unable to disclose their data but who wish to collaborate using their respective data. Thus, methods are needed that allow data to be obfuscated or encrypted in such a manner that parties can share their encrypted data for collaborative computations, yielding insights that would not otherwise be possible using disparate data.

7.2   THE CHALLENGES OF HEALTH IT: THE
CASE OF PRECISION MEDICINE

Precision medicine is an innovative approach that provides a holistic understanding of a given patient's health, disease, and condition and provides a means for choosing treatments that would be most effective for an individual. Translating initial successes to a larger scale will require a coordinated and sustained national effort. On this front, the US Precision Medicine Initiative (PMI) was announced by President Barack Obama on January 20, 2015.[9] The PMI sought to move away from the one-size-fits-all approach to healthcare delivery and instead tailor treatment and prevention strategies to people's unique characteristics, including environment, lifestyle, and genes.[10] The PMI sought to build a cohort of at least one million participants between 2016 and 2020 for the purpose of creating a resource for researchers working to understand the many aspects that influence health and disease. The PMI Cohort Program (PMI-CP) aims to collect and share samples and data from these participants, including data from electronic health records (EHRs) and from participants' devices. The overall goal is to begin building a roadmap for precision medicine in the Unites States by collecting good-quality data and samples from a large cohort of participants over several years.[11] The PMI-CP was later renamed the PMI All of Us Research Program (PMI-AURP).

To obtain a better picture of the magnitude of the PMI proposal, the project seeks to collect very detailed information from a cohort of one million volunteers, which would make it the largest longitudinal study in the history of the United States. The volunteer participants must be willing to contribute data freely, generously, regularly, and longitudinally, including agreeing to ongoing accessibility of their electronic health records; participating in and sharing the results of additional clinical and behavioral assessments; contributing DNA samples and other biologic specimens; and participating in mobile health (mHealth) data-gathering activities to collect geospatial and environmental data. This data will be made available to academic and commercial researchers and to citizen scientists.[12] The long-term goal is for these findings, once tested and confirmed, to be integrated to improve care and be used to drive more research.

To begin addressing some of the challenges related to starting the PMI-CP participant recruitment, a working group was established, which issued its report in September 2015.[13] The working group was tasked with addressing the various questions related to the launch of the PMI recruitment process. This included issues such as participant recruitment, how to set up the biobank for participants' samples, how to create the databases for holding the participants' data, the method for obtaining consent, and several questions related to IT infrastructure. The working group identified a number of roles for entities involved in the project. First, the entities taking on the role of the *biobank* will build the PMI-CP biobank and support the collection, analysis, storage, and physical distribution of biospecimens. Second, the *Data and Research Support Center* entities will acquire, organize, and provide secure access to the PMI-CP datasets and provide research support and analysis tools. Third, the *Participant Technologies Center* entities will enroll patients through direct enrollment and develop, test, and maintain the PMI-CP mobile applications—which is one of the key means of enrolling volunteers, obtaining their consent, and communicating with the participants. Finally, the *healthcare provider organizations* (HPOs) will engage their patients and enroll participants in the PMI-CP program through regional medical centers and community-based federally qualified HPOs.[14]

The concern regarding data privacy was already called out in the original White House PMI announcement.[15] Thus, following this announcement, the White House released a trust framework for PMI to ensure that PMI data is appropriately secured and protected. This framework includes principles for both privacy and data security. In February 2016, the White House announced that the Office of the National Coordinator for Health Information Technology (ONC), in collaboration with the National Institute of Standards and Technology (NIST) and the Office for Civil Rights (OCR), would develop a specific guide for precision medicine[16] following the NIST Cybersecurity Framework.[17] In order that data privacy be addressed in the PMI effort, the White House convened an interagency working group in March 2015 with the charge of developing a set of privacy principles for PMI. This group was co-led by the White House Office of Science and Technology Policy, the Department of Health and Human Services Office for Civil Rights, and the National Institutes of Health. As output, the group produced the document *Precision Medicine Initiative: Proposed Privacy and Trust Principles*.[18]

It is crucial to note here that the implementation of the PMI-CP (PMI-AURP) entails *significant changes to the relationship between patients and their healthcare*—which are evident in the new demands for patient information.[19] Convincing individuals to reconceptualize the purpose of their health information in this way requires building and maintaining public trust—something that will be difficult given the recent history of data theft in other industry sectors.[20] Several ethical, legal, and social issues also come into play.

7.3 TOWARD A PRIVACY-CENTRIC DATA ARCHITECTURE

In order for new health IT infrastructure to implement provable mechanisms for preserving data privacy, a proper privacy-centric view of data is needed that should focus on *sharing insights by design* (versus exporting data), the quality and provenance of data, the privacy protection of data during computations, and the protection of data at rest while in storage. Figure 7.1 illustrates our proposed privacy-centric data architecture.

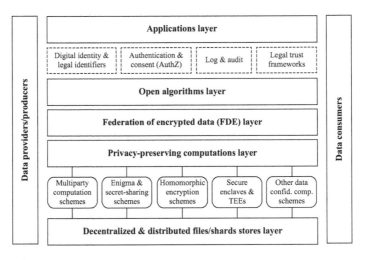

Figure 7.1
Privacy-centric data architecture for health IT.

The architecture in figure 7.1 is *layered* in the classical sense of the internet's layered architecture, whereby functions within a lower layer hide complex details from the layer above. The boundary of each layer is defined through standardized interfaces, which can be implemented in different ways (e.g., RESTful APIs, remote procedure calls (RPC)). An upper-layer function accesses services at the next layer down by using these standardized interfaces.

This layered approach provides the advantage of decoupling technologies and leads to highly modular implementations. This in turn promotes the development of new solutions for technical problems at a given layer independent of other layers. The use of standardized layer interfaces ensures that as new technologies are introduced at a given layer, other layers are not impacted (or are only minimally impacted):

- *Applications layer* Data use at this layer is driven by the specific area of application. For example, an EHR application of data will be different (and use different types of data) from a clinical-trials application.
- *Open algorithms (OPAL) layer* In this layer, the notion of open algorithms (OPAL) comes into play in the sense that it provides a logical boundary between the client (seeking insights) from the OPAL server and the data providers in the back end (see figure 7.2).
- *Federation of encrypted data (FDE) layer* The purpose of this layer is to federate data that is in encrypted form (e.g., shares, shards). Here, federation means the creation by data providers of a trust network or consortium with the goal of making available encrypted data (or shards) for collaborative privacy-preserving computing among the members of the federation.

Various technical architectures and designs, as well as business models and agreements, need to underlie the federation. Multiple federations may exist. We believe this approach may seed the creation of a future market for encrypted data shards, something that can be enabled by blockchain technology.[21]

- *Privacy-preserving data computations layer*   This layer deals with the complexity of privacy-preserving computing and collaborative confidential computing.

The goal here is that for a given open algorithms scenario and a given application, the "front-end" entities (i.e., users) are shielded from the complexity of "back-end" implementation details (e.g., via the OPAL service) of the chosen privacy-preserving scheme (e.g., homomorphic encryption, MIT Enigma, secure enclaves).

- *Decentralized and distributed files/shards layer*   This layer, among others, deals with the problem of the protection of data at rest. Notably, this includes the storage and accessibility of "raw" data files, shards/shares, and other data objects in connection with the specific privacy-preserving schemes being employed (e.g., at the layer above the current layer).

Thus, for example, if MIT Enigma[22] is employed, then shards/shares of data are dispersed throughout the peer-to-peer blockchain network of nodes. Other schemes may require that a separate share/shard management function be used, in which case solutions such as IPFS/Filecoin[23] may be used at this layer.

7.4   OPEN ALGORITHMS PRINCIPLES FOR HEALTH DATA

The concept of *open algorithms* (OPAL) evolved from several research projects over the past decade within the Human Dynamics Group

at the MIT Media Lab.[24] The general interaction flow among the
entities is summarized in figure 7.2, with a more detailed discussion
available in Hardjono and Pentland, "MIT Open Algorithms"[25] and
"Open Algorithms for Identity Federation."[26] In step 1, the querier
(either an individual or an organization) who is seeking insights (e.g.,
about a data subject) uses the client to select one or more algorithms
and their intended data. In step 2, the client delivers the algorithms
(or algorithm identifiers) to the OPAL service, which delivers them
to the corresponding data providers. In step 3, once these responses
have been received by the OPAL service, it collates the responses, performs additional filtering for personal identifiable information (PII)
leakage prevention, and then delivers the safe response to the client.

There are a number of fundamental principles underlying the
open algorithms paradigm:[27]

- *Move the algorithm to the data*   Instead of pulling data from
various repositories into a centralized location for processing, it

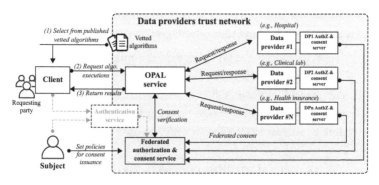

Figure 7.2
Overview of MIT open algorithms for algorithm-execution consent.

is the algorithm that should be sent to the data repositories for processing there. The goal here is to *share insights* instead of sharing raw data.

- *Data must never leave its repository*   Data must never be exported from (or copied from) its repository. This is consistent with the previous principle and enforces that principle. Exceptions to this rule are when the user requests a download of their data and when there is a legally valid court order to obtain a copy of the data.
- *Vetted algorithms*   Algorithms should be studied, reviewed, and vetted by domain experts. The goal here is to provide all entities in the ecosystem with a better understanding and assessment of the quality of algorithms from the perspective of bias, unfairness, and other possible unintended or unforeseen side effects.
- *Default to safe answers*   The OPAL service must place privacy as its main goal. Therefore, the responses from an OPAL service to the client must default to *aggregate answers*.

If subject-specific algorithms and responses are needed, then explicit consent must be obtained by the affected data subject(s) consistent with and following the General Data Protection Regulation (GDPR).[28]

There are a number of additional principles from the preceding principles that enhance the protection of data and therefore enhance privacy:

- *Data should always be encrypted*   Data must remain encrypted during computation and when in storage. The notion here is that in order to protect data repositories from attacks and theft (e.g., theft by insiders), data should never be decrypted. This means that data providers who hold subject data should employ data-at-rest protection solutions for data stores and privacy-preserving computation schemes when using the data for algorithm executions.

There are a number of emerging technologies—such as homomorphic encryption[29] and secure multiparty computation[30]—that may provide the future foundation for addressing this principle. We discuss some of these approaches.

• *Decentralized data architectures* Data providers should adopt decentralized and distributed data architectures for infrastructure security and resiliency.

Cryptographic techniques such as *secret sharing*[31] can be applied to data, which yields multiple encrypted "shards" of the data. These shards can in turn be distributed physically across a network of repositories belonging to the same data provider.[32] This approach increases the resiliency of the data provider infrastructure because an attacker would need to compromise a minimal number of repositories (N out of M nodes) in the data provider's network before the attacker could obtain access to the data item. This approach decreases the attack surface and makes the task of attacking considerably harder.

The open algorithm principle also applies to individual *personal data stores* (PDSs),[33] independent of whether the PDS is operated by the individual or by a third-party service provider (e.g., the hosted model). The basic idea is that in order to include the individual citizen in the open algorithms ecosystem, they must have sufficient interest, empowerment, and incentive to be a participant.[34] The ecosystem must therefore respect personal data stores as legitimate OPAL data repository endpoints. New models for computations across highly distributed personal data repositories need to be developed following the open algorithms principles.

Today, the open algorithms principles are being used in research projects on a national scale in Senegal and Colombia, by the Data-Pop Alliance, Imperial College London, the authors here at MIT, and the French telecom company Orange. These deployments are supported by the French Development Agency (Agence Française de Développement (AFD)), Orange, the governments of Colombia and Senegal, and telecom providers Sonatel and Telefonica.

7.5 CHALLENGES IN FEDERATED AUTHORIZATION AND CONSENT

One of the challenges in the broad area of health IT pertains to the management of consent by an individual (e.g., a patient) for a particular action to be performed on the individual's data. The problem can be complex because multiple entities and flows may be involved. For example, the authorization or consent flows may occur with the patient's proxy, such as the health provider legal entity where the patient's preferred doctor (primary care physician) is employed. The desired patient's data (e.g., imaging files) may be held by a different entity (e.g., a hospital in a different city, where the patient last resided), for example. In more health-specific language, consent means "the record of a healthcare consumer's policy choices, which permits or denies identified recipient(s) or recipient role(s) to perform one or more actions within a given policy context, for specific purposes and periods of time" (HL7 FHIR).[35]

In this section, we discuss some of the issues related to federated authorization and consent and describe a more user-centric (patient-centric) approach to consent management.

7.5.1 Policy-Based Access Control and Authorization

The issue of controlling access to multiuser resources has been an important theme since the mid-1960s with the rise of the time-share mainframe computer. Generally, the term *access control* is applied not only to physical access (to the computer systems) but also to system resources (e.g., memory, disk, files). Notable among the efforts in the early 1970s was the Multics system. In the context of government and military applications, there was the further issue of access based on a person's rank or security clearance. Here, the concept of *mandatory* and *discretionary* access control in multilevel systems came to the forefront in the form of the Bell and LaPadula (BL) model.[36]

In this model, access control is defined in terms of *subjects* possessing different *security levels*, who seek access to *objects* (i.e., system resources). Thus, for example, in the BL model, a subject (e.g., user) is permitted to access an object (e.g., file) if the subject's security level (e.g., "Top Secret") is higher than the security level of the object (e.g., "Secret"). The notion of *roles* or capacities was added to this model, leading to the *role-based access control* (RBAC) model. Here, as a further refinement of the BL model, a subject (user) may have multiple *roles* or capacities within a given organization. Thus, when the subject is seeking access to an object, he or she must indicate the role within which the request is being made. The formal model for RBAC was subsequently defined by NIST in 1992.[37]

Access control of resources is also a major concern for enterprises and corporations. This need became acute with the widespread adoption of local area network (LAN) technology by enterprise organizations in the 1990s. The same RBAC model applies also to corporate resources attached to the corporate LAN. This problem was often referred to as authentication, authorization, and audit (AAA) in the 1990s. Part of the AAA model developed during the 1990s was an abstraction of functions pertaining to *deciding* access rules from functions pertaining to *enforcing* them. Entities that decided on access rules were denoted as *policy decision points* (PDPs), while entities that enforced these access rules were denoted as *policy enforcement points* (PEPs).

The policy-based access control model is foundational to many systems deployed within enterprises today. Many solutions, such as Microsoft's Active Directory (AD), are built on the same model of policy-based access control. In the case of AD, a fairly sophisticated cross-domain architecture was developed that allows an enterprise to logically arrange itself into dozens to hundreds of interior domains (e.g., each department as a different AD group). Permissions and entitlements for subjects (employees) in AD are expressed in a comprehensive privilege attribute certificate (PAC) data structure. Interestingly, the main authentication mechanism within Microsoft AD and many similar products is the MIT Kerberos authentication system (RFC1510).[38]

7.5.2 Federation of Mediated Authorization Services

In order for authorization architectures in the consumer health space to be able to scale up, an authorization federation among the providers is needed. To place authorization federation in the proper context, we use the classic policy-based resource access control model[39] as our starting point. This is applied to a collection of *domains*, each representing distinct data controllers (holding personal data of various individuals).

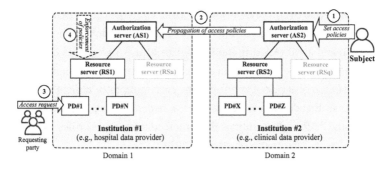

Figure 7.3
Overview of federated consent management.

For the current discussion, assume there are two domains—domain 1 and domain 2 (figure 7.3)—and both hold resources associated with an individual we refer to as the *data subject* (or simply *subject*), following the GDPR definition. As the resource owner, the subject has data located at both domain 1 and domain 2. A third party, denoted as the *requesting party*, seeks access to the subject's data located in domain 1 (e.g., to execute an algorithm on the data in domain 1).

There are at least three goals for a scalable federated authorization model:

• *Cross-domain policy propagation and enforcement* A subject (resource owner) must be able to set access policies in one domain (at AS2 in step 1 in figure 7.3) and have the policies automatically propagated (step 2) to all domains (e.g., AS1) in the federation that contain the subject's resources and have those policies enforced locally by each relevant domain.

Thus, in figure 7.3, if the subject sets access policies at AS2 in domain 2, then enforcement (step 4) must also occur at RS1 in domain 1, where the subject's resources reside.

- *Decentralization of enforcement*   Once an access policy is decided at one policy decision point (PDP) in one domain, enforcement within all domains in the federation that contain the subject's data/ resources must occur automatically without the subject's further involvement. Each policy enforcement point (PEP)—such as RS1 and RS2—in each relevant domain must operate independently of other PEPs in the same domain or other domains.

- *Legal trust framework for authorization federation*   A legal trust framework must be agreed on by all domain owners in the federation and define, among other things, the agreed behavior of PDPs and PEPs in propagating access policies and enforcing them.

7.5.3   Federation Approaches Based on Authorization Tokens
Recent advances have been made in federated authorization in health IT using model flow constructs that are used elsewhere on the internet, such as on social media platforms.[40] One popular authorization approach is the OAuth2.0 framework,[41] which today is used on most social media platforms. By using these existing authorization flows that are already familiar to end users (e.g., mobile apps), the benefit is that users (i.e., patients) can adopt the same app behavior flows for authorizations related to health data.

An important extension to the basic OAuth2.0 framework is the *user-managed access* (UMA) profiles[42] for consent over resources (e.g., files, data, service endpoints). The goal of UMA is to provide individual-centric control over "resources" (e.g., personal data, algorithms, assertions) that may be distributed across multiple locations, each employing a resource server. The basic idea of UMA is that the data subject as the *resource owner* (RO) would set access policies at one authorization provider entity (the AS in figure 7.3) and for the access policies to be propagated automatically to all resource servers (the RS in figure 7.3) who hold resources (i.e., data) belonging to the data subject and be enforced by each of the resource servers independently. When a requesting party (RqP) seeks access to a given resource protected by a resource server, the requesting party must first obtain an authorization token from the authorization provider (AS) and deliver it to the resource server with its access request. The resource server, as the policy-enforcement point, can then evaluate the token that was issued by the AS. A health-specific profile of OAuth2.0[43] and UMA[44] has begun to be developed for the health IT sector.

In the context of the PMI initiative discussed previously in section 7.2, the ONC has developed and promoted a number of standard authorization flows and APIs in support of use cases such as the PMI. One such advancement is the *Sync for Science* (S4S) APIs[45] based on the OAuth2.0 authorization framework[46] and the Health Level 7 (HL7) Fast Healthcare Interoperability Resources (FHIR) standard (Draft Standard for Trial Use 2[47]). The S4S was created for app developers following the SMART App Authorization Guide[48] (SMART meaning substitutable medical apps, reusable technology). This provides electronic access control mechanisms based on rules set to enforce a healthcare provider's organizational security policy. The S4S API uses OAuth 2.0 flows to allow a designated third-party app to have electronic, read-only access to all or a portion of health information about an individual, made available through a healthcare provider's EHR patient portal, via the individual's existing authentication credentials (e.g., username and password). The S4S API was developed with the intention that it can be used for other third-party apps, including those for medical research.[49]

7.6 PROTECTING DATA IN COLLABORATIVE COMPUTATIONS

In this section, we provide a brief overview of the various *privacy-preserving computing* paradigms that may be applicable for the use cases of data in health IT. These paradigms and their respective implementations may be relevant for the different types of health IT infrastructure that deal with different types of data. Not every paradigm may be suitable for a given data type. For example, digital imaging data (e.g., X-ray files) may not be an appropriate match for models geared toward aggregate computations, but imaging files could be analyzed or compared for differences. We focus on collaborative computation efforts that presume plaintext data located at separate data providers.

7.6.1 Shamir's Secret Sharing

One of the fundamental concepts in early cryptography research was *secret sharing*, which was pioneered by Adi Shamir.[50] In his landmark paper, Shamir asked how a secret piece of data could be "encrypted" into multiple parts in such a manner that only a subset of the parts would be needed to reconstruct the original secret. This notion subsequently became known as *threshold secret sharing*. Thus, in a given threshold secret-sharing scheme, the secret data is encrypted into M shares in such a way that a minimum threshold of N shares is required to reconstruct the secret.

The key feature here is that *any* combination of at least N unique shares suffices for reconstruction. This allows the shares to be distributed across different physical locations, making it more difficult for attackers to compromise the system, because an attacker would need to compromise at least N separate computer systems. As we will see, this feature will be central to the MIT Enigma design.

7.6.2 Multiparty Computation

The area of multiparty computation (MPC) focuses on cryptographic schemes that provide a way for a group of entities to perform "collaborative computation" or joint computations among themselves, where some of the participants are assumed to be competitors and therefore may be dishonest in their computations (i.e., honest majority assumption). Therefore, the goal of MPC schemes generally is to provide a way for these entities to "encrypt" their data in such a way that some limited computations are still possible using the encrypted data. Within a group of participating entities (e.g., health data providers), each entity has to "prepare" their data by encrypting it using the MPC cryptographic parameters agreed on by the group. They then exchange the encrypted data or "shares" among themselves. Thus, none of the entities is expected to reveal their plaintext data to one another. The goal is for all participants to obtain the same output result in the face of a possible dishonest minority of entities in the group.[51] Over the years, there have been several MPC schemes proposed, including Garbled Circuits,[52] Fairplay,[53] SPDZ,[54] and ShareMind,[55] among others.

In the context of health IT, a number of MPC schemes can be used for more collaborative computing, where the identities of the entities are known and where all entities are assumed to be honest. Thus, here MPC is used for privacy preservation instead of for the more competitive use cases.[56] For example, a group of hospitals located in a municipality or province possessing private health data of citizens could jointly compute aggregate calculations regarding their populations in the municipality or province. For instance, together they could compute the average age of patients with some illness (e.g., cancer) without ever disclosing the plaintext data about these patients. The MPC process "encrypts" the data into shares, which are then exchanged among the hospitals.

Figure 7.4 provides a high-level illustration of the use of MPC schemes as the back end to open algorithms. As in figure 7.2, the querier (requesting party) employs the client to interact with the OPAL server. The OPAL server provides the computational challenge based on the algorithm to the three data providers, A, B, and C (step 2). After the three data providers complete their MPC joint calculations (step 3), each returns the answer they calculated to the OPAL server over a secure channel.

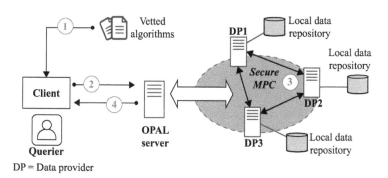

DP = Data provider

Figure 7.4
Overview of the MIT open algorithms using secure MPC on the back end.

7.6.3 MIT Enigma

The MIT Enigma paradigm[57] explores new MPC and secret-sharing[58] configurations by using nodes on a blockchain system.[59] The basic idea is to employ the computational horsepower of the decentralized nodes (e.g., mining nodes) to perform the joint MPC computations, where the computation task itself is dispersed across multiple nodes. Thus, the blockchain nodes serve as decentralized storage of the encrypted "shares" (shards) of the original data and also perform the computations. In this thinking, a data provider (data owner) may not even need to keep a local copy of its data. Knowing the location/identity of the blockchain nodes that hold its shards, the data provider can at any time fetch these shards from the relevant nodes and reconstruct the data for internal use. The nodes can be within a permissionless (public) blockchain network or a private permissioned one. One possible business model for the permissionless case is for the blockchain nodes to charge fees for the storage and processing of these shards.

There are several features of Enigma that make it a groundbreaking proposition in the context of data privacy and decentralized computation:

- *Data is sharded using a multiparty scheme* Following the classical secret-sharing and MPC models, a given data unit D is "split" using a linear secret-sharing scheme that results in, say, M shares. Only N shares will be needed to reconstruct the original data unit D (where N is less than or equal to M).
- *Shards are distributed across several nodes* Rather than locating all the M shares in one centralized database, the shares are dispersed across multiple nodes on a blockchain P2P network. This

dispersal strengthens the security of the overall scheme because an attacker would need to compromise at least N distinct nodes (assuming the attacker can locate the correct nodes).

This is shown in figure 7.5, where the entity A, for example, disperses its shares to the nodes of the blockchain denoted as 4(a). Entity B disperses its shares to nodes 4(b), and entity C disperses its shares to nodes 4(c).

- *Decentralized computing by group nodes*   When a joint computation needs to be performed by the owners of the data units (i.e., shards), the nodes on the blockchain holding these shards perform the computation in a decentralized manner.

Using the simple example in figure 7.5, we assume that entities A, B, and C (e.g., hospitals) own data units D_1, D_2, and D_3, respectively (e.g., cancer patient data). If the entities wish to perform a joint computation over the data (e.g., compute the average of D_1,

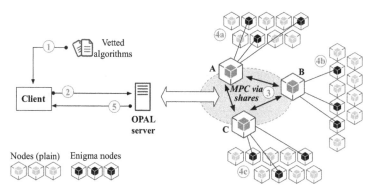

Figure 7.5
Overview of the MIT open algorithms using Enigma on the back end.

D_2, and D_3), then each of the entities must notify their respective nodes to begin engaging with the other nodes in solving the MPC computation. Thus, in figure 7.5, the nodes at 4(a), 4(b), and 4(c) will then exchange the relevant shards that they collectively require to perform the MPC computation.

It is worth noting that in figure 7.5 the "front end" remains the OPAL configuration in that the querier at the client may not even be aware that the data has been sharded and been dispersed on nodes, and that the computations are performed by nodes.

7.6.4 Hardware-Based Secure Enclaves

An alternative approach for data privacy in computation is to employ a special hardware "black box" that prevents unauthorized access to the data while it is outside the hardware. The hardware essentially provides security assistance to the applications in processing the data. The hardware assistance consists of processor extensions that establish a *secure enclave* on the platform, providing a protected execution environment. For example, the protected execution environment could be an area in the computer's memory that is shielded from interference by other processes on the same computer or from attacks by an external entity. In order to prevent unauthorized processes from accessing the protected memory, the access policies are enforced by hardware also. This permits a degree of "self-protection" on the part of the computer, retaining its own integrity and protecting the confidentiality of the data in protected memory. Examples of secure enclave hardware include the Secure Guard Extension (SGX) from Intel Corp.,[60] TrustZone from ARM Ltd.,[61] and MIT Sanctum.[62] Figure 7.6 provides an illustration of the use of secure enclaves in the context of open algorithms.

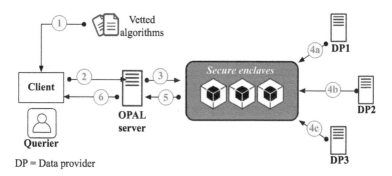

Figure 7.6
Overview of the MIT open algorithms using secure enclaves.

Figure 7.6 provides an overview of the steps involved in using secure enclaves. In essence, the secure enclave provides both sides with a guarantee of privacy of the algorithms and data while outside the enclave. This approach is attractive for cases where the algorithm owner or author does not wish the details of the algorithm (e.g., expressed in an analytics language such as the R language) to be accessible to the data provider (see figure 7.2). Correspondingly, the data provider may be prohibited from exporting data from its repository and making it available to external entities. In this case, the data provider must encrypt the data for the target secure enclave in such a way that the data is decipherable only by the secure enclave within its memory. Once in protected memory, the enclave can apply the deciphered algorithm against the deciphered data.

Figure 7.6 provides a high-level illustration of this process. When the querier on the client seeks to have an algorithm executed on the dataset held by the data provider, it queries the OPAL server as before (steps 1 and 2). In response, the OPAL server loads the algorithm to the secure enclaves (e.g., in the cloud) in step 3. If confidentiality is needed for the algorithm (i.e., the algorithm contains proprietary information), the OPAL server has the option to encrypt the algorithm prior to delivering it to the secure enclaves. After the data provider encrypts the relevant data for the target secure enclave, it delivers the encrypted data to the enclave. The enclave deciphers it within its protected memory and executes the algorithm (from step 3) on the data (shown as step 5). The secure enclave outputs the result to the OPAL server in step 6, which provides the results to the client.

7.7 USE CASES

In this section we briefly discuss some use cases for the above technologies for collaborative computations.

7.7.1 Hospital Records

OPAL and confidential computing has the potential to provide valuable, federated insights on hospital data as well as new revenue sources for hospitals sitting on large datasets. Accounting for the aforementioned limitations in data formatting, these methods of privacy-preserving computation could provide insights into optimized hospital management, patient treatment, and even general discoveries about a disease without violating the privacy of the patient.

As a proof of concept, Secure AI Labs (SAIL) worked with a pharmaceutical company to reproduce multiomic association results of microbiomes across four different hospital populations in a privacy-preserving framework based on OPAL in secure enclaves.[63] The study was led by a principal investigator at a pharmaceutical company in Boston, who provided a genomic dataset based on stool samples coming from four separate hospitals. Each patient in the dataset is associated with genomic data and one of three diagnosis phenotypes: UC (ulcerative colitis), CD (Crohn's disease), and non-IBD (noninflammatory bowel disease). SAIL normalized analysis across the four hospitals and verified that the distributions were similar for comparison by running a principal component analysis (PCA). Once comparability was confirmed, a Wilcoxon signed-rank test was run to determine which microbes are most significant for UC, CD, and IBD.

Principal component analysis   Across four hospitals, a differentially private federated learning PCA was run on the genomic dataset. After appropriate data normalization, variance-covariance matrices were computed across each dataset within four subenclaves (hardware-based secure enclaves) for each hospital. Prior to exporting the matrices from hospital environments, differential privacy noise was added to further ensure security. This noise is a matrix sampled from a multivariate normal distribution with its standard deviation scaled relative to the size of the data (figure 7.7).

The hospitals' variance-covariance matrices were gathered in a central enclave, where they were summed and primed for PCA on the combined variance-covariance matrix. Finally, dimensionality-reduced principal components were gathered for each diagnosis.

After plotting the three principal components federated and unfederated, we note a high similarity in the principal component distributions of the diagnoses regardless of the machine learning

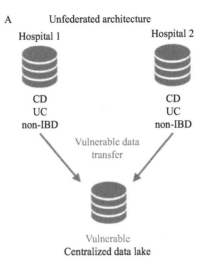

A   Unfederated architecture

Hospital 1   Hospital 2

CD   CD
UC   UC
non-IBD   non-IBD

Vulnerable data
transfer

Vulnerable
Centralized data lake

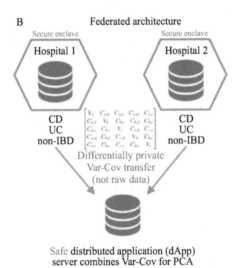

B   Federated architecture

Secure enclave   Secure enclave

Hospital 1   Hospital 2

CD   CD
UC   UC
non-IBD   non-IBD

Differentially private
Var-Cov transfer
(not raw data)

Safe distributed application (dApp)
server combines Var-Cov for PCA

Figure 7.7

Traditional methods of data analysis use unfederated architectures (a),
whereas OPAL frameworks use federated architectures (b).

setting (federated vs. unfederated), which means that using federated learning or OPAL architectures preserves the accuracy of PCA results while also preserving privacy. Both results imply a strong conclusion that there is neither technical nor biological bias. After getting confirmation from the PCA results that there was no bias between the four hospital datasets, we know the datasets are comparable for further analysis (see figure 7.8).

Wilcoxon signed-rank sum test   Researchers at the pharmaceutical company wanted also to understand which microbes were most important to which specific disease. SAIL implemented a Wilcoxon signed-rank sum test in traditional and SAIL environments. Not only were the ranking results comparable (see figure 7.8), but also the speed penalties were within reasonable tolerance (10 minutes instead of 3 minutes).

Ultimately, the conclusion of this proof of concept is that the SAIL platform is well suited for distributed data assessment (PCA) and analysis (rank sum for microbes of interest). The extension stretches beyond microbiome analysis into behavioral, multiomics, chemical, eQTL, and other clinical interests in the pharmaceutical space where timely access to more data is essential to furthering research. Data accessibility challenges in silo searching, internal review boards, anonymization, and transportation can take between 20 percent and 30 percent of a project's timeline because of restrictions in privacy, security, and compliance.[64] The vision of the SAIL platform is to streamline this process with a platform that makes privacy, security, and compliance seamless at the software level, finally closing the gap between

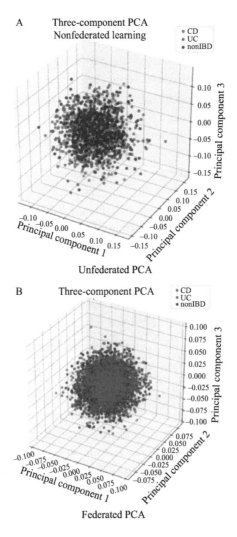

Figure 7.8

Results from traditional PCA methods (a) had the same distributions when done in a federated architecture (b).

written contract/legal agreements and the execution of code on the platform.

7.7.2 Genomic Data

Genomics-based personalized medicine began more than 10 years ago. Genetic big data has shown promise in conducting breast cancer studies, building the cancer genome atlas, and improving screening and diagnosis. Many recent studies have had prospective results with advanced machine learning and artificial intelligence (AI) technologies on genotypic and phenotypic big data. Using large amounts of federated genetic and health data to train AI models and using these models to predict diseases, drug responses, and personality traits will allow great advancements that benefit human health.

At the same time, DNA sequencing has become cheaper, better, and faster in recent years. As more people get their DNA sequenced for disease diagnoses or plain curiosity (e.g., finding their ancestry), many governments, nonprofit organizations, and commercial companies have built up their genetic databases in recent years and covet as well as protect the value of this data.

With a growing number of genetic testing companies, hospitals, and pharmaceutical firms and increasing interest in the contribution of genetic data by individuals, there is a great need for a marketplace for genetic and health data to align the interests of stakeholders big and small. However, the availability of high-quality genetic and phenotypic data remains the bottleneck of personalized healthcare. Existing databases are silos that cannot scale. Collecting useful data from different individuals, hospitals, biobanks, or other organizations is difficult, not only because of the complexity of the genetic and medical data but also because of the highly sensitive private information in the data. Regulations in both the United States and European Union make it harder for these organizations to meet the big data requirements of rapidly developing AI training applications.[65]

As a proof of concept, SAIL worked with bioinformaticians at a premier research institute to test differential privacy on a

Table 7.1

Comparison of the ranks of unfederated (a) and federated (b) results

(a) Unfederated results

Msp_name	Module_name	NonNull1	NonNull2	Statistic	*p* value
msp_0001	Core	8.0	13.0	−0.955219	0.339467
msp_0002	Core	2.0	8.0	−1.201260	0.229651
msp_0003	Core	28.0	32.0	0.506555	0.612467
msp_0004	Core	3.0	6.0	−0.571684	0.567536
msp_0005	Core	28.0	33.0	−0.738123	0.460439
msp_0006	Core	1.0	2.0	−0.151967	0.879213

(b) Federated results

	Msp_name	Module_name	Nnotnull1	Nnotnull2	Statistic	*p* value
0	msp_0001	Core	8	12	−0.723650	0.469280
1	msp_0002	Core	2	8	−1.186787	0.235312
2	msp_0003	Core	28	32	0.665758	0.505566
3	msp_0004	Core	3	5	−0.361825	0.717438
4	msp_0005	Core	28	33	−0.607866	0.543276
5	msp_0006	Core	1	2	−0.151967	0.879213
6	msp_0007	Core	28	30	1.345990	0.178306

Note: Comparing the ranks of unfederated (a) and federated (b) results, we see preserved ranks. For example, looking at msp_0002, we see that the relative ranks 2 and 8 for relative association for irritable bowel disease are preserved.

computational biology use case linking single nucleotide poly-
morphisms (SNPs) to genes driving Alzheimer's disease. Open
data sharing is one of the biggest bottlenecks to discovery in
healthcare, and in a diagnosis with over 148 failed drugs there's
a large opportunity to learn through shared data. To address this,
SAIL designed a system that protects both data and algorithms by
using differentially private (DP) machine learning.

Linear regression A simple linear regression was used to predict gene expressions based on SNP samples. Thus, SAIL implemented a differentially private simple linear regression and
compared the results to nonprivate results using *tensorflow*.

The first part of the project consists of simulating the SNP data
and gene expression to understand how a simple linear regression with differential privacy behaves. To do so, a random matrix
sampling from 0, 1, or 2 was produced to correlate to gene expressions (the mathematics behind this is elaborated in the code via
the *DataLoader* function).

The differential privacy optimizer used was set with a clip gradient and a noise multiplier parameter. The former is used to
avoid gradient divergence that could happen because of the noise
added at each iteration, and the latter is the amount of Gaussian
noise added to the gradient.

The amount of privacy budget achieved after each experiment
remains constant regardless of the size of the dataset. This is
because it only depends on the noise multiplier and the number
of iterations, which are constant in our experiment.

To ensure model correctness, multiple linear regressions were
fit using *sklearn* and compared by the R^2s of both the *sklearn* and

tensorflow results. First, the relevant parameters are set: the number of iterations and the learning rate that lead to a robust linear regression. In this case, 700 and 0.025 were used, respectively. Next, the differentially private linear regression was set with the same parameters and checked for robustness.

Differential privacy   Table 7.2 shows the results obtained in terms of R^2 with and without differential privacy. The ε column represents the privacy budget we reached. The rows with the highest non-DP R^2 (above .98) are boldfaced. Therefore, a model infused with differential privacy reacts very well and preserves the level of accuracy the non-DP model has reached. For example, on line 17, there's an R^2 of .99 for a DP R^2 of .94, so the latter model is still acceptable. In addition, it's interesting to point out that there isn't any outlier when one compares the non-DP metrics and the DP ones, regardless of the level of accuracy reached. Even in lines 1 to 12, an inaccurate model without DP still behaves the same way with DP (e.g., line 10). In conclusion, the level of accuracy between a non-DP accurate model and a DP model is retained.

7.7.3   Molecular Libraries

Another exciting extension of the OPAL architecture is for molecular libraries. As pharmaceutical companies continue to expand and develop new drug pipelines, their research and development arms generate and characterize numerous molecules. However, the vast majority of these molecules will never be used by the company. At the same time, pharmaceutical companies have a lot of difficulty capitalizing on these libraries because they cannot prove the value of their molecules without revealing the molecule and the raw data

Table 7.2

Results for different dataset sizes

	N	P	R_2	R_2_DP	R_2_adj	R_2_adj_DP	ε
0	100	10	-0.0646056	-0.0485168	-2.48539	-2.49176	1678.16
1	10,000	10	-0.267697	-0.349098	-0.959825	-0.853831	1678.16
2	100	10	-0.295457	-0.275067	-1.73812	-1.77301	1678.16
3	1,000	10	0.0458412	0.0495668	-0.0504196	-0.0500454	1678.16
4	9,000	50	0.18425	0.163755	0.00601131	-0.00132726	1678.16
5	8,000	50	0.148088	0.139863	-0.00882683	-0.0112698	1678.16
6	1,000	50	0.196575	0.201879	-0.265586	-0.262803	1678.16
7	6,000	50	0.263374	0.235547	0.0287979	0.0143091	1678.16
8	2,000	50	0.287974	0.255239	-0.0400029	-0.0601687	1678.16
9	7,000	50	0.180181	0.145559	-0.00284624	-0.0145357	1678.16
10	3,000	50	0.0557282	0.00457317	-0.0890288	-0.0923986	1678.16
11	5,000	50	0.19679	0.154595	-0.0142074	-0.0298504	1678.16
12	4,000	50	0.129962	0.110302	-0.0470312	-0.0520619	1678.16
13	**2,000**	**100**	**0.999979**	**0.937276**	**0.999942**	**0.835699**	**1678.16**
14	**5,000**	**100**	**0.984944**	**0.921579**	**0.966963**	**0.833413**	**1678.16**
15	**1,000**	**100**	**0.987018**	**0.908197**	**0.947883**	**0.646069**	**1678.16**
16	**1,000**	**200**	**0.989929**	**0.928192**	**0.959082**	**0.717311**	**1678.16**
17	**2,000**	**200**	**0.993989**	**0.949445**	**0.984135**	**0.869552**	**1678.16**

(continued)

Table 7.2 (continued)

	N	P	R_2	R_2_DP	R_2_adj	R_2_adj_DP	ε
18	5,000	200	0.984925	0.940317	0.966723	0.871213	1678.16
19	10,000	200	0.997443	0.941439	0.990374	0.785694	1678.16
20	10,000	300	0.995602	0.923871	0.988088	0.801229	1678.16
21	10,000	400	0.986459	0.933809	0.970206	0.858222	1678.16
22	10,000	1,000	0.953615	0.884144	0.831262	0.593529	1678.16
23	10,000	1,500	0.98821	0.921476	0.970204	0.797798	1678.16
24	10,000	2,000	0.998812	0.941151	0.997369	0.873415	1678.16
25	10,000	5,500	0.871685	0.812581	0.509662	0.306422	1678.16
26	10,000	6,000	0.913386	0.807328	0.775507	0.528297	1678.16

itself. Using an open trial chain architecture for collaborative learning in blinded OPAL sandboxes across molecular libraries would
allow greater innovation in the drug space.

7.7.4   Extensions and Implications

The goal of traditional randomized clinical trials is to prove safety,
dosing, and efficacy in most people. However, the underspecified
benchmark of "most people" has proven more problematic with
recent drugs that have narrower therapeutic windows. In turn,
many minority groups are completely overlooked, even in phase 3
trials, because the signal from these groups can be indistinguish-
able from statistical noise.

Integrating OPAL into the approval process would federate disparate clinical trial results for greater signal boost from these minority
groups, returning a more specific and thorough analysis of efficacy.
This would not only prevent serious adverse event disparities in
the market but also increase targeted efficacy. For example, OPAL
queries across similar arms of multiple clinical trials could not only
detect ethnic-specific signals but also boost genome-specific signals
on the horizon of personalized medicine.

The movement of data for analysis introduces many privacy
risks to regulations such as the Health Insurance Portability and
Accountability Act (HIPAA) and GDPR. However, OPAL's architecture fundamentally shifts this paradigm by moving the analysis to the data. This not only addresses the regulation at hand but
also preempts greater regulatory shifts regarding privacy in a digital world of higher granularity and sensitive data.

7.8 CONCLUSIONS

In this chapter, we have reviewed a number of strategies and possible solutions for addressing the challenges around data privacy in health IT. As society becomes increasingly data driven, health initiatives and programs such as the Precision Medicine Initiative (PMI) will require access to greater amounts of data and at a more detailed level.

We believe paradigms such as open algorithms provide a promising framework for thinking through some of the privacy challenges. The open algorithms paradigm is central to our proposed privacy-centric data architecture, which focuses on *sharing insights by design*. This is in contrast to the current prevalent model of simply exporting or copying data across institutions. Also important to open algorithms is the notion of consent for the execution of an algorithm. This is also in contrast to the current prevalent interpretation of consent as meaning permission to copy data.

If initiatives such as the contact-tracing applications for reducing the spread of COVID-19 are to gain traction in communities, then issues such as privacy need to be addressed correctly.

NOTES

1. World Economic Forum, *Rethinking Personal Data: A New Lens for Strengthening Trust*, report, May 2014, http://reports.weforum.org/rethinking-personal-data.

2. T. Cook, "You Deserve Privacy Online. Here's How You Could Actually Get It," *Time*, January 2019, https://time.com/collection-post/5502591/tim-cook-data-privacy/; R. Abelson and M. Goldstein, "Millions of Anthem

Customers Targeted in Cyberattack," *New York Times*, February 5, 2015, https://www.nytimes.com/2015/02/05/business/hackers-breached-data -of-millions-insurer-says.html; T. S. Bernard, T. Hsu, N. Perlroth, and R. Lieber, "Equifax Says Cyberattack May Have Affected 143 Million in the U.S.," *New York Times*, September 7, 2017, https://www.nytimes.com/2017 /09/07/business/equifax-cyberattack.html.

3. S. Bond, "Apple and Google Build Smartphone Tool to Track COVID-19," *National Public Radio*, April 10, 2020, https://www.npr.org/sections /coronavirus-live-updates/2020/04/10/831912284/apple-and-google -build-smartphone-tool-to-track-covid-19.

4. World Economic Forum, *Personal Data: The Emergence of a New Asset Class*, report, 2011, http://www.weforum.org/reports/personal-data -emergence-new-asset-class.

5. A. Ackerman, A. Chang, N. Diakun-Thibault, L. Forni, F. Landa, J. Mayo, R. van Riezen, and T. Hardjono, "Blockchain and Health IT: Algorithms, Privacy, and Data," MIT Fintech Future Commerce and MIT Connection Science white paper prepared for the Office of the National Coordinator for Health Information Technology, US Department of Health and Human Services (HHS), August 2016, https://www.healthit.gov/sites/default/files /1-78-blockchainandhealthitalgorithmsprivacydatawhitepaper.pdf; US Department of Health and Human Services, "ONC Announces Blockchain Challenge Winners—Use of Blockchain in Health IT and Health-Related Research Challenge," August 29, 2016, https://www.hhs.gov/about/news /2016/08/29/onc-announces-blockchain-challenge-winners.html.

6. A. Pentland, "Saving Big Data from Itself," *Scientific American* 311, no. 2 (2014): 64–67; T. Hardjono and A. Pentland, "MIT Open Algorithms," in *Trusted Data—a New Framework for Identity and Data Sharing*, ed. T. Hardjono, A. Pentland, and D. Shrier (Cambridge, MA: MIT Press, 2019), 83–107.

7. European Commission, "Regulation (EU) 2016/679 of the European Parliament and of the Council of 27 April 2016 on the Protection of Natural Persons with Regard to the Processing of Personal Data and on the

Free Movement of Such Data (General Data Protection Regulation)," *Official Journal of the European Union* L119 (2016): 1–88.

8. World Economic Forum, "Federated Data Systems: Balancing Innovation and Trust in the Use of Sensitive Data," white paper, May 2019, https://www.weforum.org/whitepapers/federated-data-systems-balancing -innovation-and-trust-in-the-use-of-sensitive-data; World Economic Forum, *Global Data Access for Solving Rare Disease: A Health Economics Value Framework*, report, February 2020, https://www.weforum.org/reports/global -access-for-solving-rare-disease-a-health-economics-value-framework.

9. The White House, *Precision Medicine Initiative: Proposed Privacy and Trust Principles*, report, July 2015, https://obamawhitehouse.archives.gov /sites/whitehouse.gov/files/documents/PMISecurityPrinciplesFramewo rkv2.pdf.

10. US Department of Health and Human Services and Office of the National Coordinator for Health Information Technology, *Precision Medicine Initiative (PMI) Data Security Principles Implementation Guide*, report, December 2016, https://www.healthit.gov/sites/default/files/pmisecurity _ig_v16-clean.pdf.

11. National Research Council, *Toward Precision Medicine: Building a Knowledge Network for Biomedical Research and a New Taxonomy of Disease* (Washington, DC: National Academies Press, 2011), https://www.nap .edu/catalog/13284/toward-precision-medicine-building-a-knowledge -network-for-biomedical-research.

12. P. L. Sankar and L. S. Parker, "The Precision Medicine Initiative's All of Us Research Program: An Agenda for Research on Its Ethical, Legal, and Social Issues," *Genetics in Medicine* 19, no. 7 (July 2017): 743–750, https://doi.org/10.1038/gim.2016.183.

13. PMI Working Group, *The Precision Medicine Initiative Cohort Program: Building a Research Foundation for 21st Century Medicine*, Precision Medicine Initiative (PMI) Working Group report to the advisory committee

to the director, NIH, September 2015, https://acd.od.nih.gov/documents /reports/DRAFT-PMI-WG-Report-9-11-2015-508.pdf.

14. Intel Corporation, Datacenter Solutions Group—Health and Life Sciences, "The US Precision Medicine Initiative Cohort Program—Investigating the Ethical and Legal Aspects Surrounding Consent," white paper, January 2017, https://www.intel.com/content/dam/www/public /us/en/documents/white-papers/precision-medicine-initiative-cohort -program-white-paper.PDF.

15. The White House, *Precision Medicine Initiative*.

16. US Department of Health and Human Services and Office of the National Coordinator for Health Information Technology, *Precision Medicine Initiative (PMI) Data Security Principles Implementation Guide*.

17. National Institute of Standards and Technology, *Framework for Improving Critical Infrastructure Cybersecurity Version 1.0*, February 2014, https:// www.nist.gov/system/files/documents/cyberframework/cybersecurity -framework-021214.pdf; National Institute of Standards and Technology, *Framework for Improving Critical Infrastructure Cybersecurity Version 1.1*, April 2018, https://doi.org/10.6028/NIST.CSWP.04162018.

18. The White House, *Precision Medicine Initiative*.

19. Sankar and Parker, "The Precision Medicine Initiative's All of Us Research Program."

20. Abelson and Goldstein, "Millions of Anthem Customers Targeted in Cyberattack"; Bernard et al., "Equifax Says Cyberattack May Have Affected 143 Million in the U.S."

21. D. Yaga, P. Mell, N. Roby, and K. Scarfone, *Blockchain Technology Overview*, National Institute of Standards and Technology Internal Report 8202, October 2018, https://doi.org/10.6028/NIST.IR.8202.

22. G. Zyskind, O. Nathan, and A. Pentland, "Decentralizing Privacy: Using Blockchain to Protect Personal Data," in *Proceedings of the 2015*

IEEE Security and Privacy Workshops (New York: IEEE, 2015), 180–184, https://doi.org/10.1109/SPW.2015.27.

23. Protocol Labs, "Inter Planetary File System (IPFS)," 2019, https://docs.ipfs.io.

24. Pentland, "Saving Big Data from Itself."

25. Hardjono and Pentland, "MIT Open Algorithms."

26. T. Hardjono and A. Pentland, "Open Algorithms for Identity Federation," in *Proceedings of the 2018 Future of Information and Communication Conference (FICC), Vol. 2,* ed. K. Arai, S. Kapoor, and R. Bhatia (Berlin: Springer-Verlag, 2018), 24–43, https://doi.org/10.1007/978-3-030-03405-4.

27. Hardjono and Pentland, "MIT Open Algorithms."

28. European Commission, "Regulation (EU) 2016/679."

29. C. Gentry, "Fully Homomorphic Encryption Using Ideal Lattices," in *Proceedings of the 41st Annual ACM Symposium on Theory of Computing (STOC'09),* ed. M. Mitzenmacher (New York: ACM, 2009), 169–178.

30. A. C. Yao, "Protocols for Secure Computations," in *Proceedings of the 23rd Annual Symposium on Foundations of Computer Science (SFCS '82)* (Washington, DC: IEEE Computer Society, 1982), 160–164; A. C.-C. Yao, "How to Generate and Exchange Secrets," in *Proceedings of the 27th Annual Symposium on Foundations of Computer Science (SFCS '86)* (Washington, DC: IEEE Computer Society, 1986), 162–167; O. Goldreich, S. Micali, and A. Wigderson, "How to Play Any Mental Game," in *Proceedings of the Nineteenth Annual ACM Symposium on Theory of Computing (STOC '87),* ed. A. V. Aho (New York: ACM, 1987), 218–229.

31. A. Shamir, "How to Share a Secret," *Communications of the ACM 22,* no. 11 (November 1979): 612–613.

32. Pentland, "Saving Big Data from Itself."

33. T. Hardjono and J. Seberry, "Strongboxes for Electronic Commerce," in *Proceedings of the Second USENIX Workshop on Electronic Commerce,* ed.

D. Tygar (Berkeley, CA: USENIX Association, 1996), 1–9; T. Hardjono and J. Seberry, "Secure Access to Electronic Strongboxes in Electronic Commerce," in *Proceedings of 2nd International Small Systems Security Conference (IFIP WG 11.2)*, ed. J. Eloff and R. von Solms (Copenhagen: IFIP, 1997), 1–13; Y. A. de Montjoye, E. Shmueli, S. Wang, and A. Pentland, "OpenPDS: Protecting the Privacy of Metadata through SafeAnswers," *PLoS One* 9, no. 7 (July 2014): 13–18, https://doi.org/10.1371/journal.pone.0098790.

34. D. Searls, *The Intention Economy* (Cambridge, MA: Harvard Business Review Press, 2012).

35. HL7 FHIR, HL7 Fast Healthcare Interoperability Resources (FHIR) Specifications (v4.0.1), n.d., http://hl7.org/fhir/.

36. D. E. Bell and L. J. LaPadula, *Secure Computer Systems: Mathematical Foundations*, MITRE Corporation Technical Report MTR-2547 I ESD-TR-73–278 (Vols. 1–2), November 1973.

37. D. F. Ferraiolo and D. R. Kuhn, "Role-Based Access Controls," in *Proceedings of the 15th National Computer Security Conference*, Baltimore, October 1992, ed. P. Gallagher and J. Burrows (NIST, 1992), 554–563, https://csrc.nist.gov/publications/detail/conference-paper/1992/10/13/proceedings-15th-national-computer-security-conference-1992.

38. J. Kohl and C. Neuman, "The Kerberos Network Authentication Service (v5)," RFC1510, IETF, September 1993, http://tools.ietf.org/rfc/rfc1510.txt.

39. Ferraiolo and Kuhn, "Role-Based Access Controls."

40. Office of the National Coordinator for Health Information Technology, *Key Privacy and Security Considerations for Healthcare APIs*, report, December 2017, https://www.healthit.gov/sites/default/files/privacy-security-api.pdf.

41. D. Hardt, "The OAuth 2.0 Authorization Framework," RFC6749, IETF, October 2012, http://tools.ietf.org/rfc/rfc6749.txt.

42. T. Hardjono, E. Maler, M. Machulak, and D. Catalano, "User-Managed Access (UMA) Profile of OAuth2.0—Specification Version 1.0,"

Kantara Initiative, Kantara published specification, April 2015, https://docs
.kantarainitiative.org/uma/rec-uma-core.html; E. Maler, M. Machulak,
and J. Richer, "User-Managed Access (UMA) 2.0," Kantara Initiative, Kantara published specification, January 2017, https://docs.kantarainitiative
.org/uma/ed/uma-core-2.0-10.html.

43. J. Richer and J. Mandel, "Health Relationship Trust Profile for Fast
Healthcare Interoperability Resources (FHIR) OAuth 2.0 Scopes," OpenID Foundation, OpenID specifications, July 2018, https://openid.net
/specs/openid-heart-fhir-oauth2-10.html.

44. J. Richer, "Health Relationship Trust Profile for Fast Healthcare
Interoperability Resources (FHIR) UMA 2 Resources," OpenID Foundation, OpenID specifications, July 2018, https://openid.net/specs/openid
-heart-fhir-uma2-10.html.

45. Office of the National Coordinator for Health Information Technology, "Key Privacy and Security Considerations for Healthcare APIs."

46. Hardt, "The OAuth 2.0 Authorization Framework."

47. HL7 FHIR, "HL7 Fast Healthcare Interoperability Resources (FHIR)
Draft Standard for Trial Use 2 (DSTU2)," https://www.hl7.org/fhir/DSTU2/.

48. SMART App Authorization Guide, http://hl7.org/fhir/smart-app-lau
nch/.

49. Office of the National Coordinator for Health Information Technology, "Key Privacy and Security Considerations for Healthcare APIs."

50. Shamir, "How to Share a Secret."

51. Yao, "Protocols for Secure Computations"; Goldreich, Micali, and
Wigderson, "How to Play Any Mental Game."

52. Yao, "Protocols for Secure Computations."

53. D. Malkhi, N. Nisan, B. Pinkas, and Y. Sella, "Fairplay—Secure Two-
Party Computation System," in *Proceedings of the 13th USENIX Security*

Symposium, August 9–13, 2004, San Diego, CA, USA, ed. M. Blaze (Berkeley, CA: USENIX, 2004), 287–302, http://www.usenix.org/publications /library/proceedings/sec04/tech/malkhi.html; A. Ben-David, N. Nisan, and B. Pinkas, "FairplayMP: A System for Secure Multi-party Computation," in *Proceedings of the 2008 ACM Conference on Computer and Communications Security, CCS 2008, Alexandria, Virginia, USA, October 27–31, 2008*, ed. P. Ning, P. F. Syverson, and S. Jha (New York: ACM, 2008), 257–266, https://doi.org/10.1145/1455770.1455804.

54. I. Damgård, M. Keller, E. Larraia, V. Pastro, P. Scholl, and N. P. Smart, "Practical Covertly Secure MPC for Dishonest Majority—or: Breaking the SPDZ Limits," in *Proceedings of Computer Security—ESORICS 2013— 18th European Symposium on Research in Computer Security, Egham, UK, September 9–13, 2013*, ed. J. Crampton, S. Jajodia, and K. Mayes, Lecture Notes in Computer Science 8134 (Berlin: Springer, 2013), 1–18, https:// doi.org/10.1007/978-3-642-40203-6; T. Araki, A. Barak, J. Furukawa, T. Lichter, Y. Lindell, A. Nof, K. Ohara, A. Watzman, and O. Weinstein, "Optimized Honest-Majority MPC for Malicious Adversaries—Breaking the 1 Billion-Gate Per Second Barrier," in *Proceedings of the 38th IEEE Symposium on Security and Privacy*, ed. K. Butler (Los Alamitos: IEEE, 2017), 843–862.

55. D. Bogdanov, S. Laur, and J. Willemson, "ShareMind: A Framework for Fast Privacy-Preserving Computations," in *Proceedings of Computer Security—ESORICS 2008, 13th European Symposium on Research in Computer Security, Málaga, Spain, October 6–8, 2008*, ed. S. Jajodia and J. López, Lecture Notes in Computer Science 5283 (Berlin: Springer, 2008), 192– 206, https://doi.org/10.1007/978-3-540-88313-5\13.

56. E. A. Abbe, A. E. Khandani, and A. W. Lo, "Privacy-Preserving Methods for Sharing Financial Risk Exposures," *American Economic Review* 102, no. 3 (2012): 65–70, http://dx.doi.org/10.1257/aer.102.3.65.

57. Zyskind, Nathan, and Pentland, "Decentralizing Privacy"; G. Zyskind and A. Pentland, "Enigma: Decentralized Computation Platform with

Guaranteed Privacy," in *New Solutions for Cybersecurity*, ed. H. Shrobe, D. Shrier, and A. Pentland (Cambridge, MA: MIT Press, 2017), 426–454; G. Zyskind, "Efficient Secure Computation Enabled by Blockchain Technology" (master's thesis, Massachusetts Institute of Technology, June 2016), https://dspace.mit.edu/bitstream/handle/1721.1/105933/964695278-MIT.pdf.

58. Shamir, "How to Share a Secret."

59. Yaga et al., *Blockchain Technology Overview.*

60. F. Mckeen, I. Alexandrovich, A. Berenzon, C. Rozas, H. Shafi, V. Shanbhogue, and U. Savagaonkar, "Innovative Instructions and Software Model for Isolated Execution," in *Proceedings of the Second Workshop on Hardware and Architectural Support for Security and Privacy (HASP2013)*, Tel Aviv, June 2013, ed. R. Lee and W. Shi (ACM: New York), 1–10, https://doi.org/10.1145/2487726.2488368; F. McKeen, I. Alexandrovich, I. Anati, D. Caspi, S. Johnson, R. Leslie-Hurd, and C. Rozas, "Intel Software Guard Extensions (Intel SGX) Support for Dynamic Memory Management Inside an Enclave," in *Proceedings of the Workshop on Hardware and Architectural Support for Security and Privacy (HASP) 2016*, Seoul, June 2016, ed. Y. Szefer, R. Lee and W. Shi, 1–9, https://doi.org/10.1145/2948618.2954331.

61. R. Coombs, "Securing the Future of Authentication with ARM TrustZone-Based Trusted Execution Environment and Fast Identity Online (FIDO)," ARM Inc. white paper, May 2015.

62. V. Costan, I. Lebedev, and S. Devadas, "Sanctum: Minimal Hardware Extensions for Strong Software Isolation," https://eprint.iacr.org/2015/564.pdf.

63. J. Lloyd-Price, C. Arze, N. Ananthakrishnan, and C. Huttenhower, "Multi-omics of the Gut Microbial Ecosystem in Inflammatory Bowel Diseases," *Nature* 569 (2019): 655–662, https://www.nature.com/articles/s41586-019-1237-9.

64. P. Holub, "Enhancing Reuse of Data and Biological Material in Medical Research: From FAIR to FAIR-Health," *Biopreservation and Biobanking* 16, no. 2 (2018): 97–105, https://www.ncbi.nlm.nih.gov/pmc/articles/PMC5906729/pdf/bio.2017.0110.pdf; D. Kondor, B. Hashemian, Y. de Montjoye, and C. Ratti, "Towards Matching User Mobility Traces in Large-Scale Datasets," *IEEE Transactions on Big Data* 16, no. 2 (September 2018),714–726, https://ieeexplore.ieee.org/document/8470173.

65. M. Kim and K. Lauter, "Private Genome Analysis through Homomorphic Encryption," *BMC Medication Information Decision Making,* 15, no. S5 (2015), https://doi.org/10.1186/1472-6947-15-S5-S3.

NARROW BANKS AND FIAT-BACKED TOKENS

Alexander Lipton, Thomas Hardjono,
and Alex Pentland

8.1 INTRODUCTION

This chapter describes the concept of a fiat-backed digital coin
(FBDC) and marries it with the idea of a narrow bank (NB). It
outlines an approach to increase FBDC acceptability and circulation from a small set of initial sponsors to a much wider (but still
limited) group of potential users, such as small- and medium-
sized enterprises (SMEs) and individuals, via a purpose-built NB.
In short, the idea is to apply distributed ledger technology (DLT)
to give a new lease on life to the old NB concept and to use an NB
as a centerpiece (glue) at the heart of a digital ecosystem. When
properly designed, an NB can be used for several related purposes,
including issuance of FBDC. While we describe the concept of an
NB in detail, it is worth mentioning that such a bank has (almost)
perfectly matching assets and liabilities, so it is impervious to
market and liquidity risks. In a nutshell, on its asset side, an NB
has only central bank cash or short-term government obligations,
while on its liability side it has deposits and equity. In the old
days, the assets would be solely in gold, later a combination of

gold and paper money, and finally, in our time, predominantly electronic balances on deposit with the central bank.

While the idea of an NB is not new, it is not clear whether a true one has ever been built. Currently, almost all banks are fractional reserve in nature and engage in maturity transformation by maintaining long-term assets and short-term liabilities, thus opening themselves to risks of potential runs and other hazards, up to and including default.

We share the view succinctly expressed by Aristotle: "But money has been introduced by convention as a kind of substitute for need or demand; and this is why we call it money, because its value is derived, not from nature, but from law, and can be altered or abolished at will."[1] In view of this quotation, we wish to design FBDC in a manner compliant with all applicable laws, including the know-your-customer (KYC) and anti-money-laundering (AML) requirements. FBDC, being a digital currency, naturally resides on a purpose-built distributed ledger. By now, building a distributed ledger system, which can function without a central authority, is well understood. Bitcoin, first described by S. Nakamoto[2] in his seminal white paper, inspired the creation of more than a thousand other cryptocurrencies, all with various degrees of novelty and utility (if any).

By construction, these currencies are native tokens, residing on a blockchain, and can therefore be controlled by the agreed consensus mechanism among agents maintaining and operating such a distributed ledger. However, until now, attempts to properly incorporate real-world assets, first and foremost fiat currencies, into a blockchain have been unsuccessful.[3] Without a satisfactory solution to this all-important problem, it is not possible to make blockchain part of the mainstream payment infrastructure.

We argue that for a consortium of sponsors (such as large banks) who are satisfactorily vetted in advance and able to pass the KYC and AML requirements, a fiat currency can be digitized with the assistance of the corresponding central bank, which agrees to convert some of the participating banks' reserves into digital tokens at a one-to-one ratio. This is the approach taken by Clearmatics, a software company based in London.[4] However, for a larger group of potential users, including, in addition to the original consortium member banks, some nonbanking financial institutions, as well as SMEs and possibly individuals, direct participation of the central bank becomes problematic. We propose a solution that boils down to building a special-purpose NB whose operations are streamlined and safeguarded as much as possible in order to limit operational risks. This bank will keep fiat currency submitted by the users and issue digital tokens in return. These tokens will circulate within the group of users in a fast and efficient manner by utilizing a distributed ledger mechanism, thus creating native tokens convertible into fiat currency at will. We emphasize that operational risks are always present, but this is true not only for the setup we are proposing but also for ordinary cash and bank deposits and, in all probability, to a larger degree.

8.2 DISTRIBUTED LEDGERS AND CRYPTOCURRENCIES

8.2.1 Background

For decades, little or no attention was paid to the infrastructure supporting the internal workings of the financial ecosystem. As a result, this infrastructure dramatically fell behind the actual demands of the marketplace. This fact became completely obvious during the global financial crisis, which put enormous stresses on the transaction infrastructure and pushed it almost to the breaking point. Currently, financial infrastructure is centered on private centralized ledgers maintained by individual banks, which are reconciled through the central banks' ledgers (see, e.g., Norman, Shaw, and Speight[5]).

Although for centuries this system served finance reasonably well, it has always been plagued with numerous issues related to both domestic and foreign transactions. In the current framework, even simple cash transfers (not to mention transactions involving securities) are slow and, under certain circumstances, risky.

In figure 8.1, we show a typical domestic bank transaction between Alice and Bob, who have accounts at two different banks. In figure 8.2, we show a typical cross-border transaction between Alice and Bob, who have accounts at two different banks located in their respective countries.

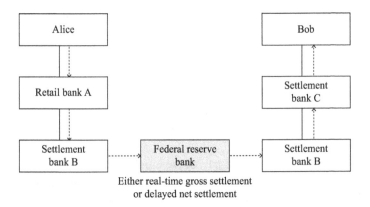

Figure 8.1
A sketch of a transaction between Alice and Bob, in which Alice sends Bob US$100.

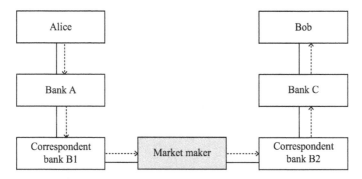

Figure 8.2
A sketch of a transaction between Alice and Bob, in which Alice sends Bob 100 pounds.

Fortunately, remarkable technological breakthroughs—mostly related to cryptocurrencies, distributed ledgers, and related concepts—simultaneously focused the attention of key decision-makers and technical experts on the glaring need to transform the financial infrastructure and, at the same time, indicated how such a transformation can be accomplished.

8.2.2 Distributed Ledger Design

Public versus private ledgers   A distributed ledger can be designed along several lines. The key question is whether a distributed ledger is needed in the first place. If the answer is affirmative, then two other questions need to be answered: Should the ledger be made permissionless or permissioned, or, equivalently, public or private? Who, and via which mechanism, maintains its integrity? We feel that the FBDC-carrying ledger should be semipermissioned so that everyone should be able to join, but participants should be known to the NB at the very least when they exchange fiat currency for tokens and, conversely, when they exchange tokens for fiat currency. In the interim, the participants probably can retain anonymity, even though the exact degree of anonymity is open to debate. It is clear that participants' identities have to be anonymous to other users; however, lawful legal authorities, under limited and well-defined conditions, should be allowed to uncover the true identities of participants.

Consensus mechanisms   Given that different actors, whose interests are not aligned, are participants of the distributed ecosystem, it is imperative to design a mechanism for achieving consensus among them. Such a mechanism has to be able to tolerate Byzantine faults, both intentional and unintentional, as discussed by Castro and Liskov,[6] Lamport, Shostak, and Pease,[7] and many others. So far, the most successful practically implemented consensus mechanism is based on the competitive proof of work (PoW) (see Nakamoto[8]). However, by its very nature, this mechanism consumes enormous amounts of energy and is not suitable for large-scale applications. Accordingly, other options, including proof of stake, proof of burn, proof of age, and random selection of validators, have to be considered (see, e.g., Buterin[9] and Chen and Micali[10]).

For the large-scale applications, we are leaning toward using validators or notaries, running full nodes, and verifying transactions along the lines of majority votes as done, for example, in the Ripple protocol.[11]

8.2.3   Background Bitcoin Setup

Recently, DLT attracted a lot of attention from both the industry and the general public. The astonishing success of Bitcoin demonstrates that a distributed ledger without central authority can function in a coherent and Byzantine fault-tolerant fashion in real life. While very impressive from a technical standpoint, Bitcoin in its original form is not suitable for high finance. The reasons are simple—the system is pseudonymous, does not solve the all-important KYC and AML requirements, is not scalable by design, as its throughput speed is no more than seven transactions per second (TpS), and consumes enormous amounts of electricity. Moreover, the volatility of Bitcoin is very high, which precludes it from being useful for transactional purposes, not to mention for lending and borrowing. Some observers even argue that the dominant raison d'être of Bitcoin is to facilitate illegal activities.[12] In addition, by construction, Bitcoin is a native token, which lives on the distributed ledger, while fiat currencies and other financial assets do not reside there. As a result, Bitcoin cannot solve the delivery versus payment problem. While in theory it is easy to move Bitcoin from one address, represented by a public key, to the next, it is not possible at all to ensure the movement of currency, goods, and services in the opposite direction. Since there are no good laws regulating these movements, the whole system is prone to all kinds of malfeasance. In figure 8.3, we show a typical transaction between Alice and Bob, who have pseudonymous Bitcoin accounts identified by their public keys.[13]

8.2.4   FBDC Setup

Despite Bitcoin's shortcomings, the Bitcoin setup can be used as a prototype for building a distributed ledger more suitable

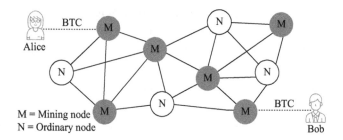

Figure 8.3

A sketch of a transaction between Alice and Bob, in which Alice sends Bob a bitcoin (BTC).

for interbank transactions and other financial purposes. Several issues need to be resolved before this goal can be achieved:

- The ledger has to be made at least semiprivate (if not private) in order to meet KYC requirements.
- The right balance has to be struck between privacy and accountability in order to satisfy the AML requirements.
- An industrial-strength and highly efficient method for maintaining consensus on the ledger, capable of handling hundreds or even thousands of transactions per second, needs to be designed.
- And, most importantly, a satisfactory method for solving the delivery versus payment problem has to be found.[14]

The validators (or notaries) responsible for the ledger's integrity should be known in advance and licensed. They should be paid a small fee for their services, say a percentage of the transaction size they approve. This fee has to be denominated in FBDC so their interest and desire to maintain the integrity of the ecosystem are properly aligned with their activities. In order to ensure

Byzantine fault tolerance of the proposed setup, validators have to create their own versions of the ledger and propose them to the rest of the validators. Several rounds of voting take place until a two-thirds majority is reached. In this regard, our approach is somewhat similar to the one used by Ripple (see Schwartz, Youngs, and Britto[15]) and can be viewed as a variation of the well-known Byzantine fault-tolerant algorithms.

To provide efficient and expedient transaction processing, individual notaries are assigned to particular subsets of all addresses. In this setup, a quorum verifies its portion of the ledger and the full ledger is reconstructed out of these portions.

The only mechanism for injecting new coins into the distributed ledger is as follows. A participant has to have a conventional fiat account, either directly in the NB or with another commercial bank. They transfer the desired amount of fiat currency to the NB. The NB in turn issues FBDC and transfers it from its public-key address to the public-key address provided by the participant. Thus, in effect, the participant becomes a shareholder in the NB rather than a depositor. Conversely, when a participant in the ledger wishes to receive fiat currency in exchange for their FBDCs, they transfer FBDCs from their public key to the public key of the bank, which in turn credits fiat currency either to the account on its own ledger or to a designated account in a different bank at a one-to-one ratio. Once an FBDC is born, it starts its journey from one address, represented by a public key, to the next. In this setup, the integrity of the distributed ledger is maintained by notaries.

In an alternative setup, coins are actually numbered and the list of numbers is maintained by the NB (although the NB is unaware of which participant holds which number) in the blind-signature framework introduced by Chaum, Fiat, and Naor.[16] Every time a coin changes hands, the new owner sends the number for checking by the NB, who compares it with the list of spent coins it maintains. If this particular coin has not been spent, it is retired, and a new coin with a new random number is issued to the designated owner. If the coin has already been spent, a transaction is rejected. The number is naturally blind-signed by the NB with its secret key in order to prevent forgery and fraud.

In figure 8.4, we show a typical transaction between Alice and Bob, both of whom have FBDC accounts. We emphasize that the FBDC is a special case of the digital Tradecoin (DTC), backed by a pool of real commodity assets, which is currently being developed at MIT (see Lipton and Pentland[17] and Lipton, Hardjono, and Pentland[18]).

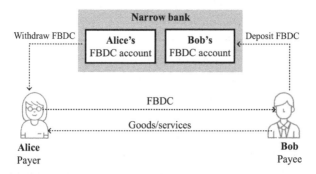

Figure 8.4

A sketch of a transaction between Alice and Bob in which Alice sends Bob 100 FBDCs.

8.3 ENTER A NARROW BANK

8.3.1 History

Modern banking originated in the High Middle Ages and blossomed during the Renaissance and the early modern period, mostly in the form of fractional reserve banking. From the beginning, fractional reserve banking firms were prone to collapse. For instance, in Florence, the Bardi, Peruzzi, and Medici companies (to mention but a few) all failed.

Not surprisingly, the narrow banking idea was pursued by visionaries, financial reformers, and regulators for hundreds of years (see, e.g., Pennacchi,[19] Dittmer,[20] Roberds and Velde,[21] narrowbanking .org,[22] and references therein). From time to time, actual attempts to build an NB have been undertaken. For instance, in 1361, Venice's senate prohibited lending out depositors' money, thus in effect making Venetian banks narrow. However, this prohibition was systematically circumvented, with associated bank failures to follow. In particular, the largest bank, that of Pisano & Tiepolo, failed in 1584, was converted into a state bank, and defaulted again in 1619. In 1609, the Bank of Amsterdam was chartered as an NB but soon after started to lend its reserves in secret. As a result, in 1791 it failed and was taken over by the city.

Eventually banks, pursuing their own self-interest, became much narrower than they were in the Renaissance or the early modern period, or are today. During the nineteenth century, British and American commercial banks followed the real bills doctrine and lent predominantly for short maturities. Bank loans mostly financed short-term working capital and provided trade credit, with maturities of two to three months, and were collateralized by the borrower's personal wealth or the goods in transit (see Boden-horn[23] and Pennacchi[24]).

In the twentieth century, however, encouraged by the creation of the Federal Reserve Bank in 1913, commercial banks drifted away from the real bills doctrine, started to lend for much longer maturities, established revolving lines of credit for some of their borrowers, and started to overemphasize their maturity transformation ability at the expense of prudence. The Great Depression of 1929 made banks' inability to meet their obligations successfully painfully obvious, which caused the idea of an NB to come to the fore.

In the United Kingdom, NBs were advocated by Soddy.[25] In the United States, a group of influential Chicago economists proposed a plan calling for the abolition of fractional reserve banks (see Knight et al.,[26] Hart,[27] Douglas et al.,[28] and Fisher[29]). Their core proposals are summarized in Phillips[30] as follows:

- Federal Reserve Banks should be owned by the government outright.
- Deposits of member banks should be completely guaranteed.
- Demands for payment by depositors should be satisfied by issuing Federal Reserve notes as legal tender.
- The gold standard should be suspended.
- The assets of all member banks should be liquidated and all existing banks dissolved.
- New NBs accepting only demand deposits subject to a 100 percent reserve requirement in cash and deposits with the Fed should be created.
- Investment trusts handling savings deposits should be created.

- Existing banking institutions should operate under Federal Reserve supervision until they are dissolved and new banks are created.

Although a practical conversion of fractional reserve banks into NBs was rejected in the 1940s under enormous political pressure from fractional reserve banks, the idea has always stayed close to the surface, and it gained considerable momentum during and after the savings and loan crisis in the 1980s and 1990s (see, e.g., Friedman,[31] Tobin,[32] Litan,[33] Bryan,[34] Burnham,[35] Pennacchi and Gorton,[36] Huber and Robertson,[37] Kobayakawa and Nakamura,[38] Al-Jarhi,[39] and Garca, Cibils, and Maino[40]).

Not surprisingly, it became extremely popular again during and after the global financial crisis (see, e.g., Kay,[41] Kotlikoff,[42] Phillips and Roselli,[43] Kumhof and Benes,[44] Chamley, Kotlikoff, and Polemarchakis,[45] Pennacchi,[46] van Dixhoorn,[47] Admati and Hellwig,[48] Cochrane,[49] Dittmer,[50] Nosal et al.,[51] and McMillan[52]).

8.3.2 A Bank That Cannot Default

The main characteristic of an NB is its asset mix, which includes solely marketable low-risk securities and central bank cash in an amount exceeding its deposit base. As a result, such a bank can only be affected by operational failures, which can be minimized, but not eliminated, by using state-of-the-art technology, thus providing a maximally safe payment system. Accordingly, NB deposits would be equivalent to currency, thus abolishing the need for deposit insurance, with all its perverse effects on the system as a whole, not to mention the associated moral hazards.

It is clear that the only way to keep one-to-one parity between the fiat currency and digital tokens is to keep the exact amount of the fiat in escrow. However, you cannot put the requisite amount in a bank and expect it to be safe at all times unless this bank is specially designed or you can open an account directly at the central bank. Indeed, bank depositors are junior unsecured creditors of a bank, so if the bank were to default, they cannot expect their deposits to stay intact. Even if a significant portion of these deposits can be recovered, the money will not be available until the bankruptcy issues are resolved, which can take a very long time. At the same time, a central bank, while happy to accommodate licensed banking institutions and a small, select group of trusted nonbanking financial firms, such as central clearing counterparties, cannot, and will not, allow a wider range of corporate or individual participants (particularly if they wish to be anonymous) to have an account with them. This is for a variety of reasons, including, but not limited to, being unable to solve the KYC/AML problem, not to mention potential political complications.

Thus, we need to build a bank that cannot default, at least not because of market and liquidity risks. One needs to be cognizant of the fact that, regardless of the amount of effort, it is not possible to build a bank that is impervious to operational risks, although proper design can minimize these risks to an acceptable degree.

8.3.3 Types of Narrow Banks

Several approaches for designing an NB have been summarized by Pennacchi:[53]

- *100 percent reserve bank (C-PeRB)* Its assets are central bank reserves and currency, and its liabilities are demand deposits and shareholder equity. Depending on the circumstances, these deposits can be either noninterest-bearing, interest paying, or interest charging. The latter setup might be necessary if the interest rate paid by the central bank is negative. C-PeRB is financed by a combination of deposits (debt) and shareholder equity.

- *Treasury money market mutual fund (TMMMF)* Its assets are Treasury bills or repurchase agreements collateralized by Treasury bills, and its liabilities are demandable equity shares having a proportional claim on the assets. A TMMMF is financed solely by equity.

- *Prime money market mutual fund (PMMMF)* Its assets are short-term federal agency securities, short-term bank certificates of deposit, bankers' acceptances, highly rated commercial paper, and repurchase agreements backed by low-risk collateral, and its liabilities are demandable equity shares having a proportional claim on the assets. As before, a PMMMF is financed solely by equity.

- *Collateralized demand deposit bank (CDDB)* Its assets are money market instruments with low credit risk and low interest-rate-risk, which are fully (over)collateralized, and its liabilities are demand deposits that have a secured claim on the collateral.

- *Utility bank (UB)* A UB is similar to a CDDB, except that collateral can include retail loans in addition to money market instruments. Putting aside operational risks inherent in the banking business, the reliability of an NB varies from completely stable (C-PeRB) to stable under most plausible circumstances (UB).

The difference between the balance sheet of a fractional reserve bank and that of an NB is shown in figure 8.5.

8.3.4 Types of Narrow Banks: The Time for an NB Is Now

While running an NB is relatively easy from a market perspective, and the capital required for doing so is comparatively small (under current Basel regulations, its size is determined by

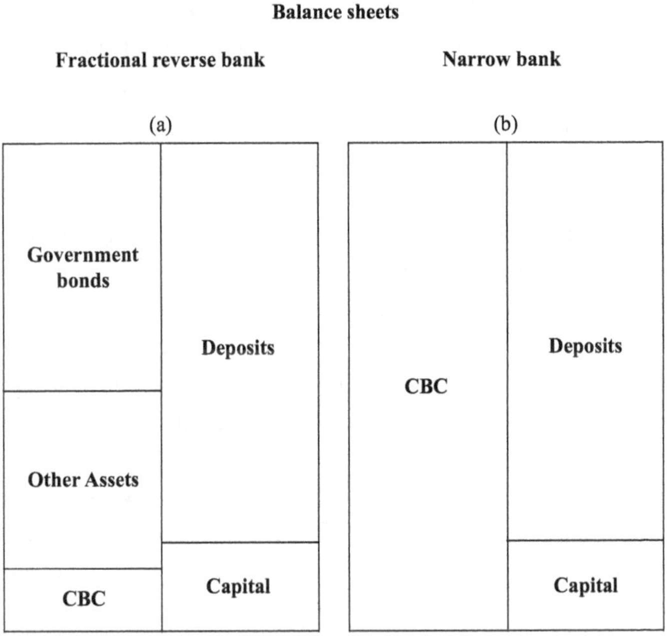

Balance sheets

Fractional reverse bank **Narrow bank**

(a) (b)

Government
bonds

Deposits Deposits

CBC

Other Assets

CBC Capital Capital

Figure 8.5
Balance sheets of a fractional reserve bank (a) and a narrow bank (b).

leverage alone), it naturally has to possess bulletproof security
and reliability. These requirements can be met by judiciously
building the corresponding ledger software and hardware. Of
course, in addition to purely operational aspects, the NB has to
satisfy the KYC/AML requirements. It is clear that a liberal use
of artificial intelligence, machine learning, and big data analytics
is necessary to accomplish this task efficiently. In this regard,
Trust::Data, a new framework for identity and data sharing

currently being developed at MIT, is particularly promising (see Pentland et al.[54]).

There is a perennial question of profitability of an NB. While a fractional reserve bank earns its living first and foremost via the net interest margin, the difference between the interest it charges its borrowers and the interest it pays its depositors, an NB seemingly is deprived of this all-important source of income. However, this is only partially true, since at present some central banks, including the Federal Reserve, do pay substantial interest on excess deposits. Besides, NBs can earn interest on securities and charge reasonable fees for transaction services. While their operating margins are certainly low (by yesteryear standards), so are their capital requirements, operating costs (because of an efficient infrastructure), and regulatory burdens. Thus, NBs could generate competitive returns on equity, which compare very favorably to those generated by their fractional reserve cousins. A quotation from Friedman captures the essence of the problem:

I shall depart from the original "Chicago Plan of Banking Reform" in only one respect, though one that I think is of great importance. I shall urge that interest be paid on the 100% reserves. This step will both improve the economic results yielded by the 100% reserve system, and, also, as a necessary consequence, render the system less subject to the difficulties of avoidance that were the bug-a-boo of the earlier proposals. This problem of how to set the rate of interest is another issue that I feel most uncertain about and that requires more attention than I have given to it.[55]

If NBs in different jurisdictions organize themselves as a network of sister banks, they can earn substantial (but fair) transaction fees on foreign exchange transactions. In principle, NBs can be affiliated with lending organizations with uninsured funding, the so-called lending affiliates. In view of this fact, lending facilities can be left to their own devices and be regulated by market forces.

It is clear that the adoption of narrow banking in its entirety would require a massive transformation of the financial ecosystem and should not be undertaken until numerous and nuanced questions dealing with the pros and cons of such a transformation are answered in sufficient detail. While we list some of the pros and cons here, we are interested in a less ambitious project—the introduction of an NB that would coexist with fractional reserve banks rather than supplant them completely. An interesting analogy jumps to mind—currently electric cars (NBs) coexist with conventional gasoline-powered cars (fractional reserve banks). While in the long run electric cars are likely to prevail over gasoline-powered cars, in the short run they can peacefully cohabit. In order to avoid academic discussions related to the transformation of the banking system from the fractional reserve to the narrow setup, we advocate creation of a few NBs as needed for achieving our specific goals. We anticipate coexistence of fractional reserve and NBs for a long time to come.

8.4 PROS AND CONS OF AN NB

8.4.1 Pros

There are many leading economists who advocate narrow banking because some of its benefits are self-evident. First, by construction, and in contrast to fractional reserve banks, assets and liabilities of NBs are perfectly aligned, so conventional stabilization mechanisms such as deposit insurance, discount window lending, rigorous regulation, and control of the balance sheet, without which fractional reserve banks could not exist, are simply not necessary. We emphasize, however, that other types of regulations are certainly needed, not least because NBs, like any other organization, are subject to operational risks, particularly from electronic attacks.

Second, since lending is performed by nonbanking institutions on an uninsured basis, governmental interference in bank lending and other activities can be dramatically reduced, if not completely eliminated. Third, deposit insurance can be reduced in size and eventually phased out.

8.4.2 Cons

Needless to say, narrow banking is not without its detractors. Some economists argue that NB will not be the silver bullet needed to kill financial instability, particularly because lending affiliates would suffer from the same issues as fractional reserve banks. Although this is true to some extent, it is clear that narrow banking can serve as a cornerstone of a stable and reliable payment system, capable of operating on its own even under the most extreme conditions, so the pressure on the financial ecosystem as a whole would be significantly less than with fractional reserve banking. To attract investors, lending affiliates would have to maintain their own strong capital cushions and look for long-term financing opportunities. Still, these measures in and of themselves might not be sufficient to ensure financial stability under all circumstances, so the "lender of last resort" in the form of a central bank would still have to be present in the system. Such a bank would provide required liquidity to uninsured lenders, including affiliates of NBs, against illiquid but sound collateral, thus avoiding a systemic credit collapse. This is compared with the current setup, where financial authorities support private banks through deposit insurance, access to the discount window, and implicit government guarantees.

Specifically, Miles argues that separation of deposit taking and lending would result in elevated agency costs and reduced stability of the supply of lending.[56] In all likelihood, this is not going to happen, since lenders would become much more efficient in order to survive without a cushion provided by depositors. Bossone emphasizes that the benefits of NBs in terms of financial stability are much smaller than the drawbacks associated with cutting the link between bank money and economic activity and creating "market incompleteness."[57] He thinks that this void will be filled by financial firms, whose operations will be as risky as the ones conducted by fractional reserve banks, so the overall stability of the financial ecosystem will not improve. Most interestingly from our standpoint, Bossone is not opposed to voluntary creation of NBs, or segregated NB subsidiaries within existing bank holding companies.[58]

The other danger is the risk of flight to quality from fractional reserve banks to NBs during times of financial instability, precisely when the former can least afford to lose their liquidity. This danger is not as acute as it might sound, because the actual amount of liquidity NBs can absorb is limited by their capital size.

8.5 NBS AS PART OF THE FINANCIAL ECOSYSTEM

8.5.1 Current Trends in Banks' Behavior

In the buildup to the global financial crisis, banks tried to stay as leveraged as possible by simultaneously reducing their capital ratio and choosing a progressively riskier asset mix. However, after 2008, their group behavior changed dramatically. The

balance sheet of the Federal Reserve is shown in figures 8.6 and
8.7. Comparison of these figures shows that the asset and liability
mix of the banking sector underwent a dramatic transformation
after the global financial crisis. One of the most striking aspects of
this change is the precipitous increase in excess reserves deposi-
tary institutions keep with the Federal Reserve. We are observing interesting and somewhat perplexing developments in that
until the onset of the global financial crisis, central banks were
run as NBs and commercial banks were run as fractional reserve
banks, while after the crisis the situation flipped, although not
completely. This fact shows that banks prefer to keep a considerable cash cushion, partly because they put an extra premium on

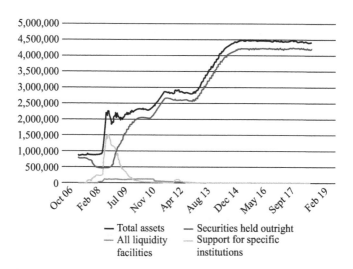

Figure 8.6
Assets of the Federal Reserve Bank. *Source*: Federal Reserve.

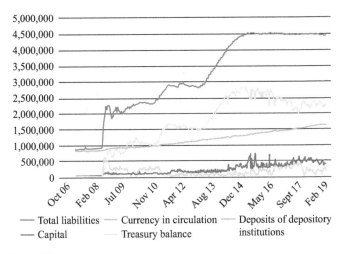

Figure 8.7

Liabilities of the Federal Reserve Bank. Excess reserves kept by commercial banks have increased enormously since 2008. *Source*: Federal Reserve.

maintaining high liquidity and partly because of lack of demand for loans. The attractive interest rate paid by the Federal Reserve on the excess deposits is clearly an additional motivation.

In view of these facts, it is clear that building an NB cannot and should not upend the overall balance of the banking ecosystem, since it is pretty much aligned with prevailing trends anyway.

8.5.2 What Can an NB Do for You?

A properly designed NB is a natural repository of funds for those who highly value their funds' stability (either by inclination, such as with wealthy individuals and organizations, or by necessity, such as among central clearing counterparties). It is also a natural emitter of FBDC. In addition, such a bank can do many other things. For instance, it can be used to hold nonoperational deposits, which conventional commercial banks do not want and cannot hold at a profit. It is also a custodian for initial margins supplied by investment banks as part of their regular over-the-counter derivatives business. These funds are naturally paid via FBDC and are kept safe by construction. Moreover, if so desired, the NB, being a neutral custodian, can provide value-added services, such as calculating the size of the required collateral and administering its allocation. An NB can also be a very useful source of digital identity.

8.5.3 Lending Affiliates: Credit Money Creators of the Future

If all banking institutions become narrow, then credit creation will be performed by lending affiliates and other lenders, for instance mutual funds or hedge funds. In fact, since the global financial crisis, a considerable portion of credit has been issued by nonbanks, while many banks keep massive excess reserves with central banks, thus becoming de facto more narrow. By reorganizing themselves into transaction-oriented NBs and lending affiliates, fractional reserve banks can become much more cost-efficient, nimble, and stable.

By construction, NBs offer their depositors a high level of safety, handle regulatory burdens with relative ease, require a low capital cushion, derive a stable and considerable flow of income from their transactional activities, and benefit from the interest paid on bank reserves by central banks. Transactional cash flow can be increased many times if foreign exchange and especially cryptocurrency issuance are included in the mix. At the same time, since NBs require a very limited capital cushion, which is needed to satisfy leverage ratio constraints and cover operational risks, they can offer a very attractive return on equity to their investors. Recall that a non-risk-based leverage ratio is calculated by dividing tier 1 capital by the bank's average total consolidated assets, which for NBs boils down to central bank reserves and short-term government paper. Under Basel III rules, banks have to maintain a leverage ratio in excess of 3 percent.

Given the simplicity of their balance sheets and the efficiency of state-of-the-art IT systems, NBs can use technological advancements, such as distributed ledgers and blockchain, to provide excellent transactional banking services and successfully compete with transaction-oriented financial technology start-ups (see Lipton,[59] Lipton, Shrier, and Pentland,[60] He et al.,[61] and Powell,[62] among others).

At the same time, uninsured lending affiliates of NBs, unencumbered by the requirement to provide utility-like transaction services, can better serve the needs of the real economy by offering traditional as well as innovative credit finance products. Given that lending affiliates would not have cheap sources of funding in the form of deposits, they would have to maintain healthy capital cushions and choose a quality of assets aligned with their risk appetite in order to attract savings and other forms of funding from investors. Lending affiliates would be stratified depending on the level of their speculative activities. Denuded of all amenities related to deposit insurance, lending affiliates will have their own skin in the game and be open to scrutiny by their investors.

Thus, splitting fractional reserve banks into NBs and lending affiliates would increase the investment value of both, much like nuclear fission releases enormous energy in nature.

8.5.4 Limited Impact of Narrow Banks on the Ecosystem at Large

Even though an NB by construction is impervious to market and liquidity shocks, it can suffer from operational risks. Hence, it requires a capital cushion. The size of this cushion is determined by the leverage ratio and is of the order 3–4 percent of its assets.

Thus, the amount of available capital effectively limits the amount of central bank money an NB can attract from fractional reserve banks. As a result, the potential systemic impact of such an institution on the financial system as a whole is limited. Besides, since an NB does not lend its funds, it is unable to create money "out of thin air," so from this angle also, its impact is limited.

Nevertheless, such a bank would have a great impact in other ways. First and foremost, it would create honest competition in the banking ecosystem and force conventional banks to pay fair interest to their depositors. Second, it would make FBDC expansion beyond its original narrow base a reality.

Finally, for the first time in recent history, such a bank would provide a venue for both retail and institutional depositors who are particularly concerned about availability and stability of their deposits even under the most extreme conditions. Among the institutional depositors, central clearing counterparties are the primary candidates, given that they have all kinds of negative externalities, including the fact that some of their largest clearing members are, at the same time, their bankers. Thus, the potential default of a clearing member can cause a double loss for such a CCP.

Narrow banking, being a radical departure from the familiar financial setup, naturally raises numerous questions for monetary policy, particularly regarding the manner of money creation and who should be responsible for it. The main issue is that to a large extent money will be created or destroyed by central banks, which would have to exercise preternatural abilities to do so properly. Money creation along these lines would be a de facto tool of central planning. Given that central planning is next to impossible to execute efficiently, the dangers can outweigh the benefits. The behavior of credit markets would be affected in a very profound way, since banks would no longer be natural sources of credit. All these effects have to be analyzed in detail before narrow banking is implemented in its entirety.

8.6 CBDC VERSUS FBDC

In principle, distributed ledgers can potentially become a truly transformative force by making central bank digital currency (CBDC) a reality, in a dramatic departure from the past. A variety of viewpoints on this subject, some of which are mutually exclusive and contradictory, can be found in Al-Jarhi,[63] Andolfatto,[64] Barrdear and Kumhof,[65] Broadbent,[66] Danezis and Meiklejohn,[67] Fung and Halaburda,[68] Koning,[69] Lipton,[70] Bordo and Levin,[71] Dyson and Hodgson,[72] Mersch,[73] Scorer,[74] and many others.

If central banks start to issue CBDC, not only can they abandon physical cash in favor of its electronic equivalent, as advocated by Rogoff,[75] but, eventually, retire a substantial portion of the government debt in its favor. This would be a very impactful development for society at large. Taken to its logical limit, CBDC can eliminate fractional banking's raison d'être and dramatically improve financial ecosystem resilience by allowing economic agents to have accounts at the central bank directly. As a result, these will dramatically reduce the ability of the banking sector to create money "out of thin air" and transfer this all-important function to central banks. However, central banks are not equipped to address the large-scale KYC/AML problem, which they would have to solve if they open their balance sheets to a large portion of economic agents rather than just licensed banks and selected financial institutions. While developments in this direction are inevitable, their timing and magnitude cannot be ascertained at present.

Realistically, we do not expect central banks' balance sheets to be open to all economic agents. Accordingly, we think that FBDC, being a private coin, is a much more convenient solution to digitization of the fiat currency than CBDC. Issued by a purpose-built NB, FBDC will be as reliable as fiat. At the same time, the corresponding bank can satisfactorily solve the KYC/AML problem and navigate the complicated political landscape. Moreover, NBs, organized as a network of sister banks incorporated in different jurisdictions, can simplify and cheapen foreign exchange transactions.

8.7 DIGITAL IDENTITY AND KYC/AML

With the emergence of blockchain and DLT, and their use for cryptocurrencies, the question of digital identity in the context of KYC/AML has come to the foreground. A major shortcoming in current identity systems on the internet is the lack of privacy with respect to transactions performed using these identities. This deficiency is also true in the context of blockchain-based currencies, such as Bitcoin, namely in the disclosure of identities through the reverse engineering and analytics of the public keys used in transactions recorded on the blockchain.

We believe a new breed of "cryptoidentities" may need to be devised that not only provides transaction confidentiality but more importantly also exhibits the features necessary to make it compliant with KYC/AML regulations. These cryptoidentities must be based on and derive from the appropriate combination of highly private and accurate personal data and must yield truthful assertions or claims regarding the owner relevant to the KYC/AML requirements. Additionally, for transaction confidentiality, these identities must be conditionally anonymity-verifiable, meaning that the identities must seem anonymous to nonparticipants and be reversible by KYC/AML processes. In this way, a chain of provenance (or chain of verifiability) can be established for a given digital identity from the transaction on the blockchain to the legal owners of the digital identity.

The area blockchain and DLT is currently still nascent, and additional infrastructure technologies will be needed in order for the full benefits of blockchain to be realized in a transformative manner in connection to digital identities. The report by Hardjono and Maler provides a broad industry review of identity technology and the relevance of blockchain to identity management.[76]

8.8 MORAL HAZARD

One of the greatest hazards of a widely used digital currency is that it could enable a repressive surveillance state. If the government can track all its citizens' payments, then it can exert unprecedented control over their lives. Nor is this situation just some science fiction fantasy; in parts of northern China, virtually all payments—for transportation, food, entertainment, communication, everything— are logged by just two companies, both of which collaborate closely and share data with the government.

To avoid this situation, small financial transactions, such as are currently performed with cash, must be anonymous. Exceptions to this anonymity should be few and far between. For instance, in serious criminal investigations or similar situations where there is an overriding social imperative, society may decide that it should be possible to override this anonymity using carefully vetted and expensive methods such as legal court orders.

Fortunately, there are a range of cryptographic methods to enforce levels of anonymity, ranging from technologies that allow complete unbreakable anonymity, to methods that provide anonymity for payers but not for sellers, to frameworks that provide anonymity except for court orders. For instance, a narrow bank can follow the Chaumian scheme and issue numbered and blind-signed currency units onto a distributed ledger, whose trust is maintained either by designated notaries or by the bank itself. KYC/AML requirements could be limited to large deposits or withdrawals, much as cash transactions are today.

8.9 CONCLUSIONS

In this chapter, we have outlined an efficient framework that can be used to extend the domain of applicability of the FBDC from an initial group of bank sponsors to a much wider group of potential users, including SMEs. We have argued that a purpose-built NB is necessary (and, we hope, sufficient) to achieve this goal. It can be used not only to securely hold collateral but also to solve the all-important KYC/AML problem. The FBDC, being a stable cryptocurrency, can facilitate both domestic and foreign trade and offer numerous possibilities for streamlining and facilitating commercial and retail transactions.

NOTES

1. Aristotle, *Nicomachean Ethics.*

2. S. Nakamoto, "Bitcoin: A Peer-to-Peer Electronic Cash System," 2008. https://bitcoin.org/bitcoin.pdf.

3. Tether is a representative example of such an attempt.

4. The lead author is a member of their advisory board.

5. B. Norman, R. Shaw, and G. Speight, "The History of Interbank Settlement Arrangements: Exploring Central Banks' Role in the Payment System," Bank of England Working Paper 412, June 2011.

6. M. Castro and B. Liskov, "Practical Byzantine Fault Tolerance," , in *Proceedings of the Third Symposium on Operating Systems Design and Implementation (OSDI), New Orleans, USA, February 1999,* 173–183, http://www.pmg.lcs.mit.edu/papers/osdi99.pdf.

7. L. Lamport, R. Shostak, and M. Pease, "The Byzantine Generals Problem," *ACM Transactions on Programming and Language Systems* 4, no. 3 (July 1982): 382–401.

8. Nakamoto, "Bitcoin."

9. V. Buterin, "What Proof of Stake Is and Why It Matters," *Bitcoin Magazine,* August 2013, https://bitcoinmagazine.com/articles/what-proof-of -stake-is-and-why-it-matters-1377531463.

10. J. Chen and S. Micali, "Algorand: The Efficient and Democratic Ledger," July 2016, http://arxiv.org/abs/1607.01341.

11. D. Schwartz, N. Youngs, and A. Britto, *The Ripple Protocol Consensus Algorithm*, Ripple Inc. technical report, 2014.

12. Given that records of Bitcoin transactions are preserved in perpetuity, it might not be as good as believed for such activities.

13. In real life, even movements from native Bitcoin addresses are performed with the assistance of digital currency exchanges, such as Coinbase, which is orthogonal to the very idea of decentralization.

14. Here, FBDC is coming into play. FBDCs, being fully fiat-backed tokens, reside on the ledger. Since they are backed by the fiat currency at a one-to-one ratio, the corresponding delivery versus payment problem is solved naturally.

15. Schwartz, Youngs, and Britto, *The Ripple Protocol Consensus Algorithm*.

16. D. L. Chaum, A. Fiat, and M. Naor, "Untraceable Electronic Cash," in *Proceedings on Advances in Cryptology (CRYPTO'88)*, ed. S. Goldwasser, Lecture Notes in Computer Science 403 (New York: Springer-Verlag, 1990), 319–327, http://dl.acm.org/citation.cfm?id=88314.88969.

17. A. Lipton and A. Pentland, "Breaking the Bank," *Scientific American* 318, no. 1 (2018): 26–31.

18. A. Lipton, T. Hardjono, and A. Pentland, "Digital Trade Coin (DTC): Towards a More Stable Digital Currency," *Journal of the Royal Society Open Science (RSOS)* 5, no. 7 (August 2018): 180155, https://doi.org/10.1098/rsos.180155.

19. G. Pennacchi, "Narrow Banking," *Annual Review of Financial Economics* 4, no. 1 (October 2012): 141–159, https://ideas.repec.org/a/anr/refeco/v4y2012p141-159.html.

20. K. Dittmer, "100 Percent Reserve Banking: A Critical Review of Green Perspectives," *Ecological Economics* 109, no. C (2015): 9–16, https://ideas.repec.org/a/eee/ecolec/v109y2015icp9-16.html.

21. W. Roberds and F. R. Velde, "Early Public Banks," Federal Reserve Bank of Atlanta Working Paper, August 2014.

22. NarrowBanking, www.narrowbanking.org.

23. H. Bodenhorn, *A History of Banking in Antebellum America*(Cambridge: Cambridge University Press, 2000), https://ideas.repec.org/b/cup/cbooks /9780521662857.html.

24. Pennacchi, "Narrow Banking."

25. F. Soddy, *Wealth, Virtual Wealth, and Debt*, American ed. (New York: E. P. Dutton, 1933).

26. F. Knight, G. Cox, A. Director, P. Douglas, A. Hart, L. Mints, H. Schultz, and H. Simons, "Memorandum on Banking Reform," Franklin D. Roosevelt Presidential Library, President's Personal File 431, 1933.

27. A. G. Hart, "The 'Chicago Plan' of Banking Reform, I: A Proposal for Making Monetary Management Effective in the United States," *Review of Economic Studies* 2, no. 2 (1935): 104–116.

28. P. Douglas, I. Fisher, F. D. Graham, E. J. Hamilton, W. I. King, and C. R. Whittlesey, "A Program for Monetary Reform," 1939, available at Chicago Booth, https://faculty.chicagobooth.edu/amir.sufi/research/MonetaryRe form_1939.pdf .

29. I. Fisher, *100% Money; Designed to Keep Checking Banks 100% Liquid; to Prevent Inflation and Deflation; Largely to Cure or Prevent Depressions: and to Wipe Out Much of the National Debt* (New York: Adelphi Press, 1945).

30. R. J. Phillips, "The 'Chicago Plan' and New Deal Banking Reform," in *Stability in the Financial System*, ed. D. Papadimitriou (London: Palgrave Macmillan UK, 1996), 94–114.

31. M. Friedman, *A Program for Monetary Stability* (New York: Fordham University Press, 1959).

32. J. Tobin, *Financial Innovation and Deregulation in Perspective—Issue 635 of Cowles Foundation Paper* (New Haven, CT: Cowles Foundation for Research in Economics at Yale University, 1986).

33. R. E. Litan, *What Should Banks Do?* (Washington, DC: Brookings Institution Press, 1987).

34. L. Bryan, "Core Banking," *McKinsey Quarterly* 1 (1991): 61–74.

35. J. B. Burnham, "Deposit Insurance: The Case for the Narrow Bank in Regulation," *Cato Review of Business and Government* 14, no. 2 (1991): 35–43, https://www.cato.org/sites/cato.org/files/serials/files/regulation/1991/4/v14n2-4.pdf .

36. G. Pennacchi and G. Gorton, "Money Market Funds and Finance Companies: Are They the Banks of the Future?," in *Structural Change in Banking*, ed. M. Klausner and L. White (Irwin Publishing, 1993).

37. J. Huber and J. Robertson, *Creating New Money: A Monetary Reform for the Information Age* (London: New Economics Foundation, 2000).

38. S. Kobayakawa and H. Nakamura, "A Theoretical Analysis of Narrow Banking Proposals," *Monetary and Economic Studies* 18, no. 1 (May 2000): 105–118.

39. M. A. Al-Jarhi, "Remedy for Banking Crises: What Chicago and Islam Have in Common: A Comment," *Islamic Economic Studies* 11, no. 2 (2004): 24–42.

40. V. F. Garca, V. F. Cibils, and R. Maino, "Remedy for Banking Crises: What Chicago and Islam Have in Common," *Islamic Economic Studies* 11, no. 2 (2004): 2–22, https://ideas.repec.org/a/ris/isecst/0067.html.

41. J. Kay, "Should We Have 'Narrow Banking'?," in *The Future of Finance: The LSE Report*, ed. A. Turner (London: London School of Economics, 2010), 217–234.

42. L. J. Kotlikoff, *Jimmy Stewart Is Dead: Ending the World's Ongoing Financial Plague with Limited Purpose Banking* (Hoboken, NJ: John Wiley and Sons, 2011).

43. R. J. Phillips and A. Roselli, "How to Avoid the Next Taxpayer Bailout of the Financial System: The Narrow Banking Proposal," in *Financial Market Regulation: Legislation and Implications*, ed. J. A. Tatom (New York: Springer, 2011), 149–161.

44. M. Kumhof and J. Benes, "The Chicago Plan Revisited," International Monetary Fund Working Paper 12/202, August 2012, https://ideas .repec.org/p/imf/imfwpa/12-202.html.

45. C. Chamley, L. J. Kotlikoff, and H. M. Polemarchakis, "Limited-Purpose Banking–Moving from 'Trust Me' to 'Show Me' Banking," *American Economic Review* 102, no. 3 (2012): 113–119.

46. Pennacchi, "Narrow Banking."

47. C. van Dixhoorn, "Full Reserve Banking: An Analysis of Four Monetary Reform Plans," Sustainable Finance Lab, 2013, https://sustainablefinancelab .nl/wp-content/uploads/sites/334/2019/02/Full-Reserve-Banking -Dixhoorn-SFL.pdf.

48. A. Admati and M. Hellwig, *The Bankers' New Clothes: What's Wrong with Banking and What to Do about It* (Princeton, NJ: Princeton University Press, 2013), https://ideas.repec.org/b/pup/pbooks/9929.html.

49. J. H. Cochrane, "Toward a Run-Free Financial System," in *Across the Great Divide: New Perspectives on the Financial Crisis*, ed. M. N. Baily and J. B. Taylor (Stanford, CA: Hoover Institution, Stanford University, 2014), 1–53, https://www.hoover.org/sites/default/files/across-the-great-divide-ch10.pdf.

50. Dittmer, "100 Percent Reserve Banking."

51. E. Nosal, R. Garratt, J. J. McAndrews, and A. Martin, *Segregated Balance Accounts*, Federal Reserve Bank of New York Staff Report 730, May 2015, https://ideas.repec.org/p/fip/fednsr/730.html.

52. J. McMillan, *The End of Banking: Money, Credit, and the Digital Revolution* (Zurich: Zero/One Economics, 2015).

53. Pennacchi, "Narrow Banking."

54. A. Pentland, D. Shrier, T. Hardjono, and I. Wladawsky-Berger, "Towards an Internet of Trusted Data," in *Trusted Data—a New Framework for Identity and Data Sharing*, ed. T. Hardjono, A. Pentland, and D. Shrier (Cambridge, MA: MIT Press, 2019), 15–40.

55. Friedman, *A Program for Monetary Stability*.

56. W. Miles, "Can Narrow Banking Provide a Substitute for Depository Intermediaries?," Federal Reserve Bank of St. Louis, First Annual Missouri Economics Conference, May 4–5, 2001, 1–25, https://files.stlouisfed .org/files/htdocs/conferences/moconf/papers/miles.pdf.

57. B. Bossone, "Should Banks Be Narrowed? An Evaluation of a Plan to Reduce Financial Instability," Levy Economics Institute, Economics Public Policy Brief Archive 69, 2002, https://ideas.repec.org/p/lev/levppb /ppb69.html.

58. Bossone, "Should Banks Be Narrowed?"

59. A. Lipton, "Banks Must Embrace Their Digital Destiny," *Risk Magazine*, July 2016, https://www.risk.net/derivatives/2466314/banks-must-embrace -their-digital-destiny.

60. A. Lipton, D. Shrier, and A. Pentland, "Digital Banking Manifesto: The End of Banks," MIT Connection Science, 2016, https://www.getsmarter .com/blog/wp-content/uploads/2017/07/mit_digital_bank_manifesto _report.pdf.

61. D. He, R. B. Leckow, V. Haksar, T. M. Griffoli, N. Jenkinson, M. Kashima, T. Khiaonarong, C. Rochon, and H. Tourpe, "Fintech and Financial Services; Initial Considerations," International Monetary Fund Staff Discussion Notes 17/05, June 2017, https://ideas.repec.org/p/imf /imfsdn/17-05.html.

62. J. H. Powell, "Innovation, Technology, and the Payments System" (speech at Blockchain: The Future of Finance and Capital Markets?, New Haven, CT, March 2017), https://www.federalreserve.gov/newsevents/spee ch/powell20170303a.htm.

63. Al-Jarhi, "Remedy For Banking Crises: A Comment."

64. D. Andolfatto, "Fedcoin: On the Desirability of a Government Crypto-currency," February 2015, http://andolfatto.blogspot.com/2015/02/fedcoin -on-desirability-of-government.html.

65. J. Barrdear and M. Kumhof, "The Macroeconomics of Central Bank Issued Digital Currencies," Bank of England Working Paper 605, July 2016, https://ideas.repec.org/p/boe/boeewp/0605.html.

66. B. Broadbent, "Central Banks and Digital Currencies" (speech by Mr. Ben Broadbent, Deputy Governor for Monetary Policy of the Bank of England, at the London School of Economics, London, March 2, 2016), https://www.bis.org/review/r160303e.pdf.

67. G. Danezis and S. Meiklejohn, "Centrally Banked Cryptocurrencies," December 2015, https://arxiv.org/abs/1505.06895.

68. B. Fung and H. Halaburda, "Central Bank Digital Currencies: A Framework for Assessing Why and How," Bank of Canada Discussion Paper 16–22, 2016, https://ideas.repec.org/p/bca/bocadp/16-22.html.

69. J. P. Koning, *Fedcoin: A Central Bank-Issued Cryptocurrency*, R3 Consortium Technical Report, November 2016, https://www.r3.com/wp-content /uploads/2017/06/fedcoincentral-bankR3.pdf.

70. A. Lipton, "The Decline of the Cash Empire," *Risk Magazine*, October 2016, https://www.risk.net/risk-management/2475663/decline-cash -empire.

71. M. D. Bordo and A. T. Levin, "Central Bank Digital Currency and the Future of Monetary Policy," NBER Working Paper 23711, National Bureau

of Economic Research, Cambridge, MA, August 2017, https://ideas.repec.org/p/nbr/nberwo/23711.html.

72. B. Dyson and G. Hodgson, "Digital Cash: Why Central Banks Should Start Issuing Electronic Money," Positive Money, 2016, https://positivemoney.org/publications/digital-cash/.

73. Y. Mersch, "Digital Base Money: An Assessment from the ECB's Perspective" (speech at the farewell ceremony for Pentti Hakkarainen, Finlands Bank, Helsinki, January 16, 2017), https://www.ecb.europa.eu/press/key/date/2017/html/sp170116.en.html.

74. S. Scorer, "Central Bank Digital Currency: DLT, or not DLT? That Is the Question," Bank Underground, June 2017, https://bankunderground.co.uk/2017/06/05/central-bank-digital-currency-dlt-or-not-dlt-that-is-the-question/.

75. K. S. Rogoff, *The Curse of Cash* (Princeton, NJ: Princeton University Press, 2016).

76. T. Hardjono and E. Maler, *Blockchain and Smart Contracts Report,* Kantara Initiative Report, June 2017, https://kantarainitiative.org/confluence/display/BSC/Home.

STABLE NETWORK DYNAMICS IN A TOKENIZED
FINANCIAL ECOSYSTEM

Shahar Somin, Goren Gordon, Alex Pentland,
Erez Shmueli, and Yaniv Altshuler

9.1 INTRODUCTION

A central concern with any economic system is its stability and resilience. Use of distributed data resources and distributed encryption methods helps with many security problems. However, as the wild price history of Bitcoin shows, use of distributed functions and secure methods does little to guarantee stability. A further concern is centralization and monopoly. During the last decade, a handful of companies have contributed to an alarmingly centralized World Wide Web. Google and Facebook directly influence over 70 percent of internet traffic.[1]

Moreover, dominance on the internet affects the entire economy. For instance, in digital advertising, almost 60 percent of spending went to Google and Facebook in 2016. Amazon accounted for 43 percent of e-commerce sales in the United States that same year. Such digital monopolies also have important implications for journalism, politics, and society.[2] Such centralization, associated data scandals, and other side effects have led to suggestions that breaking up these large network monopolies may ultimately be the only solution.[3]

But how can one tell that a company is too large or when the network is becoming unstable? At what point should regulators interfere and how? We need answers to these and similar questions, using a framework that is largely independent of the system under scrutiny. At the heart of all these networks is the ubiquitous law of proportional growth, stating that a firm's growth rate is proportional to its size. More specifically, we consider a system of agents whereby the rate at which any given agent establishes connections to other agents is proportional to its already existing number of connections and its intrinsic fitness. This representation is known to apply to a large class of interacting systems[4] and carries a risk of centralization[5] in the sense that removal of a few dominant agents would collapse the entire system.

9.1.1 Dynamics of a Digital Economy

Most of today's network economies include distributed communication networks (e.g., the internet), but transactions occur in centralized and conventional enterprise management software, and humans are part of the accounting and audit systems. The purest examples of network economies today have both communication and transaction execution on the distributed network, including standard accounting and audit functions. Efficiency, transparency, cost, and security are pushing all economic ecosystems toward this more distributed, all-digital network technology, leaving only proprietary, private, or legal functions on the periphery.

Such fully distributed digital systems are often called distributed ledger or blockchain technologies. This category includes systems such as Estonia's long-standing government infrastructure, China's new "smart city" infrastructure, Singapore's Project Ubin trade and logistics infrastructure, national digital currencies being deployed by China and Singapore, and grassroots systems such as Bitcoin. These systems are proliferating throughout the globe and giving birth to new types of economic ecosystems. These new ecosystems present new types of challenges for policymakers and regulators because of their potential economic and social impacts, which could fundamentally alter traditional financial and social structures.

Perhaps the archetypal example of such a new economy is a system called Ethereum, which was launched in July 2015[6] and today has 1.4 million users and a $25 billion capitalization. The Ethereum network includes a public ledger that keeps records of all Ethereum-related transactions. The Ethereum ledger is able to store not only ownership, similar to Bitcoin, but also execution code, in the form of "smart contracts." This has led to the creation of a large number of new types of "tokens," which are tradable securities offered by a wide variety of service providers, with all transactions carried out by their corresponding smart contracts and all publicly accessible, although encrypted, on the Ethereum ledger. As a result, the Ethereum network ecosystem constitutes a unique example of a large-scale, highly varied financial ecosystem, whose entire transaction history is publicly available from its inception.

In this chapter, we will analyze the dynamical properties of the Ethereum financial ecosystem, with an eye toward understanding its stability and resilience. We show that the Ethereum financial ecosystem, despite being hugely heterogeneous in terms of users, services, tradable certificates (called tokens), and accounts (called wallets), still satisfies the key stability and resilience properties that characterize older financial networks. We will make use of all Ethereum network transactions between February 2016 and June 2018, resulting in 88,985,493 token trades performed by 17,611,649 unique wallets.

To accomplish this task, we will observe γ, the power of the degree distribution (e.g., the exponent that characterizes the distribution of transaction connections between actors within the Ethereum network). We will show how this metaparameter is able to describe the dynamics and consolidation process of the network through time, despite exponential growth of the network and the churn of services, investments, and users. In particular, we demonstrate that the dynamics of the Ethereum economy, as captured by γ, can be modeled as a damped harmonic oscillator, enabling the prediction of an economic network's *future* dynamics.

The ability to predict the future dynamics of the Ethereum network (or other digital economies) can provide policymakers with a useful tool for designing regulations and mechanisms to control instabilities within the network. Finally, drawing on further work by Lera, Pentland, and Sornette,[7] we will describe the intervention required to control monopolies and will argue that this same method can be applied to other financial networks as a better method for antitrust regulators to use to prevent monopolies.

9.2 BACKGROUND AND RELATED WORK

The Ethereum network is perhaps the first to support execution of smart contracts.[8] Smart contracts are computer programs formalizing digital agreements that automatically enforce agreed conditions, thereby allowing the execution of contractual agreements while enforcing their correctness. The development of "digital law" for regulation of such contracts is discussed in chapter 14 and at http://law.mit.edu.

There has been a recent surge in attempts to model social dynamics via statistical physics tools.[9] Frisch,[10] who started this trend, has suggested using a damped oscillator to model the postwar economy or disasters, based on the assumption that there is an equilibrium state that has been perturbed. Network science has added a new dimension to our understanding of these dynamics by modeling the transaction graph connecting individual actors. This type of analysis has been usefully applied to social networks,[11] computer communication networks,[12] biological systems,[13] transportation,[14] emergency detection,[15] and financial trading systems.[16]

Because the first objective of this chapter is to explore the dynamics of the diverse Ethereum network over time, we begin by observing weekly rolling window snapshots of the network's transaction data. This data is shown in figure 9.1, where it is

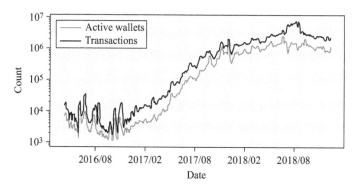

Figure 9.1

Number of weekly active wallets and transaction volume.

obvious that there is exponential growth within a highly unpredictable ecosystem. This erratic behavior, across multiple properties, might suggest that the Ethereum network is unstable.

However, traditional metrics such as number of transactions or number of wallets are only a surface representation of the economic network. We are instead interested in its dynamics and in predicting its stability. To accomplish this goal, we first explore the network's degree of distribution and verify that the Ethereum network has the same network properties as other real-world networks. We therefore construct a directed graph consisting of all transactions during the two-and-a-half-year period examined.

The resulting graph consists of 6,890,237 vertices and 17,392,610 edges. Outgoing edges depict transactions in which wallet u sold a token to other wallets and incoming edges to u are formed as a result of transactions in which u bought any token from others. The Outgoing degree of vertex u represents the number of unique wallets buying tokens from u, and its incoming degree depicts the number of unique wallets selling tokens to it.

Surprisingly, despite the great heterogeneity of tokens and exponential growth, the degree of distribution very accurately follows the standard power-law pattern of other financial networks, such as those of Newman[17] and Altshuler, Pan, and Pentland.[18] As shown in figure 9.2, the Ethereum network has a few very connected nodes (wallets) with exponentially fewer and fewer connections present in more and more nodes (wallets).

In order to apply network theory to modeling the Ethereum network's dynamics over time, we also verify that temporal snapshots of this network adhere to a power-law model. We therefore form and analyze *weekly transaction graphs*, each of which is based on one

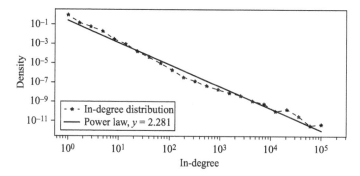

Figure 9.2

Analysis of Ethereum network dynamics for a two-year period from February 2016 to June 2018. The network nodes are wallets, and edges are formed by buy and sell transactions. The outgoing degree of a node reflects the number of unique wallets receiving tradable securities (tokens) from that node, and vice versa for the incoming degree. Both outgoing and incoming degrees have a power-law distribution, similar to what was demonstrated in the analysis of mobile phone, citation data, and many other real-world networks (see, e.g., M. E. Newman, "The Structure and Function of Complex Networks," *SIAM Review* 45, no. 2 (2003): 167–256).

week of all Ethereum transactions. Similar to the overall power-law fit shown in figure 9.2, each of the weekly graphs also follows power-law patterns, and their *goodness-of-fit*, measured by their R^2, is lower bounded by 0.8 and converges to 1.0 (a perfect fit).

9.3 THE DAMPED OSCILLATOR MODEL

We can also calculate the γ exponents separately for both incoming and outgoing degree distributions for each of these weekly graphs. The exponents of both γ_t^{in} and γ_t^{out} are shown in figure 9.3, and it is clear that the time evolution of both the incoming-degree exponent and the outgoing-degree exponent can be modeled as a harmonic damped oscillator.

The damped oscillator model has a constant *stable state* and is governed by five parameters: (1) λ, the exponential decay; (2), the angular frequency; (3) γ_∞, the stable state to which the system

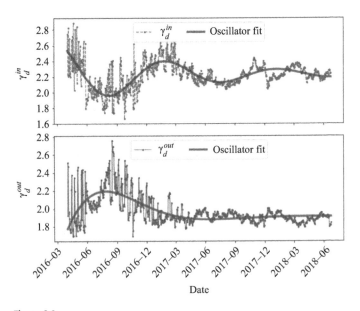

Figure 9.3
Ethereum transaction network temporal development, demonstrating the underlying consolidation process the network undergoes. Evolution of the incoming degree distribution, γ_t^{in}, is shown in the upper panel, and the outgoing degree distribution, γ_t^{out}, is displayed in the lower panel. Both converge toward stable states following a harmonic damped oscillator model.

converges; (4) A, the maximum amplitude of the oscillation; and (5) ϕ, the phase of the oscillation.

As illustrated in figure 9.3, our analysis demonstrates the underlying temporal consolidation process of the Ethereum ecosystem during the 30 months, reaching an equilibrium with respect to the essential network characteristics, γ_t^{out} and γ_t^{in}. Though unpredictable in many surface aspects, such as exchange rates, number of active wallets, and activity volume, when observed as a dynamic process it is clear that the Ethereum network undergoes a steady consolidation process, reaching an equilibrium, which it has maintained to this day.

We conclude that the Ethereum network conforms to the statistics of other social networks.[19] There is no a priori theoretical justification as to why a highly heterogeneous amalgamation of unrelated tokens, each with a different source and functionality, will result in a cohesive, single network behaving according to the well-established principles of other human networks unless all the elements of the transaction network share a common dynamics originating from the character of the underlying market. Our results therefore support the idea that the Ethereum network has condensed into a single community.

9.4 INTERPRETATION

To better understand the character of the Ethereum network's oscillating dynamics, it is useful to understand the meaning of γ, the exponent of the power-law degree distribution. The degree distribution's slope (on the log-log scale) intuitively describes the ratio between the number of sparsely connected wallets at the network's edge and the number of connections of the network's largest hub. For instance, a *small* γ means the ratio between the number of sparsely connected wallets and the size of the largest hub is small.

We note that the Ethereum network's dynamics can be roughly divided into two phases, with a transition occurring around April 2017, when exponential growth of the number of "edge" wallets began because of a rush of new human users. During the first phase, with a relatively small number of participants, the number of buyers and sellers in the network and the sizes of the associated hubs were all quite comparable; however, both γ^{in} and γ^{out} show large antiphase oscillations, signifying an "overshoot" of the system beyond its equilibrium state. This is the hallmark of a potentially dangerous underdamped oscillator. This overshoot in γ^{in} and γ^{out} may represent "herd" behavior of many individuals/ wallets entering the community and making a small number of buying transactions.

During the second phase, however, the number of sellers and buyers started undergoing exponential growth. During this period, the largest selling hub became excessively large, accompanied by a substantially lower number of active sellers in the network, correlating with its rather low γ^{out} and corresponding to the much more damped oscillations in that period. We further note that γ^{in} continued presenting oscillatory behavior in the second phase, with γ^{in} values higher than 2, as the ratio between buyers in the network and the size of the largest buying hub remained high.

9.5   PREDICTION

Once the damped oscillator modeling parameters of the Ethereum network's dynamics are established, the resulting analytic model can also be used for predictive purposes. We can, for instance, predict future values of γ based on fitting to a damped oscillator during the first 18 months of data and then extending that fit to predict the second year.

The prediction for γ^{in} is shown in figure 9.4 (upper panel) and shows that damped oscillations during the last year of data can be accurately predicted by the oscillator model trained during the first phase of network growth. Figure 9.4 (bottom panel) shows that future γ^{out} dynamics are predicted fairly well but not as well as for γ^{in}.

One explanation for the greater precision of γ^{in} predictions is that the vertical line marks the beginning of the period of exponential growth in the number of wallets. This characteristic of γ^{out} is described by Barabási,[20] where it is claimed that networks are anomalous among naturally occurring scale-free networks, since their largest hub grows faster than the network's size, N.

9.6   REGULATION OF FINANCIAL NETWORKS

The analysis so far shows that the Ethereum network converged to stable dynamics once the level of transaction activity became large. Can we use this example to better understand what sorts of regulatory policies will enforce this sort of stability and prevent monopolies? The answer is yes; this network perspective gives us a new way to understand how to make better predictions of

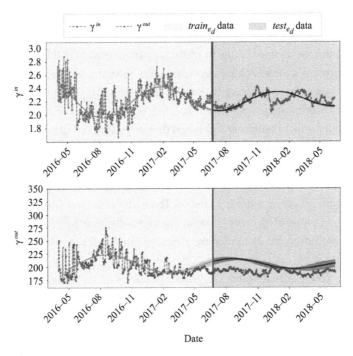

Figure 9.4

Prediction of γ dynamics for both incoming degree (top panel) and outgoing degree (bottom panel). Training was performed until the estimation date e_d = June 25, 2017, denoted by the vertical line. The test data contains γ^{in} and γ^{out} values from the last year of data, starting from the vertical line up until June 2018.

impending financial problems and what sort of financial regulation will be most effective at preventing these problems.

For instance, Lera, Pentland, and Sornette[21] used a model similar to that used in the Ethereum analysis shown here and developed a way to map a system of interacting agents into a phase space in which the "distance" from a regime of unhealthy centralization can be measured. This allows anticipation of the emergence of overly dominant agents ex ante and construction of methods for early intervention. This distance they develop is quite similar to the oscillation damping factor for γ^{in} and γ^{out} that we have shown for the Ethereum network.

Lera, Pentland, and Sornette show that in a sufficiently active economic system, seemingly overly fit traders may temporarily emerge essentially out of a streak of luck and then vanish as quickly as they appeared. In other words, the dynamics of the fitnesses themselves change quickly enough that no systematic instability can grow explosively. However, in a slower-paced economic system, such a self-correction does not necessarily happen.

This change in system dynamics can be seen between the first phase of growth in the Ethereum network, where there were relatively few transactions and correspondingly large oscillations in the degree distribution, and the second phase, where the system became much more active and the dangerous oscillations subsided. In such situations, an external regulator (e.g., the state) may wish to interfere and assert system stability. However, ad hoc punishment of individual, particularly fit agents not only seems "unfair" but is in the end useless, because the emergence of winner-takes-all (WTA) situations is a consequence of the distribution of fitnesses as a whole.

In fact, the dynamics of growth gives rise to two distinct asymptotic regimes: the fit-get-richer (FGR) regime and the WTA regime. In the latter, the system is largely dependent and controlled by just a few agents. In statistical quantum mechanics, this regime corresponds to a Bose-Einstein condensate.[22] In the socioeconomic context, the dominant agents have been termed dragon kings.[23]

The quantitative difference between the two regimes can be well understood in terms of how the network degree distributions in γ^{in} and γ^{out} change over time. The FGR regime corresponds to a power-law degree distribution, with agents' influences distributed over a wide range of values. In the WTA regime, the distribution exhibits a truncated power law, with one or more agents that have degree larger than the point of truncation and dominate the system disproportionately.

This result implies that the common countermeasure of stopping the most dominant agents from growing further does not solve the problem sustainably. Instead, it is the weakest agents that need to be supported to generate an overall more balanced fitness landscape and thus a healthier, more stable system.

Currently, governments address centralization issues with progressive taxes, antitrust laws, and similar legislation. However, this analysis of network dynamics reveals that this naive approach addresses only the symptom of disproportionately dominant firms rather than the underlying cause, which is that the structure of the financial network is fundamentally imbalanced. Instead of punishing the most competitive firms, one should foster competition that is more balanced by improving the relative fitness of underperforming agents.

The important implication for practical purposes is that controlling the system by taming the few largest or fittest agents is not effective. Dampening or rewiring of dominant nodes might delay but not prevent WTA dominance, akin to similar observations in the context of explosive percolation.[24] Instead, to effectively prevent the formation of winner-takes-all situations, the fitness landscape as a whole must be considered.

NOTES

1. A. Staltz, "The Web Began Dying in 2014. Here's How," staltz.com, 2017, https://staltz.com/the-web-began-dying-in-2014-heres-how.html.

2. M. Moore and D. Tambini, *Digital Dominance: The Power of Google, Amazon, Facebook, and Apple* (Oxford: Oxford University Press, 2018).

3. G. Faulconbridge and P. Sandle , "Father of Web Says Tech Giants May Have to Be Split Up," *Reuters*, November 1, 2018, https://www.reuters .com/article/us-technology-www/father-of-web-says-tech-giants-may -have-to-be-split-up-idUSKCN1N63MV.

4. M. Bell, S. Perera, M. Piraveenan, M. Bliemer, T. Latty, and C. Reid, "Network Growth Models: A Behavioural Basis for Attachment Proportional to Fitness," *Scientific Reports* 7, 42431 (2017), https://doi.org/10.1038 /srep42431.

5. G. Bianconi and A. L. Barabasi, "Bose-Einstein Condensation in Complex Networks," *Physical Review Letters* 86, no. 24 (2001):5632–5635.

6. V. Buterin, "A Next-Generation Smart Contract and Decentralized Application Platform," Ethereum Foundation white paper, 2014.

7. S. Lera, A. Pentland, and D. Sornette, "Prediction and Prevention of Disproportionally Dominant Agents," *PNAS* 117, no. 44 (2020): 27090–27095, https://doi.org/10.1073/pnas.2003632117.

8. Buterin, "A Next-Generation Smart Contract and Decentralized Application Platform."

9. C. Castellano, S. Fortunato, and V. Loreto, "Statistical Physics of Social Dynamics," *Reviews of Modern Physics* 81, no. 2 (2009): 591-646, https://doi.org/10.1103/RevModPhys.81.591.

10. R. Frisch, "Propagation Problems and Impulse Problems in Dynamic Economics," in *Economic Essays in Honour of Gustav Cassel* (London: Allen & Unwin, 1933), 171–173, 181–190, 197–203); reprinted in D. Hendry and M. Morgan, *The Foundations of Econometric Analysis* (Cambridge: Cambridge University Press, 1995), 333–346, https://doi.org/10.1017/CBO9781139170116.032.

11. M. E. Newman, "The Structure and Function of Complex Networks," *SIAM Review* 45, no. 2 (2003): 167–256.

12. R. Pastor-Satorras and A. Vespignani, *Evolution and Structure of the Internet: A Statistical Physics Approach* (Cambridge: Cambridge University Press, 2007).

13. A.-L. Barabasi and Z. N. Oltvai, "Network Biology: Understanding the Cell's Functional Organization," *Nature Reviews Genetics* 5, no. 2 (2004): 101–113, https://doi.org/10.1038/nrg1272.

14. Y. Altshuler, R. Puzis, Y. Elovici, S. Bekhor, and A. Pentland, "On the Rationality and Optimality of Transportation Networks Defense: A Network Centrality Approach," in *Securing Transportation Systems*, ed. S. Hakim, G. Albert, and Y. Shiftan (New York: John Wiley & Sons, 2015), 35–63.

15. Y. Altshuler, M. Fire, E. Shmueli, Y. Elovici, A. Bruckstein, A. S. Pentland, and D. Lazer, "The Social Amplifier—Reaction of Human Communities to Emergencies," *Journal of Statistical Physics* 152, no. 3 (2013): 399–418.

16. Y. Altshuler, W. Pan, and A. Pentland, "Trends Prediction Using Social Diffusion Models," in *Social Computing, Behavioral-Cultural Modeling and Prediction*, ed. S. J. Yang, A. M. Greenberg, and M. Endsley,

SBP 2012, Lecture Notes in Computer Science vol. 7227 (Berlin: Springer, 2012), 97–104. https://doi.org/10.1007/978-3-642-29047-3_12.

17. Newman, "The Structure and Function of Complex Networks."

18. Altshuler, Pan, and Pentland, "Trends Prediction Using Social Diffusion Models."

19. Newman, "The Structure and Function of Complex Networks"; Pastor-Satorras and Vespignani, *Evolution and Structure of the Internet*; Barabasi and Oltvai, "Network Biology"; Altshuler et al., "On the Rationality and Optimality of Transportation Networks Defense."

20. A.-L. Barabási, *Network Science* (Cambridge: Cambridge University Press, 2016).

21. Lera, Pentland, and Sornette, "Prediction and Prevention of Disproportionally Dominant Agents."

22. Bianconi and Barabasi, "Bose-Einstein Condensation in Complex Networks."

23. D. Sornette and G. Ouillon, "Dragon-Kings: Mechanisms, Statistical Methods and Empirical Evidence," *European Physical Journal Special Topics* 205, no. 1 (2012): 1–26.

24. R. D'Souza and J. Nagler, "Anomalous Critical and Supercritical Phenomena in Explosive Percolation," *Nature Physics* 11, no. 7 (2015): 531–538, https://doi.org/10.1038/nphys3378.

III

DATA AND AI: A NEW ECOLOGY

TOWARD AN ECOSYSTEM OF TRUSTED DATA AND AI

Alex Pentland and Thomas Hardjono

10.1 INTRODUCTION

As the economy and society move from a world where interactions are physical and based on paper documents toward a world that is primarily governed by digital data and artificial intelligence (AI), our existing methods of managing security, transparency, and accountability are proving inadequate. Large-scale fraud, data breaches, and concerns about uses of AI are common. If we can create an ecosystem of trusted data and trusted AI that provides safe, secure, and human-centric services for everyone, then huge societal benefits can be unlocked, including better health, greater financial inclusion, and a population that is more engaged with and better supported by its government.[1]

To avoid having our critical systems suffer increasing rates of damage and compromise, bias and unfairness, and ultimately failure, we need to move decisively toward pervasive data minimization and general auditing of data use and AI computation. Current firewall, event sharing, and attack detection approaches are simply not feasible as long-run solutions for cybersecurity, nor is current ad hoc evaluation of AI's unintended effects suf-ficient. We need to adopt an inherently more robust approach.

Dramatically better technology for an inherently safe, equitable data and AI ecosystem has already been built and is being deployed at scattered locations around the world, as will be described in this chapter. For instance, the European Union's data protection authorities are supporting a simplified, easy-to-deploy version called OPAL (which stands for open algorithms[2]) for pilot testing within certain countries (see https://mit-opal.mit.edu and http://opalproject.org). The concept behind OPAL is that instead of copying or sharing data, algorithms are sent to existing databases, executed behind existing firewalls, and only the encrypted results are shared. This minimizes opportunities to attack databases or divert data for unapproved use, and OPAL may be combined with differential privacy, homomorphic encryption, or secure multi-party computation in order to provably ensure that data remains safe.[3]

Perhaps just as importantly, having an OPAL-style system means that the use of data and the performance of the algorithms can be continuously logged and audited. Consequently, the per-formance of AI algorithms concerning fairness, privacy, and secu-rity can be monitored according to agreed standards. Moreover, if new questions about use and performance arise, the data to answer those questions is immediately available in the logs of the OPAL system.

However, technical solutions such as OPAL are inadequate without human-centric governance. There must be user-centric data ownership and management as well as the development of secure and privacy-preserving machine learning algorithms; the deployment of transparent and accountable algorithms; and the introduction of machine learning fairness principles and methodologies to overcome biases and discriminatory effects. Humans must be placed at the center of the discussion, as humans are ultimately both the actors and the subjects of the decisions made via algorithms. If we are able to ensure that these requirements are met, we should be able to realize the positive potential of AI-driven decision-making while minimizing the risks and possible negative unintended consequences on individuals and on society as a whole.

This book has argued that the best way to achieve human-centric governance is through the notion of a data cooperative, which is a voluntary collaborative agreement by individuals that their personal data may be used to derive insights for the benefit of their community. These insights can be in the form of simple maps or statistics or generated by state-of-the-art AI methods. Importantly, a data cooperative does *not* require that individuals give up ownership of their data, only that their data may be used for specific agreed uses.

There are several key aspects of a data cooperative. First, members of a data cooperative member have legal ownership of their data, which can be collected into their personal data store (PDS),[4] and they can add and remove data from the PDS as well as suspend access to the data repository. Members have the option to maintain their single or multiple personal data stores at the cooperative or on private data servers.

However, if the data store is hosted at the cooperative, then data protection (e.g., data encryption) and curation are performed by the cooperative itself for the benefit of its members. Moreover, the data cooperative has a legal fiduciary obligation to its members.[5] This means that the cooperative organization is owned and controlled by the members. Finally, the ultimate goal of the data cooperative is to benefit and empower its members. As highlighted in previous chapters of this book, credit and labor unions can provide an inspiration for data cooperatives as collective institutions able to represent the data rights of individuals.

Such personal data platform cooperatives are a means for avoiding asymmetries and inequalities in the data economy and realizing the concept of property-owning democracy, introduced by political and moral philosopher John Rawls.[6] In particular, Loi, Dehaye, and Hafen[7] argue that a society characterized by multiple personal data platform cooperatives is more likely to realize Rawls's principle of fair equality of opportunity, where individuals have equal access to the resources—data in this case—needed to develop their talents.

10.2   THE DATA COOPERATIVE ECOSYSTEM

The data cooperative ecosystem is summarized in figure 10.1. The main entities are the data cooperative as a legal entity, the individuals who make up the membership and elect the leadership of the cooperative, and the external entities who interact with the data cooperative, referred to as *queriers*. The cooperative as an organization may choose to operate its own IT infrastructure or to outsource these IT functions to an external operator or IT services provider. In the case of outsourcing, the service level agreement and contracts must include the prohibition for the operators to access or copy the member's data. Furthermore,

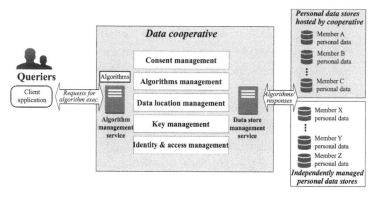

Figure 10.1
Overview of the data cooperative ecosystem.

the prohibition must extend to all other third-party entities from which the outsourcing operator purchases or subcontracts parts of its own services.

A good analogy can be gleaned from credit unions throughout the United States. Many of the small credit unions band together to share IT costs by outsourcing IT services from a common provider, known in the industry as *credit union service organizations* (CUSOs). Thus, a credit union in Vermont may band together with one in Texas and another in California to contract a CUSO to provide basic IT services. This includes a common computing platform on the cloud, shared storage on the cloud, shared applications, and so on. The credit union may not have any equipment on-premises other than the personal computers used to connect to the platform operated by the CUSO. Here, despite that the three credit unions use a common platform, the CUSO may tailor the appearance of the user interface differently for each credit union in order to provide some degree of differentiation to its members. However, the CUSO in turn may be subcontracting functions or applications from a third party. For example, the CUSO may be running its platform using virtualization technology on Amazon Web Services. It may purchase storage from yet a different entity. This approach of subcontracting functions or services from other service providers is currently very common.

In the context of the data cooperative that chooses to outsource IT services, the service contract with the IT services provider must include prohibitions by third-party cloud providers from accessing data belonging to the cooperative's members.

10.3   PRESERVING DATA PRIVACY OF MEMBERS

We propose to use the MIT *open algorithms* (OPAL) approach to ensure the privacy of the member's data held within the personal data stores.[8] In essence, the OPAL paradigm requires that data never be moved or copied out of its data store and that the algorithms be instead transmitted to the data stores for execution.

The following key concepts and principles underlie the open algorithms paradigm:

- *Move the algorithm to the data*   Instead of "pulling" data into a centralized location for processing, it is the algorithm that must be transmitted to the data repositories' endpoints and be processed there.
- *Data must never leave its repository*   Data must never be exported or copied from its repository. Additional local data-loss protection

could be applied, such as encryption (e.g., homomorphic encryption), to prevent backdoor theft of the data.

- *Vetted algorithms*   Algorithms must be vetted to be "safe" from bias, discrimination, privacy violations, and other unintended consequences.
- *Provide only safe answers*   When returning results from executing one or more algorithms, return *aggregate answers* only as the default granularity of the response. Any algorithm that is intended to yield answers that are specific to a data subject (individual) must only be executed after obtaining the subject's fully informed consent.[9]

To ensure that data analysis does not reveal personal data, the AI community over the years has developed a range of privacy-preserving machine learning methods. These methods are inspired by research efforts in cryptography and have the goal of protecting the privacy of the input data and/or the models used in the learning task. Examples of this approach are differential privacy,[10] federated learning,[11] and encrypted computation.[12]

Differential privacy is a methodology for publicly sharing information about a given dataset by providing a description of the patterns related to the groups represented in the dataset while at the same time keeping the information about the individuals private. For example, government agencies use differential privacy algorithms to publish statistical aggregates while ensuring that individual survey responses are kept confidential. In order to work, differential privacy adds some amount of statistical noise, thus obscuring the contributions of specific individuals in the dataset.

Federated learning is a machine learning approach where different entities or organizations collaboratively train a model while keeping the training data decentralized in local nodes. Hence, the raw data samples of each entity are stored locally and never exchanged, while parameters of the learning algorithm are exchanged in order to generate a global model. It is worth noting that federated learning does not provide a full guarantee of the privacy of sensitive data (e.g., personal data), as some characteristics of the raw data could be memorized during the training of the algorithm and thus be extracted. For this reason, differential privacy can complement federated learning by keeping private the contribution of single organizations or nodes in the federated setting.[13]

Finally, encrypted computation aims at protecting the learning model itself by allowing it to train on and evaluate encrypted data. Thus, the organization training the model is not able to see or leak the data in its nonencrypted form. Examples of methods for encrypted computation are homomorphic encryption, functional encryption, secure multiparty computation, and influence matching.

10.4 CONSENT FOR ALGORITHM EXECUTION

One of the contributions of the EU General Data Protection Regulation (GDPR) is the formal recognition at the regulatory level of the need for *informed consent* to be obtained from subjects.[14] More specifically, the GDPR calls for the entity processing the data to have the ability to "demonstrate that the data subject has consented to processing of his or her personal data" (Article 7). Related to this, a given "data subject shall have the right to withdraw his or her consent at any time" (Article 7). In terms of minimizing the practice of copying data unnecessarily, the GDPR calls out in clear terms the need to access data "limited to what is necessary

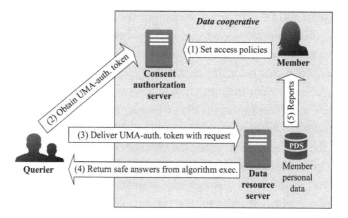

Figure 10.2

Overview of consent management using user-managed access (UMA).

in relation to the purposes for which they are processed (data minimisation)" (Article 5).

In the context of the GDPR, we believe that the MIT open algorithms approach substantially addresses the various issues raised by the GDPR by virtue of data never being moved from or copied from its repository.

Furthermore, because OPAL requires that algorithms be selected and transmitted to the data endpoints for execution, the matter of consent in OPAL becomes one of *requesting permission from the subject for the execution of one or more vetted algorithms on the subject's data*. The data cooperative, as a member organization, has the task of explaining in lay terms the meaning and purpose of each algorithm and conveying to the members the benefits from executing the algorithm on the member's data.

In terms of the consent management system's implementation by a data cooperative, there are additional requirements that pertain to *indirect access* by service providers and operators that may be hosting data belonging to members of the cooperative. More specifically, when an entity employs a service operated by a third party (e.g., client or application running in the cloud) and that service handles data, algorithms, and computation results related to the cooperative's activities, then we believe authorization must be expressly obtained by that third party.

In the context of possible implementations of authorization and consent management, the current popular access authorization framework used by most hosted application and services providers today is based on the *OAuth2.0* authorization framework.[15] The OAuth2.0 model is relatively simple in that it recognizes three basic entities in the authorization workflow. The first entity is the *resource owner*, which in our case translates to the cooperative on behalf of its members. The second entity is the *authorization service*, which could map to either the cooperative or an outsourced provider. The third entity is the requesting party using a *client* (application), which maps roughly to our querier (person or organization seeking insights). In the case where the data cooperative is performing internal analytics for its own purposes, the querier is the cooperative itself.

While the OAuth2.0 model has gained traction in industry over the past decade (e.g., in mobile apps), its simplistic view of the three-party world does not take into account today's reality of the popularity of hosted applications and services. In reality, each of the three parties in OAuth2.0 (the client, the authorization server, and the resource) could be operated by separate legal entities. For example, the client application could be running in the cloud, and thus any information or data passing through the client application would become accessible to the cloud provider.

Early awareness of the inherent limitations of OAuth2.0 has led to additional efforts being directed at expanding the three-party configuration to become a five- or six-party arrangement (figure 10.3) while retaining the same OAuth2.0 token and messaging formats. This work has been conducted in the Kantara Initiative standards organization since 2009, under the umbrella of *user-managed access* (UMA). As implied by its name, UMA seeks to provide ordinary users as resource (data) owners with the ability to manage access policy in a consistent manner across the user's resources, which may be physically distributed throughout different repositories on the internet. The UMA entities follow closely and extend the entities defined in the OAuth2.0 framework. More importantly, the UMA

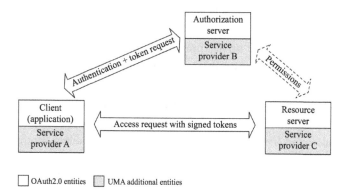

☐ OAuth2.0 entities ☐ UMA additional entities

Figure 10.3
Overview of UMA entities as an extension of the OAuth2.0 model.

model introduces new functions and tokens that allow it to address complex scenarios that explicitly identify hosted service providers and cloud operators as entities that must abide by the same consent terms of service.

Recognition of service operators as third-party legal entities The UMA architecture explicitly calls out entities that provide services to the basic OAuth2.0 entities. The goal is to extend the legal obligations to these entities as well, which is crucial for implementing informed consent in the sense of the GDPR.

Thus, for example, in the UMA workflow in figure 10.3, the client is recognized as consisting of two separate entities: the querier (e.g., person), which operates the hosted client application, and service provider A, which makes the client application available on its infrastructure. When the querier is authenticated by the authorization server and is issued an access token, service provider A must also be separately authenticated and be issued a unique access token.

This means that service provider A, which operates the client application, must accept the terms of service and data usage agreements presented by the authorization server in the same manner that the querier (person or organization) must accept them.

Multiround handshake as a progressive legally binding mechanism Another important contribution of the UMA architecture is the recognition that a given endpoint (e.g., API at the authorization server) provides the opportunity to successively engage the caller to agree to terms of service and data usage agreements (referred to as *binding obligations* in UMA).

More specifically, UMA uses the multiround protocol run between the client and the authorization server to *progressively bind* the client in a lockstep manner. When the client (client-operator) chooses to proceed with the handshake by sending the next message in the protocol to the endpoint of the authorization server, the client has implicitly agreed to the terms of service at that endpoint. This is akin to the client agreeing step-by-step to additional clauses in a contract each time the client proceeds with the next stage of the handshake.

10.5 IDENTITY-RELATED ALGORITHM-BASED ASSERTIONS

A potential role for a data cooperative is to make available the summary results of analytic computations to external entities regarding a member (subject) upon request by the member. Here the workflow must be initiated by the member, who is using his or her data (in their personal data store) as the basis for generating the assertions about them, based on executing one or more of the cooperative-vetted algorithms. In this case, the cooperative behaves as an *attribute provider* or *assertion provider* for its members[16] by issuing a signed assertion in a standard format (e.g., SAML2.0[17] or Claims[18]). This is particularly useful when the member is seeking to obtain goods and services from an external *service provider*.

As an example, a particular member (individual) could be seeking a loan (e.g., car loan) from a financial institution. The financial institution requires proof of the member's income and expenditures over some time (e.g., the last five years) as part of its risk-assessment process. It needs an authoritative and truthful source of information regarding the member's financial behavior over the last five years. Today, in the United States, this role is fulfilled by the so-called credit scoring or credit reporting companies, such as Equifax, TransUnion, and Experian.

However, in this case, the member could turn to its cooperative and request that the cooperative run various algorithms—including algorithms private to the cooperative—on the various datasets regarding the member that are located in the member's personal data store. At the end of these computations, the cooperative could issue an authoritative and truthful assertion, which it signs using its private key. The digital signature signifies that the cooperative stands behind its assertions regarding the given member. Then the cooperative or the member could transmit the signed assertion to the financial institution. Note that this cycle of executing algorithms, followed by assertion creation and transmittal to the financial institution, can be repeated as many times as needed until the financial institution is satisfied. This is shown in figure 10.4.

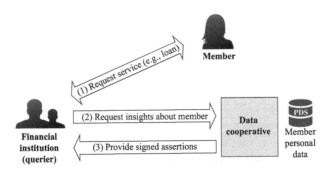

Figure 10.4
Overview of obtaining assertions from the data cooperative.

There are a number of important aspects regarding this approach of relying on the data cooperative:

- *Member driven* The algorithmic computation on the member's data and the assertion issuance must be invoked or initiated by the member. The data cooperative must not perform this computation and issue assertions (about a member) without express directive from the member.
- *Short-lived assertions* The assertion's validity period should be limited to the duration of time specified by the service provider. This reduces the window of opportunity for the service provider to hoard or resell to a third party the assertions obtained from the cooperative.
- *Limited to a specific purpose* The assertion should carry an additional legal clause, indicating that the assertion is to be used for a given purpose only (e.g., member's application for a specific loan type and loan amount).
- *Signature of cooperative* The data cooperative, as the issuer of the assertions or claims, must digitally sign the assertions. This conveys the consent of the member (for the issuance of assertion) and conveys the authority of the cooperative as the entity that executes algorithms over the member's data.
- *Portability of assertions* The structure of the assertion data should be independent (stand-alone), portable, and not tied to any specific infrastructure.
- *Incorporate terms of use* The assertion container (e.g., SAML2.0 or Claims) issued by the cooperative must carry unambiguous legal statements regarding the terms of use of the information contained in the assertion. The container itself may even carry a

copyright notice from the cooperative to discourage service providers from propagating the signed assertions to third parties.

Once the assertion has been issued by the cooperative, there are numerous ways to make it available to external third parties—depending on the privacy limitations of the entities concerned. In the preceding case, a member (subject) may wish for the assertion to be available only to the specific service provider (e.g., loan provider) because the event pertains to a private transaction. In the case where the service provider needs to maintain copies of assertions from the cooperative for legal reasons (e.g., taxation purposes), the service provider could return a signed digital receipt agreeing to the terms of use of the assertions.[19]

In other cases, a member may wish for some types of assertions containing static personal attributes (e.g., age or year of birth) to be readily available without the privacy limitations. For example, the member might use such attribute-based assertions to purchase merchandise tied to age limits (e.g., alcohol). In this case, the signed assertion can be readable from a well-known endpoint at the cooperative, be readable from the member's personal website, or be carried inside the member's mobile device. Therefore, the portability of the assertion structure is important.

10.6 CONCLUSIONS

Today, we are in a situation where individual assets—people's personal data—are being exploited by AI algorithms without sufficient value being returned to the individual. This is analogous to the situation in the late 1800s and early 1900s that led to the creation of collective institutions such as credit unions and labor unions, so the time seems ripe for the creation of collective institutions to represent the data rights of individuals.

We have argued that data cooperatives with fiduciary obligations to members provide a promising direction for the empowerment of individuals through collective use of their own personal data. A data cooperative not only can give members access to expert, community-based advice on how to manage, curate, and protect access to their personal data but can also run internal analytics that benefit the collective membership. Such collective insights provide a powerful tool for negotiating better services and discounts for the collective's members.

NOTES

1. World Economic Forum, *Personal Data: The Emergence of a New Asset Class*, report, 2011, http://www.weforum.org/reports/personal-data-emergence-new-asset-class.

2. T. Hardjono, D. Shrier, and A. Pentland, eds., *Trusted Data—a New Framework for Identity and Data Sharing* (Cambridge, MA: MIT Press, 2019).

3. Hardjono, Shrier, and Pentland, *Trusted Data*.

4. Y. A. de Montjoye, E. Shmueli, S. Wang, and A. Pentland, "OpenPDS: Protecting the Privacy of Metadata through SafeAnswers," *PLoS One* 9, no. 7 (July 2014): 13–18, https://doi.org/10.1371/journal.pone.0098790.

5. J. M. Balkin, "Information Fiduciaries and the First Amendment," *UC Davis Law Review* 49, no. 4 (2016): 1183–1234.

6. J. Rawls, *Justice as Fairness: A Restatement* (Cambridge, MA: Harvard University Press, 2001).

7. M. Loi, P.-O. Dehaye, and E. Hafen, "Towards Rawlsian 'Property-Owning Democracy' through Personal Data Platform Cooperatives,"

Critical Review of International Social and Political Philosophy (2020): 1–19, https://doi.org/10.1080/13698230.2020.1782046.

8. Hardjono, Shrier, and Pentland, *Trusted Data*.

9. Loi, Dehaye, and Hafen, "Towards Rawlsian 'Property-Owning Democracy' through Personal Data Platform Cooperatives."

10. C. Dwork and A. Roth, "The Algorithmic Foundations of Differential Privacy," *Foundations and Trends in Theoretical Computer Science* 9, nos. 3–4 (2014): 211–407.

11. A. Dubey and A. Pentland, "Private and Byzantine-Proof Federated Decision Making," in *Proceedings of the International Conference on Autonomous Agents and MultiAgent Systems (AAMAS 2020)*, ed. A. Seghrouchni and G. Sukthankar (New York: ACM, 2020), 357–365.

12. N. Dowlin, R. Gilad-Bachrach, K. Laine, K. Lauter, M. Naehrig, and J. Wernsing, "Cryptonets: Applying Neural Networks to Encrypted Data with High Throughput and Accuracy," in *ICML16: Proceedings of 33rd International Conference on Machine Learning*, vol. 48 (New York: JMLR Press, 2016), 201–210.

13. M. Brundage, "Toward Trustworthy AI Development: Mechanisms for Supporting Verifiable Claims," 2020, https://arxiv.org/abs/2004.07213.

14. European Commission, "Regulation (EU) 2016/679 of the European Parliament and of the Council of 27 April 2016 on the Protection of Natural Persons with Regard to the Processing of Personal Data and on the Free Movement of Such Data (General Data Protection Regulation)," *Official Journal of the European Union* L119 (2016): 1–88.

15. D. Hardt, "The OAuth 2.0 Authorization Framework," RFC6749, IETF, October 2012, http://tools.ietf.org/rfc/rfc6749.txt.

16. American Bar Association, "An Overview of Identity Management: Submission for UNCITRAL Commission 45th Session," ABA Identity Management Legal Task Force, May 2012, http://meetings.abanet.org

/webupload/commupload/CL320041/relatedresources/ABA-Submission
-to-UNCITRAL.pdf.

17. OASIS, "Assertions and Protocols for the OASIS Security Assertion
Markup Language (SAML) V2.0," March 2005, http://docs.oasisopen.org
/security/saml/v2.0/ saml-core-2.0-os.pdf.

18. M. Sporny, D. Longley, and D. Chadwick, "Verifiable Credentials Data
Model 1.0," W3C, W3C Candidate Recommendation, March 2019, https://
www.w3.org/TR/verifiable-claims-data-model; D. Reed and M. Sporny,
"Decentralized Identifiers (DIDs) v0.11," W3C, Draft Community Group
Report, July 9, 2018, https://w3c-ccg.github.io/did-spec/.

19. M. Lizar and D. Turner, "Consent Receipt Specification Version 1.0,"
Kantara Initiative, March 2017, https://kantarainitiative.org/confluence
/display/infosharing/Home.

11

STABLECOINS

Alexander Lipton, Aetienne Sardon, Fabian Schär,
and Christian Schüpbach

11.1 INTRODUCTION

What started as a niche phenomenon within the cryptocurrency community has now reached the realms of multinational conglomerates, policymakers, and central banks.

From J.P. Morgan's Jamie Dimon to Facebook's Mark Zuckerberg, stable coins have made their way onto the agenda of today's top CEOs. As projects such as Libra have enjoyed broad media coverage, they are also increasingly being scrutinized by regulatory authorities,[1] and as the term *stablecoin* spread, its meaning started to blur. This is problematic because an unclear definition may make us susceptible to deceptive innovation; that is, reintroducing existing services but with a different appearance. We ought to ask ourselves whether stablecoins are here to stay or whether they are simply old wine in new bottles.

This chapter aims to educate on stablecoins by providing historical context on their origin and by describing which key factors have been driving their adoption. Moreover, we review existing terminologies and taxonomies on stablecoins and examine their disruptive potential. Based on this, we propose a novel definition of stablecoins and outline an alternative taxonomy. We briefly discuss the different use cases of stablecoins as well as the underlying economic incentives for creating them. We also touch on regulatory considerations and briefly summarize key factors driving the future development of stablecoins.

11.2 MOTIVATION

Money is omnipresent in modern life, but we rarely dare to question it. It has existed for more than 5,000 years, so one is prone to misconceive it as a fixed concept when in fact it has been continuously changing. And as our society evolves, so does the way we interact with and transact with money. With new forms of money on the rise, we are being challenged to question our understanding of money and ask ourselves what the future of money will look like.

Stablecoins have been discussed as a potential candidate for a new, faster, more accessible, and transparent form of money. With Facebook's engagement in the Libra stablecoin, there has been substantial attention to the topic, but the emergence of new technologies, such as distributed ledger technology (DLT), has subtly diverted our focus away from how we can create value to how we can use this technology.

In order to keep from falling prey to deceptive innovation, policymakers, incumbents, challengers, and the general public alike should be interested in developing a sound understanding of stablecoins.

11.3 WIR: A STABLECOIN PRECURSOR

The concept of devising a supplementary currency system is not new. One of the most successful examples is the Swiss WIR Bank, formerly known as the Swiss Economic Circle. It was founded in 1934 by Werner Zimmermann and Paul Enz.[2] WIR is the abbreviation for *Wirtschaftsring-Genossenschaft* (meaning "mutual economic support circle") but also means "we" in German.[3] WIR was driven by the ambition to alleviate the negative effects of the Great Depression, solve the associated middle-class crisis, and reform the monetary system on the basis of the *Freigeld* (meaning "free money") theory.[4] To achieve these goals, WIR initiated its own WIR currency (CHW) allowing participants to exchange goods and services without using conventional fiat currencies.

Today, the WIR network comprises over 62,000 small and medium-sized enterprises (SMEs), reporting a turnover of almost 2 billion WIR in 2012. While the WIR network is now also open to private clients, its focus remains on SMEs. The main benefits of joining the WIR network are threefold. First, companies joining experience on average a 5 percent increase in business, most likely because of loyalty effects.[5] Second, participants in the WIR network can obtain loans at a lower interest rate compared to traditional bank loans. Third, members of the WIR network experience a greater sense of solidarity and community.[6]

Companies participating in the WIR system commit to accepting CHW for their goods and services at a one-to-one ratio with the corresponding Swiss franc amount. In order to join the WIR system, companies can apply for a zero-interest loan of up to

10,000 CHW.[7] If a company wishes to leave the system, surplus CHW must be spent within the system. While the WIR system bears similarities with the idea of a stablecoin, there also is a notable difference in that buying or selling CHW on a secondary market is strictly prohibited.[8] In section 11.4, we will identify the presence of a secondary market as one of the key characteristics of a stablecoin.

11.4 A BRIEF HISTORY OF STABLECOINS

It is impossible to have a well-rounded discussion on stablecoins without examining their origins. Although numerous stablecoin projects exist today, there is one stablecoin that stands out in its significance: Tether.[9] As one of the first and to this day most widely used stablecoins, Tether has played a significant, albeit controversial, role in the development of stablecoins.

As of December 2019, there were more than 4.1 billion Tether tokens in circulation. Each token is supposed to be worth $1. The issuing company, Tether Limited, claims that Tether tokens are 100 percent backed by liquid reserves. However, numerous parties have raised allegations that there is a shortfall in its reserves. These allegations have been fueled by severe deficiencies in the auditing process.[10] Doubts about Tether's reserves have repeatedly manifested themselves in lower secondary market prices. For example, at the beginning of 2017, Tether's secondary market price dropped to as low as $0.91 (see figure 11.1). Nonetheless, Tether is still by far the most actively traded stablecoin. In fact, in terms of trading volume, it can easily compete with other cryptoassets such as Bitcoin or Ethereum.[11]

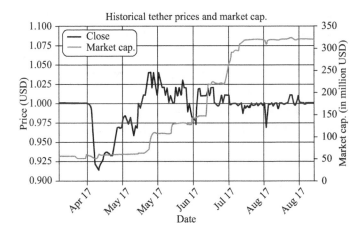

Figure 11.1
Tether prices and market capitalization.

Tether, known initially as Realcoin, was founded in 2014 by Brock Pierce, Craig Sellars, and Reeve Collins. Before founding Tether, two of the three cofounders worked on a project called Mastercoin (later rebranded as Omni). Mastercoin's mission was to allow users to create their own virtual currencies on top of the Bitcoin protocol.[12] For this purpose, the Mastercoin Foundation developed an additional layer on top of Bitcoin, which would later serve as the technological foundation for issuing the first Tether tokens, in October 2014.

One of the key drivers for Tether's growth was its listing on and distribution through cryptocurrency exchanges. Bitfinex, as one of the largest cryptocurrency exchanges, played a pivotal role in promoting Tether. Although denied by both companies' officials, multiple indications suggest that Bitfinex and Tether have been closely affiliated.[13]

When Tether tokens first started trading on Bitfinex in 2015, their turnover was rather insignificant. However, as cryptocurrencies gained traction, so did the Tether stablecoin. By mid-2017, Tether's market capitalization had surpassed $100 million (see figure 11.1). At the same time, Bitfinex users were starting to experience substantial delays in their US dollar withdrawal requests.[14] Shortly thereafter, rumors spread that Bitfinex had been cut off from its US dollar wire transfers.[15] At the same time, numerous cryptocurrency exchanges, such as Kraken, Binance, and Huobi, decided to list Tether trading pairs.[16] This support allowed Tether tokens to spread quickly across the cryptocurrency trading ecosystem. Tether allowed users to circumvent traditional wire transfers by providing an alternative settlement mechanism. Although token users were unable to withdraw their US dollars, Tether allowed them to transfer their tokens pegged to the US dollar between exchanges without being exposed to the price volatility of cryptocurrencies.

After the 2018 cryptocurrency crash, a paper was published claiming that Tether was used to inflate and manipulate Bitcoin prices.[17] It has been suggested that cryptocurrency exchanges may have had a vested interest in continuing the distribution of Tether and generally promoting the use of stablecoins to increase trading volumes. Moreover, stablecoins posed an opportunity for cryptocurrency exchanges to become less dependent on unstable banking relationships.[18]

Given the strong demand for a stablecoin like Tether, it comes as no surprise that new players rushed into the market from late 2017 onward. For example, in 2018, TrustToken, Paxos, Gemini, and Circle all launched stablecoins pegged to the US dollar. These projects promoted their stablecoins as being more reliable and trustworthy, providing higher transparency in their reserve management.[19] Note that all these stablecoins were primarily designed to work within the cryptocurrency space. The surge in projects also sparked creativity in terms of how to design a stabilization mechanism for a stablecoin. For example, a project called Maker DAO built a decentralized stablecoin (DAI) whose reserve would be comprised of other cryptocurrencies and completely governed on-chain through Ethereum smart contracts. Another project, called Basis, raised $133 million with the goal of launching an algorithmic cryptocurrency protocol that claimed to create a stable digital currency without requiring any asset backing whatsoever. However, it is noteworthy that the Basis team decided to shut down the project because it would have faced US securities regulation.[20]

In parallel with the stablecoin developments from the cryptocurrency community, large corporations started to experiment with blockchain technology—mainly for large-scale transactions. For example, UBS published a paper introducing the so-called Utility Settlement Coin in 2016, which financial institutions could use to facilitate cross-border payments and settlement.[21] In 2018, MIT developed the idea of Tradecoin, in which multiple "sponsors" form a consortium where they can tokenize their assets and build a system of digital cash on top of that. The sponsors contribute assets to a collectively owned asset pool and in exchange receive tradecoins from the consortium. The safekeeping of the consortium's asset pool is managed by a narrow bank to guarantee that the tradecoins are fully backed by the actual asset base. The consortium can then use its tradecoins as an asset base to issue e-cash tokens to retail users.[22] At the beginning of 2019, J. P. Morgan announced that it would become the first US bank to create a digital coin representing a fiat currency. While these projects are not necessarily comparable to a stablecoin like Tether, they do appear to have been fueled by the associated rising interest in novel digital currency forms.

In June 2019, Facebook officially revealed its plans to launch a new global digital currency called Libra.[23] The Libra project immediately triggered strong headwinds from regulators. For example, France's finance minister, Bruno Le Maire, said that "no private entity can claim monetary power, which is inherent to the sovereignty of nations."[24] Publications from the European Central Bank (ECB) and Bank for International Settlement discussing potential risks associated with stablecoins followed shortly, in August and October 2019, respectively.

11.5 TERMINOLOGY

In this section, we first briefly discuss the etymology of stablecoins and then review the strengths and weaknesses of standard stablecoin definitions. We then point out some of the difficulties surrounding stablecoin terminology. We continue by briefly reviewing Christensen's theory of disruptive innovation in the context of stablecoins and finally provide a new definition of stablecoins.

11.5.1 Etymology: From Bitcoin to Stablecoin

Before 2008, the term *coin* was unambiguously associated with actual physical coins. The advent of Bitcoin, however, led to a recontextualization of the word. One can only wonder why Bitcoin was not named Bitcash or Bitmoney at the time,[25] but as

Bitcoin emerged, the word *coin* experienced a semantic change. Its usage was now broadened to the digital economy.

As the number of cryptocurrency projects increased, so did the excitement for digital coin jargon. From Litecoin to Dogecoin, digital coin minting proved very popular. With a plethora of inherently volatile digital coins, the blockchain community started exploring whether blockchain could also be used to create more stable cryptocurrencies or, in other words, *stable coins.*

Data from Google Trends shows that the term *stablecoin* first emerged in late 2013. Its appearance coincided with a spike in searches for Mastercoin (see figure 11.2). As described in the previous section, Mastercoin laid the groundwork for Tether and

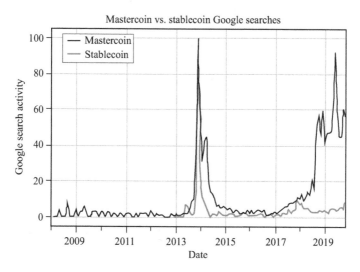

Figure 11.2
Google searches going from "Mastercoin" to "stablecoin."

made the previously vague concept of a stablecoin a reality. Thus, Mastercoin and stablecoins are closely intertwined, both from a conceptual and from an etymological viewpoint.

11.5.2 Introduction to Stablecoin Terminology

While many different definitions of stablecoins exist, we highlight the one given by the ECB: "[Stablecoins are defined as] digital units of value that are not a form of any specific currency (or basket thereof) but rely on a set of stabilization tools which are supposed to minimize fluctuations of their price in such currency(ies)."[26]

Although a rather broad definition, it reflects three important aspects:

1. First, it is technology neutral and excludes already existing distinct forms of currencies that simply use DLT for recording purposes. This fact helps differentiate between stablecoins as a genuinely new form of money (e.g., DAI) and commercial bank money that is powered by new technology (e.g., JPM Coin).

2. Second, it highlights that there must be some form of stabilization mechanism to reduce volatility relative to an existing currency.

3. Third, it points out that a stablecoin has a market price of its own, implying that its price expressed in the target quoted currency is not necessarily equal to one.

Other definitions are often phrased in a way that blurs the lines between the stablecoin and the "linked" asset. For example, the Bank for International Settlement states that "stablecoins have many of the features of cryptoassets but seek to stabilize the price of the 'coin' by linking its value to that of a pool of assets." The word *link* suggests a form of equivalence between the stablecoin and the "linked" asset when in fact both need to be conceived of as separate assets and can potentially be decoupled. In this respect, a stablecoin is to its "linked" asset as a derivative is to its underlying asset. In particular, most stablecoins introduce some counterparty risk.

11.5.3 Motivation: Why New Terminology?

As already pointed out, there is a blurring line between stablecoins that are a genuinely new type of asset and those that represent existing forms of currency. We advocate avoiding introduction of new terminology for already well-understood and existing concepts (e.g., commercial bank money). Instead, we endorse using the term *stablecoin* to label and identify genuinely innovative forms of money that are outside the established monetary system (potentially beyond the control of central banks) but have the potential to fundamentally change and disrupt it.[27]

Christensen's theory of disruptive innovation provides a useful tool to help identify potentially disruptive stable coins and distinguish them from rebranded traditional financial services. According to Christensen's theory, there are two forms of innovation: sustaining innovation and disruptive innovation.[28]

Sustaining innovation is aimed at improving existing products for an incumbent's established customer base. Typically, higher-quality products are introduced to satisfy the high end of the market, where profitability is highest.

Disruptive innovation, on the other hand, is initially considered inferior by most of an incumbent's customers. It either starts in low-end or new markets. In the first case, a disruptor introduces a good enough product for otherwise underserved low-end customers. In the second case, a disruptor introduces a genuinely new product in a market where none existed, basically turning nonconsumers into consumers. As shown in figure 11.3, the disruptor then moves upmarket, providing the quality that mainstream customers require while preserving the advantages that drove its early success. When mainstream customers start adopting the new product, disruption has occurred.

Putting Christensen's theory of disruptive innovation into practice, let us consider four examples: Tether, J. P. Morgan Coin, Tradecoin, and Libra.

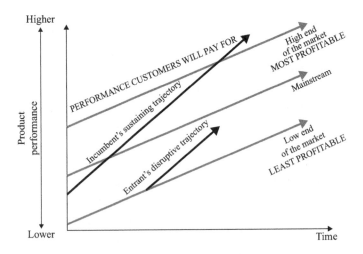

Figure 11.3
Disruptive versus sustaining innovation trajectories. *Source*: C. M. Christensen, M. E. Raynor, and R. McDonald, "What Is Disruptive Innovation?," *Harvard Business Review*, December 2015, https://hbr.org/2015/12/what-is-disruptive-innovation.

1. Tether exhibits characteristics of a disruptive innovation. The reasons are as follows. First, it originated in a low-end market that was otherwise neglected by incumbents (see section 11.4). Tether provided a good enough product to help cryptocurrency users transact in something that is close enough to the US dollar without requiring access to traditional payment systems or banking services. Second, Tether started moving upmarket. Because it is listed on over 100 exchanges, including conservative ones such as Coinbase, both mainstream and high-end institutional customers (e.g., proprietary trading firms) have started using Tether. Tether is also scaling up to support additional blockchain networks (e.g., Ethereum, Liquid, Tron) and currencies (e.g., euro, Chinese yuan).

2. JPM Coin displays the qualities of a sustaining innovation. There are two reasons to support this view. First, the coin is aimed at improving interbank clearing and settlement. Such services were available before JPM Coin, but the coin was introduced to make the process faster and more efficient. Second, the target customer base is clearly in the high end of the market (as JPM Coin is available exclusively to institutional clients) and not geared toward mainstream or low-end customers. Therefore, JPM Coin follows an incumbent's sustaining innovation trajectory (see figure 11.3).

3. Tradecoin represents a disruptive innovation. Its main objective is to give asset-backed currencies a new lease on life. In its mature state, the DTC can serve as a much-needed counterpart to fiat reserve currencies of today.

4. Libra's innovation quality depends on its go-to-market strategy. It may be considered a disruptive innovation if it indeed

initially focuses on the low-end market and subsequently moves upmarket. According to its website, Libra's vision is to provide payment services for the 1.7 billion people who are unbanked. The unbanked population is a low-end market that traditionally has been neglected by incumbents. With each of Libra's founding members having a global reach and substantial financial resources, they are best equipped to turn their vision into reality. If Libra delivers on its promise and someday dominates the unbanked market, it has strong potential to move upmarket and eventually disrupt traditional payment services.

While missing out on a potential sustaining innovation may only have minor repercussions, failing to detect a disruptive innovation poses an existential threat to an incumbent's business. With the rise of DLT, the financial services space has been overcrowded with seemingly innovative payment solutions. At the same time, it has become increasingly difficult to separate genuinely new payment solutions from reengineered legacy systems under the guise of innovation. We therefore advocate using the term *stablecoin* more carefully to label genuinely new forms of money that possess disruptive potential. At the same time, we suggest avoiding use of the term to relabel existing products or minimally improved ones.

11.5.4   A Novel Definition

We aim to provide a compact definition for stablecoins that captures their essential characteristics and is easy to use. We identify three fundamental properties that characterize a stablecoin and set it apart from other forms of money.

A stablecoin is a digital unit of value with the following three properties:

1. It is not a form of currency.
2. It can be used without any direct interaction with the issuer.
3. It is tradable on a secondary market and has a low price volatility in terms of a target quoted currency.

There are three advantages of using this definition. First, it is technology neutral, focusing on the underlying conceptual elements of a stablecoin instead of its implementation details. Second, it is mutually exclusive with existing forms of currency (similar to the ECB definition). This property makes the definition useful in identifying genuinely new forms of money with disruptive potential. Third, it highlights the unique features that make stablecoins distinct from previously known payment systems. Stablecoins can be used without requiring any direct interaction with the issuer (e.g., for peer-to-peer transfers) and can be exchanged on a secondary market at a somewhat reliable and "stable" price.[29]

11.6 TAXONOMY

In the following we briefly discuss existing taxonomies and provide a tripartite classification.

11.6.1 Review

Most taxonomies classify stablecoins based on differences in their collateralization mechanics. For example, some authors suggest differentiating between fiat-, commodity-, crypto- and uncollateralized stablecoins.[30] Others suggest grouping them as on-chain-, off-chain-, and uncollateralized stablecoins.[31] Still others distinguish between fully fiat collateralized, partially fiat collateralized, crypto-overcollateralized, dynamically stabilized, and asset-collateralized stablecoins.[32] Since taxonomies focused on collateralization types are already well known, we will refrain from repeating them. Instead of focusing on collateralization setups, we point to a simple yet revealing dichotomy of stablecoins: whether the stablecoin represents a legal claim and therefore requires a functioning legal system or whether it works even in the absence of any institutions. The former are issued as an IOU, and the issuers may be held responsible if they fail to deliver on their promise. The latter are self-sustained in the sense that the stabilization mechanism does not rely on any institutions or a functioning legal system. Frequently examined features such as the degree of decentralization and openness of a stablecoin system are highly correlated with the existence or absence of a coin holder's legal claim. For example, if there is no legal claim associated with a coin, the system is most likely to be decentralized, with low accountability and high openness. As a stablecoin system works through its network effects, it is unlikely to be restricted for its own sake but rather because of regulatory and legal constraints. If, on the other hand, the legal and regulatory structure allows the system to be open, it most likely will be.

11.6.2 A Tripartite Classification

The fair value of a stablecoin should be equal to its expected redeemable amount. The trust in the redeemability of a stablecoin may be based on different rationales. As an expansion of existing taxonomies, we provide an additional classification to reflect these different redeemability rationales, grouping stable-coins into three categories:

1. *Claim based*   These coins can come in two forms. First, coin holders can have a direct legally enforceable right to personally redeem their coins against a predefined amount or value of a reference asset (e.g., fiat money or commodity). For exam-ple, Circle states in its terms for USDC that "sending USDC to another address automatically transfers and assigns to that Holder, and any subsequent Holder, the right to redeem USDC for U.S. Dollar funds."[33] Moreover, coins that are structured as electronic money or commercial bank money in prepaid pay-ment systems would also fall under this category. Second, coin holders may benefit from a transitive claim, meaning they may not be entitled to redeem the coin themselves but instead have to go through a third party. For example, two-tiered stablecoin systems, such as proposed by Libra, where some privileged users ("authorized resellers") have a right to redeem while other users do not, are based on the idea of a transitive claim.

2. *Good faith based*   These are coins where the holder believes in the good business practices of the issuer, assuming redeem-ability of its coins without having any legal right. The issuer typically promotes the coins as being backed by reserves but excludes any right of redemption in its terms and conditions. For example, TrustToken states in its legal terms that "the Company itself does not guarantee any right of redemption or exchange of TrueCurrency tokens for fiat currency."[34]

3. *Technology based*   These are coins where technology is used to autonomously induce price stabilization (e.g., using smart

contracts to store and manage cryptoasset collateral). These systems do not rely on a legal claim or a user's faith in the good intentions of the issuing entity. Instead, the user's expectations of redeemability are driven by their trust in the underlying technology and implementation. For example, on-chain collateralized and algorithmic stablecoins belong to this category.

To put our view into a broader context, we refer to the International Monetary Fund's money tree (see figure 11.4). The money tree identifies five different means of payment: B-money, E-money, I-money, central bank money, and cryptocurrency. According to our definition (see section 11.4) and taxonomy, claim- and good-faith-based stablecoins would comprise I-money and partly E-money. Technology-based stable coins are congruent to the IMF's definition of "managed coins."[35] We can see that our framework is at least partially congruent with the IMF's categorization—in particular with respect to differentiation based on the existence or absence of a claim.

11.7 USE CASES

Of the many use cases that have been discussed for stablecoins, the following have materialized so far:

- *Cross-border payments and arbitrage* Stablecoins have been used for cross-border payments, especially between cryptocurrency exchanges, giving traders a tool to take advantage of arbitrage opportunities and thereby improve market efficiency.
- *Trading and settlement* Stablecoins have been used as a trading instrument to quickly convert from volatile cryptocurrencies

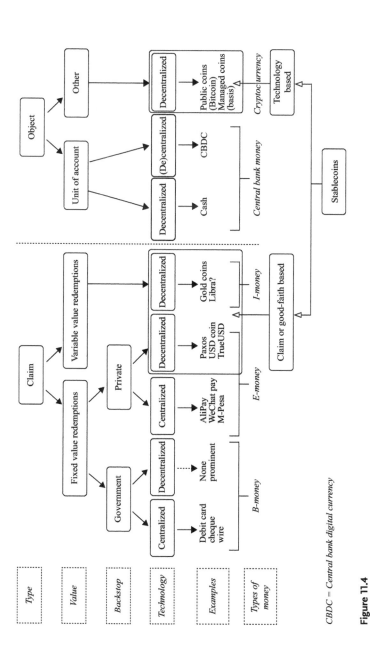

CBDC = Central bank digital currency

Figure 11.4

Placing stablecoins into the IMF's "money tree." *Source:* T. Adrian and T. Mancini-Griffoli, "The Rise of Digital Money," July 2019.

into more stable currency substitutes and vice versa. Conversely, from the perspective of the cryptocurrency exchanges, stablecoins allowed the exchanges to offer their users trading and settlement functionalities like that of the US dollar but without depending on traditional wire transfers. Therefore, stablecoins enabled exchanges to become less reliant on often fragile banking partnerships. It is noteworthy that most stablecoin wallets are controlled by cryptocurrency exchanges, suggesting that users mainly transfer stablecoins between exchange omnibus wallets and rarely withdraw them. For example, a recent report found that only about 300 entities control over 80 percent of Tether tokens, with many of these being cryptocurrency exchanges.[36]

- *Decentralized finance applications* These offer a broad variety of use cases, including decentralized exchanges, lending markets, derivatives, and on-chain asset management.[37] For all these applications, stablecoins play an important role. Additionally, stablecoins like DAI allow users to take on leveraged trading positions.[38] Moreover, users can also lock up their DAI tokens to earn interest (e.g., on Aave, Compound, and dYdX).

Other use cases, such as payment, payroll, and remittance, have not received much attention so far. Similarly, integration of stablecoins into decentralized applications or as a cash leg handling in financial contracts based on smart contracts has yet to find wider adoption.

11.8   REVENUE STREAMS AND COST STRUCTURE

Stablecoin issuers may profit from multiple revenue streams. The composition of revenues may vary greatly depending on the exact stablecoin setup. For example, technology and claim-based stablecoins are likely to exhibit very different revenue stream structures. Regardless of the different stablecoin types and their different revenue focuses, we identify the following five revenue streams:

- *Interest earnings* Stablecoin issuers typically allocate all interest earnings generated from the reserve fund to themselves. Issuers are not required and, in some instances, are even prohibited from passing on interest earnings to coin holders. For example, electronic money institutions (EMIs), such as Circle, are prohibited from paying interest. Depending on the legal structure of the stablecoin, issuers may have varying degrees of freedom in reserve fund management. Generally, issuers have an incentive to issue stablecoins for currencies that offer positive interest rates. For example, TrustToken supports stablecoins for US dollars, British pounds, Australian dollars, Canadian dollars, and Hong Kong dollars, all of which used to provide positive interest rates, ranging between 0.75 percent and 3.95 percent.[39] However, most of these rates have been cut to almost zero lately. Depending on the size of the reserve funds, interest earnings may be substantial. For example, let us assume Tether has $4.1 billion in reserves. According to Tether, "The composition of the Reserves used to back Tether Tokens is within the sole control and at the sole and absolute discretion of Tether."[40] Let us further assume that Tether's liquidity management allocates 80 percent of its reserves into US dollar money market funds with an annual percentage rate of 1.7 percent. The float would generate earnings of $55.8 million per year.[41]

- *Transaction fees* Stablecoin issuers may charge fees for every transfer. For example, Tether's smart contract has a feature that allows it to charge up to 20 basis points of the transaction value with a maximum fee of $50 per transaction.[42] Let us assume an average daily number of transactions of 100,000, with an average size of $5,000.[43] If Tether were to charge a 1 basis point transaction fee, this would result in revenues of $18.2 million per year. However, Tether has not charged any transaction fees so far, because doing so would disincentivize using Tether coins, potentially leading to a shrinking reserve fund and diminishing interest earnings. Moreover, the transaction fee would only apply to on-chain transactions (excluding any intraexchange transactions). So far, interest earnings seem to have outweighed potential earnings from transaction fees. As commented in their code, Tether most likely sees transaction fees as a means of last resort ("if transaction fees ever became necessary"[44]).

- *Issuance and redemption fees*   Stablecoin issuers may charge fees for the issuance (minting) and redemption (burning) of stablecoins. For example, Tether charges 0.1 percent per deposit and the greater of 0.1 percent or $1,000 per withdrawal.[45] Obviously, the issuer may use fees to steer the inflows and outflows to its stablecoin. This may become necessary if the issuer has limitations in terms of the reserve fund size or balance sheet (e.g., considering capital requirements for EMIs or restrictions given by an issuer's banking partner). Similarly, in the case of liquidity shortages, an issuer may discourage outflows by imposing higher withdrawal fees.

- *Cross-selling*   Stablecoin issuers may cross-sell additional services that build on their stablecoin. For example, some cryptocurrency exchanges are closely affiliated with stablecoin issuers (e.g., Bitfinex and Tether, as described in section 11.4). Stablecoins may serve as a means to attract and facilitate trading on their platforms. Moreover, exchanges may also make a market in their own stablecoins, providing additional revenue potential.

▪ *Secondary tokens* Technology-based stablecoin systems are often designed as a twofold token model, where one token serves as the stablecoin and the second provides some special functionality to interact with the stablecoin system. The second token is typically designed to increase in value with stablecoin usage. The initiators of the stablecoin system regularly allocate a proportion of these tokens to themselves so they benefit from such value appreciation. For example, DAI has a special governance token (MKR), which is also needed to close a collateral debt position (see section 11.7). Whenever users want to regain access to their locked cryptoassets, they need to pay interest in the form of MKR tokens, which subsequently get burned. As the supply of MKR tokens decreases over time, there will be a lower supply that may ceteris paribus lead to higher prices.

As with revenue streams, a stablecoin's cost structure differs across stablecoin types. In particular, the cost structure will heavily depend on whether the issuing entity is regulated. In general, we identify the following seven cost components:

▪ *Legal, regulatory, and compliance* Various legal and regulatory clarifications may become necessary. Depending on the regulatory status of the issuer (e.g., EMI), licensing costs may be incurred. Licenses may be necessary for every jurisdiction in which the stablecoin will be made available. Moreover, compliance efforts (e.g., to ensure adherence with know-your-customer (KYC) regulations and applicable anti-money-laundering (AML) requirements) need to be considered.

- *IT development* When a public DLT is used, the stablecoin issuer benefits from the openness and interoperability of the underlying DLT. Development costs would mostly comprise setting up the smart contract. In contrast, integration into third-party systems such as wallets or exchanges does not involve additional efforts (e.g., by adhering to standards such as ERC-20 token standard on the Ethereum platform).

- *IT audits* When a stablecoin is based on a public DLT, the proper functioning of the corresponding smart contract is of critical importance. Typically, a stablecoin issuer mandates that security experts audit the smart contracts in order to assure that the contracts do not have any security flaws and work as expected.

- *Financial audits* Depending on the regulatory status of the stablecoin issuer, audits of its financial statements may be mandatory. Some issuers may voluntarily conduct financial audits to assure users that the reserves are managed responsibly.

- *Banking services* Depending on the nature of the stablecoin, the issuer may rely on banking services to store its reserves.

- *Key management* The issuance and redemption of stablecoins involve some form of approval workflow. Especially for stablecoins that use a public DLT, secure management of potential administrator/issuer keys is of utmost importance.

- *Insurance* When a stablecoin is backed by physical assets, such as gold or bank notes, the corresponding storage would typically require insurance coverage.

Depending on the stablecoin category, the cost structure may tend to involve higher fixed costs than variable costs, providing an attractive, scalable business model. It comes as no surprise that some stablecoin issuers are incorporated in offshore locations to evade regulatory requirements while still benefiting from the global scale that borderless DLT systems provide.

From a regulatory standpoint, no unified definition of stable-coins exists so far. In order to reflect the current situation, we briefly review the Swiss Financial Market Supervisory Authority's (FINMA) statement on stablecoins, the United States' proposed Managed Stablecoins Are Securities Act of 2019, and the ECB's position.

FINMA points out that no specific regulation currently covers stablecoins. However, following a technology-neutral approach, FINMA states that many proposed stablecoin projects give rise to licensing requirements under the Banking Act or the Collective Investment Schemes Act. Moreover, because stablecoins are regularly intended to serve as a means of payment, the Anti–Money Laundering Act is almost always applicable, resulting in strict KYC requirements, transaction monitoring, and other safeguards. Lastly, if a payment system of significant importance is to be created, a licensing requirement under the Financial Market Infrastructure Act is probable. FINMA identifies eight categories of stablecoins, with most falling under existing regulations. For example, if a stablecoin is linked to a fiat currency, this likely constitutes a deposit-taking business under banking law (e.g., Tether). If a stablecoin is linked to a basket of fiat currencies, as proposed by Libra, the applicable regulation depends on who bears the market risk associated with management of the currency basket. If the issuer bears it, this constitutes a deposit-taking business under banking law. If the token holder bears it, the stablecoin is considered a collective investment scheme.[46] The fact that FINMA subsumes most of the stablecoins under existing regulations substantiates our view that in many instances stablecoins are not a new form of currency (see subsections 11.5.4 and 11.5.3 and section 11.6). Similar to FINMA's substance over form attitude, US policymakers have advocated a "same risks, same rules" approach toward stablecoins. In the newly proposed Managed Stablecoins Are Securities Act of 2019, they define "managed stablecoins" as a digital asset whose value is determined by reference to the value of a basket of assets and where the holder is entitled to obtain payment based on the value of that basket. These "managed stablecoins" will be considered securities under the existing Securities Act of 1933.[47]

Lastly, the ECB has formulated a stance toward the regulatory treatment of stablecoins that is similar to that of FINMA and US policymakers. While the ECB does acknowledge that some stablecoins may fall outside current regulatory regimes, in many cases the risks that they entail are "the same as for their non-DLT competitors." In particular, the ECB states that stablecoins issued as tokenized funds are likely to qualify as electronic money and as such are already covered by the existing second Electronic Money Directive (EMD2) in the European Union. The ECB also points out that the use of a new technology may often be mistaken for the introduction of a new asset class. However, those stablecoins that are truly part of the new phenomenon of cryptoassets may still involve major uncertainties related to their governance and regulatory treatment.[48]

It is noteworthy that the regulatory treatment of stablecoins is not only relevant for potential licensing requirements but may also have an impact on their accounting treatment. For example, concerning the asset side of a bank's balance sheet, FINMA has suggested applying an 800 percent risk weight to cryptocurrency assets regardless of whether these assets are held in the bank or in a trading book.[49] Depending on its specific nature, a stablecoin may be seen as a cryptocurrency and thus induce higher capital requirements. Since no official statement has been given so far, it seems that every bank intending to transact in stablecoins is best advised to check the coin's regulatory qualification with the regulator. Similarly, from the perspective of a stablecoin issuer, the accounting treatment on the liability side of the balance sheet may vary greatly depending on the exact nature of the stablecoin. While stablecoins construed as electronic money may be straightforward to account for, more exotic stablecoin formats may be rather challenging.

11.10 POSSIBLE SCENARIOS AND OUTLOOK

Factors from within and outside the stablecoin universe are going to drive further development of stablecoins. Incumbents and policymakers, as well as challengers and users, are going to influence stablecoin evolution.

Within the cryptocurrency universe, the creation of a new prominent decentralized application (DApp) or cryptoasset may lead to a sudden demand shock in stablecoins. For example, if stablecoins are required to interact with such a DApp or represent the only access point to purchase a promising new cryptoasset, the demand for stablecoins would likely surge. Similarly, the adoption of decentralized exchanges may also lead to increasing demand for stablecoins in order to facilitate trading. In contrast, in the case of a major incident such as the detection of a critical vulnerability in a DLT system or a large-scale security breach on one of the dominant cryptocurrency exchanges, stablecoin use would likely diminish. Depending on the severity of such an incident, policymakers may see themselves forced to impose stricter rules on businesses interacting with stablecoins. A policy shock, such as the introduction of specific licensing requirements, may make stablecoin projects less attractive and, in the worst case, bring further development to a halt. Aside from the regulatory circumstances, the overall economic environment may impact stablecoin adoption. For example, if interest rates were to normalize, the demand for more risky asset classes could recede and lead to higher opportunity costs for users when holding stablecoins bearing zero interest. On the other hand, in the case of a financial crisis, users may suddenly find themselves attracted to alternative forms of currency such as cryptocurrencies. Increased trading activity on cryptocurrency exchanges could positively affect the popularity of stablecoins. Lastly, the overall monetary system may be fundamentally changed through the introduction of a central bank digital currency (CBDC), potentially upstaging stablecoins.

11.11   SUMMARY AND CONCLUSION

Stablecoins are an ambiguous concept of money. While they first originated in the world of cryptocurrencies, they have now become an independent concept of their own. Nonetheless, in order to develop a deeper understanding of what problems they currently solve and may address in the future, it is vital to understand how and why they first came into existence.

As described in section 11.4, stablecoins developed initially from the idea of democratizing the issuance of private currencies. At the same time, cryptocurrency exchanges needed a fiat currency substitute that would allow them to become less reliant on typically fragile banking partnerships. Stablecoins proved to be an elegant solution for growing the cryptocurrency trading ecosystem while minimizing dependence on traditional banking services. As Tether grew popular, so did the general enthusiasm for stablecoins, and as the usage of the term stablecoin spread, its meaning started to blur.

Imprecise terminology may make us susceptible to deceptive innovation, overestimating the significance of reengineered legacy payment systems and potentially overlooking more profound changes in our monetary system. As described in section 11.5, Christensen's theory of disruptive innovation provides a useful tool for distinguishing between stablecoins as a genuinely new asset type and old wine in new bottles. Building on those insights, we provide a new definition that distills the essential characteristics of a stablecoin. Specifically, we claim that it is not an existing form of currency, it does not require any direct relationship with the issuer, and it is tradable on a secondary market at a relatively stable and predictable price.

In section 11.6, we proposed an easy-to-use yet expressive taxonomy that focuses on the absence or existence of a legal claim, distinguishing between claim-, faith-, and technology-based stablecoins. We also put this classification into a broader context by comparing it with existing taxonomies and found a strong congruence with the IMF's money tree.

In section 11.7, we briefly reviewed current use cases of stablecoins, highlighting cross-border payments, cross-cryptocurrency exchange settlement, and decentralized finance applications. We claimed that the idea of stablecoins has outgrown its cryptocurrency origins. However, their use is still very much rooted in the cryptocurrency space.

In section 11.8, we examined the revenue and cost structure of stablecoins. We found that interest earnings on the reserve funds provide substantial upside potential for stablecoin issuers. Given their predominantly fixed-cost structure, stablecoins constitute highly scalable business models. Unsurprisingly, to reduce costs, many issuers are incorporated in offshore locations while still benefiting from the global reach of today's DLT platforms.

In section 11.9, we briefly considered the regulators' perspectives by reviewing statements given by the FINMA, US policymakers, and the ECB. We found that most regulators have a technology-neutral view, aiming to subsume stablecoins under existing regulations.

In section 11.10, we completed our stablecoin examination by briefly outlining potential future scenarios. We find that claim- and faith-based stablecoins build on existing money forms, whereas technology-based stablecoins are decoupled from the traditional money creation circle.

All in all, we conclude that stablecoins are a moving target with tremendous potential to fundamentally change the financial system. With DLT providing a borderless and easy-to-integrate infrastructure, stablecoins have the potential to scale rapidly on a global scale and disrupt existing payment systems. Stablecoins are challenging our notion of money, creating a paradoxical situation in which they may be used like a currency without actually being labeled one. It remains to be seen whether stablecoins are going to coexist, complement, or take over existing payments, but in any case we should aim to use a more concise technology-neutral language, allowing us to focus on the truly disruptive potential of future money forms and on applying new technologies such as DLT in a more purpose-driven way.

NOTES

1. Council of the European Union, "Joint Statement by the Council and the Commission on 'Stablecoins,'" December 5, 2019, https://www.consilium .europa.eu/de/press/press-releases/2019/12/05/joint-statement-by-the -council-and-the-commission-on-stablecoins; S. R. Garcia, Managed Stablecoins Are Securities Act of 2019, November 20, 2019, https://www.congress .gov/bill/116th-congress/house-bill/5197/text; FINMA, "FINMA Publishes Stable Coin Guidelines," September 11, 2019, https://www.finma.ch /en/news/2019/09/20190911-mm-stable-coins.

2. D. Orrell and R. Chlupat, *The Evolution of Money* (New York: Columbia University Press, 2016).

3. N. Vardi, L. Scipione, V. Santoro, C. Mertzanis, C. Gortsos, C. D. Anca, V. Cattelan, M. B. Beros, A. Borron, and A. Jaczuk-Gorywoda, *Money, Payment Systems and the European Union*, ed. G. Gimigliano (Newcastle: Cambridge Scholars Publishing, 2016).

4. P. Vuillaume, *WIR: Eine konomische analyse der komplementrwhrung zum schweizer franken*, 2015, https://wwz.unibas.ch/fileadmin/user_upload /wwz/00_Professuren/Berentsen_Wirtschaftstheorie/Lecture_Material /Master_s_Thesis/Completed_Master_s_Theses/vuillaume.pdf.

5. Orrell and Chlupat, *The Evolution of Money*.

6. Vuillaume, *WIR*.

7. WIR, *Wir-kmu-paket*, 2020,https://www.wir.ch/firmenkunden/wir-ihr -weg-zum-erfolg/wir-kmu-paket/#eintrag-9374.

8. WIR, *Fragen und antworten (FAQ)*, 2020, https://www.wir.ch/ueber
-uns/fragen-antworten-faq/#eintrag-3199.

9. ConsenSys, *The State of Stablecoins*, 2019, https://media.consensys.net
/the-state-of-stablecoins-2019-40c3eca990f4.

10. Tether, "Terms of Service," February 2019, https://tether.to/legal;
F. Coppola, "Tether's U.S. Dollar Peg Is No Longer Credible," *Forbes*,
March 14, 2019, https://www.forbes.com/sites/francescoppola/2019/03
/14/tethers-u-s-dollar-peg-is-no-longer-credible/\#11956405451b.

11. CoinMarketCap, "Top 100 Cryptocurrencies by Market Capitalization," March 2020, https://coinmarketcap.com.

12. D. Zynis, "A Brief History of Mastercoin," Omni Foundation, November 29, 2013, https://blog.omni.foundation/2013/11/29/a-brief-history-of
-mastercoin/; C. Sellars, "Craig Mastercoin Foundation CTO. AMA!," Omni
Foundation, August 7, 2014, https://blog.omni.foundation/2014/08/07
/craig-mastercoin-foundation-cto-ama; J. Roth, F. Schär, and A. Schöpfer,
"The Tokenization of Assets: Using Blockchains for Equity Crowdfunding,"
SSRN, September 19, 2019, https://ssrn.com/abstract=3443382.

13. For example, the Paradise Papers leak revealed that Bitfinex officials
were responsible for setting up Tether Holdings Limited in the British Virgin
Islands in 2014. Moreover, Tether Limited and Bitfinex both share the same
CEO, CFO, and general counsel. See S. Haig, "Paradise Papers Reveal Bitfinex's Devasini and Potter Established Tether Already Back in 2014," *Bitcoin
News*, November 23, 2017, https://news.bitcoin.com/paradise-papers-reveal
-bitfinexs-devasini-and-potter-established-tether-already-back-in-2014/.

14. M. Leising, L. Katz, and Y. Rivera, "One of the Biggest Crypto Exchanges
Is Heading to the Caribbean," Bitfinex, May 2018, https://blog.bitfinex.com
/category/profiles.

15. As it later turned out, Bitfinex's bank accounts had been frozen by Wells
Fargo. See S. Higgins, "Bitfinex Sues Wells Fargo over Bank Transfer Freeze,"

Coindesk, April 11, 2017, https://www.coindesk.com/bitcoin-exchange-bitf inex-sues-wells-fargo-over-bank-transfer-freeze.

16. Kraken, "Kraken Announces Support for 'Crypto Dollar' Tether (USDT)," March 2017, https://blog.kraken.com/post/206/kraken-announces-support -for-crypto-dollar; Binance, "Binance Will Add USDT Market Soon," 2017, https://www.binance.com/en/support/articles/115001094331; Huobi, "Huobi Pro Will Launch Tether (USDT) on October 24th, 2017," October 2017, https:// medium.com/huobi-global/huobi-pro-will-launch-tether-usdt-on-october -24th-2017–7b4af9e56491.

17. J. M. Griffin and A. Shams, "Is Bitcoin Really Un-tethered?," October 2019, unpublished.

18. S. Upson, "Why Tether's Collapse Would Be Bad for Cryptocurrencies," *Wired*, January 2018, https://www.wired.com/story/why-tethers-collapse -would-be-bad-for-cryptocurrencies.

19. Gemini, "Gemini Dollar," 2020, https://gemini.com/dollar; Coinbase, "Coinbase and Circle Announce the Launch of USDC—a Digital Dollar," October 2018, https://blog.coinbase.com/coinbase-and-circle-announce-the -launch-of-usdc-a-digital-dollar-2cd6548d237; S. Miah, "Huobi Introduces HUSD—the Universal Stablecoin Providing Maximum Stability," Medium .com, October 23, 2018, https://medium.com/swlh/huobi-introduces-husd -the-universal-stablecoin-providing-maximum-stability-272c9bf24831.

20. N. Al-Naji, "Basis," Basis, December 2018, https://www.basis.io.

21. UBS, *Building the Trust Engine*, 2016, https://www.ubs.com/microsites /blockchain-report/en/home.html.

22. A. Lipton, A. Pentland, and T. Hardjono, "Narrow Banks and Fiat Backed Digital Coins," *Capco Institute Journal* 47 (2018): 101–116; A. Lipton, T. Hardjono, and A. Pentland, "Digital Trade Coin (DTC): Towards a More Stable Digital Currency," *Journal of the Royal Society Open Science (RSOS)* 5, no. 7 (August 2018): 180155, https://doi.org/10.1098/rsos

.180155; A. Lipton and A. Pentland, "Breaking the Bank," *Scientific American* 318, no. 1 (2018): 26–31.

23. J. Horwitz and P. Olson, "Facebook Unveils Cryptocurrency Libra in Bid to Reshape Finance," *Wall Street Journal*, June 18, 2019, https://www.wsj.com /articles/facebook-unveils-crypto-wallet-based-on-currency-libra-11560850141.

24. Reuters, "France and Germany Agree to Block Facebook's Libra," *Reuters*, September 13, 2019, https://www.reuters.com/article/us-facebook -cryptocurrency-france-german/france-and-germany-agree-to-block -facebooks-libra-idUSKCN1VY1XU.

25. Perhaps archaic words were more aligned with the ideological tendencies of declinism and cryptoanarchism within the cryptocurrency community. Note that both Bitcash and Bitmoney exist today but were launched long after Bitcoin in early 2019 and late 2018, respectively.

26. D. Bullmann, J. Klemm, and A. Pinna, "In Search for Stability in Crypto-assets, Are Stablecoins the Solution?," ECB Occasional Paper No. 230, Social Science Research Network (SSRN), August 2019, https://ssrn .com/abstract=3444847.

27. For a more detailed comparison between the various already existing forms of money and genuine cryptocurrencies, we refer the reader to the monetary control structure cube proposed in A. Berentsen and F. Schär, "The Case for Central Bank Electronic Money and the Non-case for Central Bank Cryptocurrencies," *Federal Reserve Bank of St. Louis* 100, no. 2 (2018): 79–106.

28. C. M. Christensen, M. E. Raynor, and R. McDonald, "What Is Disruptive Innovation?," *Harvard Business Review*, December 2015, https://hbr .org/2015/12/what-is-disruptive-innovation.

29. In fact, some stablecoins require an efficient secondary market for their stabilization mechanism to work. Such stablecoin systems are constructed in such a way that, by design, arbitrage opportunities arise as soon as the market price deviates from the target par value.

30. D. Hays, *Gold Stablecoins*, Crypto Research, August 27, 2019, https://cryptoresearch.report/crypto-research/gold-stablecoins.

31. A. Berentsen and F. Schär, "Stablecoins: The Quest for a Low-Volatility Cryptocurrency," in *The Economics of Fintech and Digital Currencies*, ed. A. Fatás (London: CEPR Press, 2019), 65–71, https://voxeu.org/content/economics-fintech-and-digital-currencies.

32. A. Lipton, "Towards a Stable Tokenized Medium of Exchange," in *Cryptoassets: Legal, Regulatory, and Monetary Perspectives* (Oxford: Oxford University Press, 2019), 89–116, https://doi.org/10.1093/oso/9780190077310.003.0005.

33. Circle, "Circle USDC User Agreement," December 2019, https://support.usdc.circle.com/hc/en-us/articles/360001233386.

34. TrustToken, "Truecoin Terms of Use," August 2019, https://www.trusttoken.com/terms-of-use. Similarly, stablecoins that promote buybacks to stabilize market prices would fall under this category as well because such buybacks would typically occur at the issuer's discretion without the issuer being legally bound to them.

35. T. Adrian and T. Mancini-Griffoli, "The Rise of Digital Money," International Monetary Fund (IMF), FinTech Notes, July 15, 2019, https://www.imf.org/en/Publications/fintech-notes/Issues/2019/07/12/The-Rise-of-Digital-Money-47097.

36. O. Kharif, "Just 318 Crypto Addresses Control 80% of Tether," *Bloomberg*, August 7, 2019, https://www.bloomberg.com/news/articles/2019-08-07/tether-mafia-318-crypto-addresses-control-most-of-stablecoin.

37. F. Schär, "Decentralized Finance: On Blockchain- and Smart Contract-Based Financial Markets," *SSRN*, March 8, 2020, https://ssrn.com/abstract=3571335.

38. For example, DAI currently uses an overcollateralization rate of 150 percent, meaning that for $100 worth of DAI $150 worth of cryptoassets need to be locked in a so-called collateral debt position (or vault). A trader wanting to leverage his ETH position could lock $100 worth of ETH and

receive $100/150 = $66.66 worth of DAI. He could then buy $66.66 worth of ETH, lock these assets in the collateral debt position, and repeat this process again and again, yielding a total leveraged position of $300.

39. TrustToken, "Explore All of Our Currencies," March 2020, https://www.trusttoken.com/currencies.

40. Tether, "Terms of Service."

41. Swiss Fund Data, "Credit Suisse Money Market Fund—USD B," 2020, https://www.swissfunddata.ch/sfdpub/de/funds/show/29451.

42. Etherscan, "Tether USD (USDT)," March 2020, https://etherscan.io/address/0xdac17f958d2ee523a2206206994597c13d831ec7/\#code.

43. Etherscan, "Tether USD (USDT)—Analytics," March 2020, https://etherscan.io/token/0xdac17f958d2ee523a2206206994597c13d831ec7/\#tokenAnalytics.

44. Etherscan, "Tether USD (USDT)—Contract Source Code," March 2020, https://etherscan.io/address/0xdac17f958d2ee523a2206206994597c13d831ec7/\#code.

45. Tether, "Fees," March 2020, https://tether.to/fees.

46. FINMA, *Supplement to the Guidelines for Enquiries Regarding the Regulatory Framework for Initial Coin Offerings (ICOs)*, November 2019.

47. Garcia, Managed Stablecoins Are Securities Act of 2019.

48. Bullmann, Klemm, and Pinna, "In Search for Stability in Crypto-assets, Are Stablecoins the Solution?"

49. Y. Mauchle and S. Guidoum, "Flat Risk Weight of 800%—? FINMA Clarifies Prudential Consequences of Cryptoassets Trading by Swiss Banks and Securities Dealers," Baker & McKenzie, December 6, 2018, https://blockchain.bakermckenzie.com/2018/12/06/flat-risk-weight-of-800-finma-clarifies-prudential-consequences-of-cryptoassets-trading-by-swiss-bank.

INTEROPERABILITY OF DISTRIBUTED SYSTEMS

Thomas Hardjono, Alexander Lipton,
and Alex Pentland

12.1 INTRODUCTION

One of the key issues facing the nascent area of blockchain and
distributed ledger technology (DLT) is the lack of interoperability
across various blockchain networks.[1] The original blockchain idea
of Haber and Stornetta[2] is now a fundamental construct within
most blockchain systems, starting with the Bitcoin system, which
first adopted the idea and deployed it in a digital currency context. Given the history of the development of the internet and of
computer networks in general (e.g., LANs, WANs), it is unlikely
that the world will settle on one global blockchain system operating universally. The emerging picture will most likely consist of
islands of blockchain systems, which—like autonomous systems
that make up the internet—must be stitched together in some
fashion to make a coherent union.

One of the main features of a blockchain network that distin-
guishes it from an internet routing domain is the perceived economic *value* of the signed information contained in the records
of the shared ledger of the blockchain. In the case of an internet

protocol (IP) routing domain, the goal of the routing protocols and the network elements (e.g., routers) is to route the data packet through the domain in the shortest time possible. Data packets or PDUs (protocol data units) are therefore seen as being ephemeral and carry no value in themselves. Indeed, some routing protocols may even duplicate some data packets and pass them through different routes in order to speed up the delivery of the total application-layer message.

In the world of blockchain technology, many leading developers of blockchain protocols and networks seek to be the sole platform where transactions occur. We believe this outlook is too short term and even naive, given the history of the purpose of internet development. Many leading voices in the blockchain world often fail to understand the fundamental goals of the internet architecture as promoted and led by the Defense Advanced Research Projects Agency (DARPA) and thus fail to fully appreciate how these goals have shaped the internet to be as successful as it is today. There was a pressing need in the Cold War period of the 1960s and 1970s to develop a new communications network architecture that would allow communications to survive in the face of attacks. In section 12.2, we review and discuss these goals.

The goal of this chapter is to bring to the forefront the notion of *interoperability*, *survivability*, and *manageability* for blockchain systems using lessons learned from the three decades of development of the internet. Our overall goal is to develop a design philosophy for an interoperable blockchain architecture and to identify some design principles that promote interoperability.[3]

12.2 INTERNET ARCHITECTURE

In considering the future direction for blockchain systems generally, it is useful to recall and understand goals of the internet architecture defined in the early 1970s as a project funded by DARPA. The definition of the internet in the late 1980s was that it is "a packet switched communications facility in which a number of distinguishable networks are connected together using packet switched communications processors called gateways which implement a store and forward packet-forwarding algorithm."[4]

12.2.1 Fundamental Goals

It is important to remember that the design of the Advanced Research Projects Agency Network (ARPANET, the internet's predecessor) and the internet favored military values (e.g., survivability, flexibility, and high performance) over commercial goals (e.g., low cost, simplicity, or consumer appeal),[5] which in turn has affected how the internet has evolved and been used. This emphasis was understandable given the Cold War backdrop to the packet-switching discourse throughout the 1960s and 1970s. The ARPANET was an early packet-switching network. It was the first network to implement the TCP/IP protocol suite.

The DARPA view at the time was that there were seven goals of the internet architecture, with the first three being fundamental to the design and the remaining four being second-level goals. The following are the fundamental goals of the internet in their order of importance:[6]

1. *Survivability*   Internet communications must continue despite the loss of networks or gateways.

This was the most important goal of the internet, especially if it was to be the blueprint for military packet-switched communications facilities. This meant that if two entities were communicating over the internet and some failure caused the internet to be temporarily disrupted and reconfigured to reconstitute the service, then the entities communicating should be able to continue without having to reestablish or reset the high-level state of their conversation. Therefore, to achieve this goal, the state information that describes the ongoing conversation must be protected.

More importantly, in practice, this explicitly means that it is acceptable to lose the state information associated with an entity if at the same time the entity itself is lost. This notion of the state of conversation is related to the end-to-end principle discussed later.

2. *Variety of service types* The internet must support multiple types of communications services.

    "Multiple types" meant that at the transport level the internet architecture should support different types of services distinguished by different requirements for speed, latency, and reliability. Indeed, it was this goal that resulted in the separation into two layers of the TCP layer and IP layer, and the use of bytes (not packets) at the TCP layer for flow control and acknowledgment.

3. *Variety of networks* The internet must accommodate a variety of networks.

    The internet architecture must be able to incorporate and utilize a wide variety of network technologies, including military and commercial facilities.

The remaining four goals of the internet architecture are distributed management of resources, cost-effectiveness, ease of attaching hosts, and accountability in resource usage. Over the ensuing three decades, these second-level goals have been addressed in different ways. For example, accountability in resource usage evolved from the use of rudimentary management information bases into the current sophisticated traffic management protocols and tools. Cost-effectiveness was always an important aspect of the business model for consumer internet service providers (ISPs) and corporate networks.

12.2.2 The End-to-End Principle

One of the critical debates throughout the development of the internet architecture in the 1980s was in regard to the placement of functions that dealt with the reliability of message delivery (e.g., duplicate message detection, message sequencing, guaranteed message delivery, encryption). In essence, the argument revolved around the amount of effort put into reliability measures within the data communication system and was seen as an engineering trade-off based on performance; that is, how much low-level function (for reliability) needed to be implemented by the networks rather than by the applications at the endpoints.

The line of reasoning against low-level function implementation in the network became known as the *end-to-end argument* or principle. The basic argument is that a lower-level subsystem that supports a distributed application may be wasting its effort by providing a function that must be implemented at the application level anyway.[7] Thus, for example, for duplicate message suppression, the task must be accomplished by the application itself, seeing that the application is most knowledgeable regarding how to detect its own duplicate messages.

Another case in point relates to data encryption. If encryption and decryption are to be performed by the network, then the network and its data transmission systems must be trusted to securely manage the required encryption keys. Also, when data enters the network (to be encrypted there), the data will be in plaintext and therefore susceptible to theft and attacks. Finally, the recipient application of the encrypted message will still need to verify the source authenticity of the message. The application will still need to perform key management. Therefore, the best place to perform data encryption and decryption is at the application endpoints. There is no need for the communication subsystem to provide automatic encryption of all traffic; that is, encryption is an end-to-end function.

The end-to-end principle was a fundamental design principle of the security architecture of the internet. Among other things, it influenced the direction of the subsequent security features of the internet, including the development of the IP-security sublayer[8] and its attendant key management function.[9] Today, the entire virtual private network (VPN) subsegment of the networking industry is based on this end-to-end principle. (The global VPN market alone is forecast to reach $70 billion in the next few years.) The current day-to-day use of the secure sockets layer (TLS)[10] to protect HTTP (hypertext transfer protocol) web traffic (i.e., browsers) is also built on the premise that client-server data encryption is an end-to-end function performed by the browser (client) and by the HTTP server.

12.2.3 The Autonomous Systems Principle
Another key concept in the development of the internet is that of an *autonomous system* (AS) (or routing domain) as a connectivity

unit that provides scale-up capabilities. More specifically, the classic definition of an AS is a connected group of one or more networks (distinguishable via IP prefixes) run by one or more network operators that has a single, clearly defined routing policy.[11] The notion of autonomous systems provides a way to *hierarchically aggregate routing information* so that the distribution of routing information itself becomes a manageable task. This division into domains provides independence for each domain owner/operator to employ the routing mechanisms of its choice (see figure 12.1). IP packet routing inside an autonomous system is therefore referred to as *intradomain* routing, while routing between (across) autonomous systems is referred to as *interdomain* or *cross-domain* routing. The common goal of many providers of routing services (consumer ISPs, backbone ISPs, and participating corporations) is to support different types of services (in the sense of speed, latency, and reliability).

In the case of intradomain routing, the aim is to share best-route information among routers using an intradomain routing protocol (e.g., distance vector such as RIP[12] or link state such as OSPF[13]). The routing protocol of choice must address numerous issues, including possible loops and imbalances in traffic distribution. Today, routers are typically owned and operated by the legal owner of the autonomous system (e.g., ISP or corporation). These owners then enter into *peering agreements* with each other in order to achieve end-to-end reachability of destinations across multiple hops or domains. The primary revenue model in the ISP industry revolves around different tiers of services appropriate to different groups of customers.

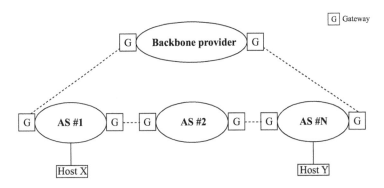

Figure 12.1

Autonomous systems as a set of networks and gateways (after V. G. Cerf and R. E. Khan, "A Protocol for Packet Network Intercommunication," *IEEE Transactions on Communications* 22 (1974): 637–648).

There are several important points regarding the autonomous systems paradigm and the positive impact this paradigm has had on the development of the internet for the past four decades:

- *Autonomous systems paradigm leads to scale*   The autonomous system paradigm, the connectionless routing model, and the distributed network topology of the internet allow each unit (the AS) to solve performance issues locally. This in turn promotes service scale in the sense of throughput (end to end) and reach (the large number of connected endpoints). Therefore, it is important to see the global internet today as a connected set of islands of autonomous systems stitched together through peering agreements.
- *Domain-level control with distributed topology*   Each autonomous system typically possesses multiple routers operating the same

intradomain routing protocol. The availability of multiple routers implies availability of multiple routing paths through the domain. Despite this distributed network topology, these routers are centrally controlled (e.g., by the network administrator of the domain). The autonomous system as a control unit provides manageability, visibility, and peering capabilities centrally administered by the owner of the domain.

- *Each entity or device is uniquely identifiable in its domain* All routers (and other devices, such as bridges and switches) in an autonomous system are uniquely identifiable and visible to the network operator. This is a precondition of routing. The identifiability and visibility of devices in a domain are usually limited to that domain. Entities outside the domain may not even be aware of the existence of individual routers in the domain.

- *Autonomous system reachability* Autonomous systems interact with each other through special kinds of routers—called gateways— that are designed and configured for cross-domain packet routing. These operate specific kinds of protocols (such as an exterior border gateway protocol[14]), which provides transfer of packets across domains. For various reasons (including privacy and security), these exterior-facing gateway protocols typically advertise only reachability status information regarding routers and hosts in the domain but do not publish internal routing conditions.

- *Autonomous systems are owned and operated by legal entities* All routing autonomous systems (routing domains) today are owned, operated, and controlled by known entities. Internet service providers (ISPs) provide their autonomous system numbers and routing prefixes to internet routing registries (IRRs). IRRs can be used by ISPs to develop routing plans. An example of an IRR is the American Registry for Internet Numbers (ARIN),[15] which is one of several IRRs around the world.

In the next section, we remap the fundamental goals of the internet architecture in the context of blockchain systems, with the goal of identifying some fundamental requirements for blockchain interoperability.

12.3   A DESIGN PHILOSOPHY FOR BLOCKCHAIN SYSTEMS

During the 1970s and 1980s, several local area network (LAN) systems were in development and were marketed for enterprises (e.g., IBM SNA,[16] DECnet[17]). However, these LANs were distinct enough in their technological approaches (e.g., PHY layer protocols) that they did not interoperate with each other.[18] Today, we are seeing a very similar situation, in which multiple blockchain designs are being proposed (e.g., Bitcoin,[19] Ethereum,[20] Hyperledger,[21] CORDA[22]), each having different technological designs and approaches. Most share some common terminology (e.g., "transaction," "mining node"), but there is little or no interoperability among these systems.

Following from the first fundamental goal of the internet architecture, the lesson learned there was that *interoperability is key to survivability*. Thus, interoperability is central to the entire value proposition of blockchain technology. Interoperability across blockchain systems must be a requirement—at both the *mechanical level* and the *value level*—if blockchain systems and technologies are to become the fundamental infrastructure of future global commerce.[23]

This chapter focuses primarily on interoperability across blockchain systems at the mechanical level as the basis for achieving a measurable degree of *technical trust* across these systems. In turn, technical trust is needed by the upper-level functions to achieve interoperability at the value level so *legal frameworks* can be created that are able to quantify risks based on the technological choices used to implement technical trust. Poorly designed blockchain systems should present a higher risk for commerce, and vice versa. Finally, *business trust* can be built on these legal frameworks to allow business transactions to occur seamlessly across multiple blockchain systems globally.

In this section, we identify and discuss some of the challenges to blockchain interoperability, using the internet architecture as a guide and using the fundamental goals as the basis for developing a design philosophy for interoperable blockchains.

In order to clarify the meaning of *interoperability* in the context of blockchain systems, we offer the following definition of an *interoperable blockchain architecture* using the NIST definition of *blockchain*: "An interoperable blockchain architecture is a composition of distinguishable blockchain systems, each representing a unique distributed data ledger, where atomic transaction execution may span multiple heterogeneous blockchain systems, and where data recorded in one blockchain is reachable, verifiable and referenceable by another possibly foreign transaction in a semantically compatible manner."[24] In the following, we recast the aspects of survivability, variety of service types, and variety of systems in the context of blockchain systems.

12.3.1 Survivability

As mentioned previously, interoperability is key to survivability. In the internet architecture, survivability as viewed by DARPA[25] meant that communications must continue despite the loss of networks and gateways. In practical engineering terms, this meant the use of the packet-switching model as a realization of the *connectionless* routing paradigm.

In the context of blockchain systems generally, survivability should also mean continued operations in the face of various kinds of attacks. The possible types of attacks on a blockchain system have been discussed elsewhere and consist of a broad spectrum. These range from classic network-level attacks (e.g., network partitions, denial of services, DDOS), to more sophisticated attacks targeting the particular constructs (e.g., consensus implementation[26]), to targeting specific implementations of mining nodes (e.g., code vulnerabilities, viruses). Similar to the case for applications on the internet, we can also view survivability more specifically from the perspective of the application (and its user) that is transacting on the blockchain. A user's transaction should proceed as far as possible despite the blockchain being under attack.

For blockchain systems, we propose to reinterpret the term *survivability* to mean the completion (confirmation) of an application-level transaction independent of blockchain systems involved in achieving the completion of the transaction. Furthermore, the transaction may be composed of *subtransactions*, in the same sense that a message on the internet may consist of multiple IP datagrams. Thus, in the blockchain case, an application-level transaction may consist of multiple ledger-level transactions (subtransaction), where each could be intended for (and be confirmed at) different blockchain systems (e.g., subtransaction for asset transfer in blockchain A simultaneously with a subtransaction for payments and a subtransaction for taxes in blockchain B).

Here, the notion that packets routing through multiple domains are opaque to the user's communications application (e.g., email applications, browsers) is now recast as the notion of *subtransactions confirmed on a spread of blockchain systems generally opaque to the user application*. Thus, the challenge of reliability and "best effort delivery" becomes the challenge of ensuring that an application-level transaction is completed within a reasonable time, possibly with the application itself being oblivious to the actual blockchains where different ledger-level subtransactions are finally confirmed.

To illustrate the challenges of survivability as interpreted in this manner, we start with the simplest case, in which an application sends a "data" transaction (signed hash value) to a blockchain for the purpose of recording it on the ledger of the blockchain (figure 12.2). We ignore for the moment the dichotomy of permissionless and permissioned blockchains and ignore the specific logic syntax of the blockchain. Here the application does not care which blockchain records the data as long as once the transaction is confirmed, the application (and other entities) can later find the transaction/block and verify that the data has been recorded immutably. Figure 12.2 illustrates the scenario. The application transmits data bytes (hash) to blockchain system 1 and waits for confirmation to become available on the blockchain. After waiting unsuccessfully for some predetermined time (i.e., timeout), the application transmits the same data bytes to a different blockchain system, blockchain system 2. The application continues this process until it is able to obtain the desired confirmation.

Although the example in figure 12.2 may appear overly simplistic and inefficient, and has the undesirable side effect of confirmations on multiple blockchains, it highlights a number of questions similar to those posed in the early days of the internet architecture's development:

- *Application degree of awareness*   To what degree must an application be aware of the internal constructs of a blockchain system in order to interact with it and make use of the blockchain? Most wallet applications today must maintain configuration information regarding which blockchain system a key applies to. As a point of comparison, an email client application today is not aware of constructs of packets, MPDUs (media access control protocol data units), routing, and so on. It interacts with the mail server according to a high-level protocol (e.g., POP3, IMAP, SMTP) and a well-defined API. The email client needs only to know the destination email address.

- *Distinguishability and addressability of blockchain systems*   For an interoperable blockchain architecture, each blockchain autonomous system must be distinguishable from a naming perspective as well as from an addressing/routing perspective. This introduces some new challenges, such as the situation where a node is

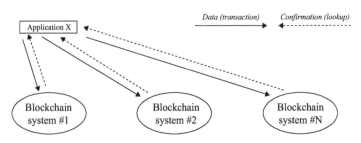

Figure 12.2
Example of the reliability of a simple transaction.

permitted to participate in several blockchain systems simultaneously. From a key management perspective, there is also the question regarding multiple uses of the same public-key pair across several distinct blockchain systems.

- *Placement of reliability functions*   What is the correct notion of "reliability" in the context of interoperable blockchain systems, and where should the function of reliability be placed? That is, should the function of retransmitting the same data bytes (transaction) be part of the application, part of the blockchain system, or part of a yet to be defined "middle layer"? As a comparison, within the TCP/IP stack, the TCP protocol has a number of flow control features that hide reliability issues from the higher-level applications.

- *Semantic interoperability*   If in the future there emerge blockchain autonomous systems with different applications (e.g., registry of assets, currency trading), what mechanisms will be needed to convey to an external system the functional goal of a blockchain and its application-specific semantics? As a comparison, the HTTP protocol and RPC interprocess communications both run on the TCP/IP layer. However, these represent different resource access paradigms for different types of applications.

- *Objective benchmarks for speed and performance*   How do external entities obtain information about the current performance/throughput of a blockchain system, and what measure can be used for comparisons across systems?

12.3.2   Variety of Service Types

The second goal of the internet architecture was the support for different types of services, distinguished by different speeds, latencies, and reliabilities. The bidirectional reliable data delivery model was suitable for a variety of "applications" on the internet, but each application required different speeds and bandwidth consumption (e.g., remote login, file transfer). This understanding led to the realization early in the design of the internet that more than one transport service would be needed and that the architecture must simultaneously support transports wishing to tailor reliability, delay, or bandwidth usage. This resulted in the separation of TCP (which provided a reliable sequenced data stream) from the IP protocol that provided "best effort" delivery using the common building block of the *datagram*. The user datagram protocol (UDP)[27] was created to address the need for certain applications that wished to trade reliability for direct access to the datagram construct.

For blockchain systems, we propose to reinterpret the notion of service types from the perspective of the different needs of various applications. We distinguish three basic types of service:

- *Immediate direct confirmation* This refers to applications that require the fastest confirmation from a specific destination blockchain system. The confirmation of the transaction must occur at the destination blockchain. Therefore, speed and latency are the primary concerns for these types of applications. This is summarized in figure 12.3(a). This situation is an analog of the classic TCP-based login service, in which the user performs a login to a specific computer system and needs confirmation with as little delay as possible (e.g., milliseconds, seconds). Digital currency applications (e.g., currency trading systems) are a typical example of cases needing direct and immediate confirmation with low latency.

- *Delayed mediated confirmation* This refers to applications that are satisfied with a "temporary" confirmation produced by a mediating blockchain system, which will then seek to "move" the transaction to its intended destination blockchain system. This is summarized in figure 12.3(b). The application will obtain two confirmations. The first is a temporary confirmation from the mediating blockchain system, while the final confirmation will occur at the destination blockchain system at a later time. Therefore, there are two latency values, corresponding to the two confirmations. The understanding here is that the application deems the first latency to be acceptable from a practical perspective and that the second latency can be of a longer period of time (e.g., minutes). This is akin to the store-and-forward method used by classic electronic mail systems. An example of this type of application is noncritical notarization applications that seek to record static (unchanging) data (e.g., birth date on a birth certificate) and do not require low-latency confirmations.
- *Multi-chain mediated confirmation* This scenario is a multi-chain variation of the single-party mediated case mentioned earlier. Here, two or more applications are seeking to complete a common transaction at an agreed destination blockchain system, with the aid of settlement logic that executes at the destination blockchain system. Each application is willing to accept a "temporary" confirmation produced by a mediating blockchain system, with the understanding that they will obtain a final confirmation from the destination blockchain system. This is summarized in figure 12.3(c). This situation is akin to TCP-based messaging or chat servers (e.g., XMPP), in which two (or more) parties converge on a common server even though each may have its own local servers.

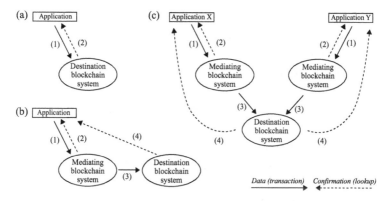

Figure 12.3
Service types based on different confirmation models: (a) immediate direct confirmation; (b) delayed mediated confirmation; (c) multi-chain mediated confirmation.

12.3.3 Variety of Blockchain Systems

The third fundamental goal of the internet architecture was to support a variety of networks, which included networks employing different transmission technologies at the physical layer (e.g., X.25, SNA), local networks and long-haul networks, and networks operated or owned by different legal entities. The *minimum assumption* of the internet architecture—which is central to the success of the internet as an interoperable system of networks—was that each network must be able to transport a *datagram* as the lowest-unit common denominator. Furthermore, this was to be performed "best effort"—namely with reasonable but not perfect reliability.

For blockchain systems, we propose a reinterpretation of the minimal assumption as consisting of

1. a common *standardized transaction format and syntax* that will be understood by all blockchain systems regardless of their respective technological implementation and

2. a common *standardized minimal set of operations* that will be implemented on all blockchain systems regardless of their technological choices.

The notion of a common transaction format is akin to the definition of the minimal IP datagram, which was first published in the 1974 milestone paper by Vint Cerf and Bob Kahn.[28] The operation involved in the datagram case is simple and is implicit in the datagram construct itself, namely that a set of bytes needs to be transmitted from one IP address to another. The situation is somewhat more complex in blockchain systems. Aside from the current common fields found in transactions in current systems (e.g., sender and receiver public keys, time stamp, pointers), there is the question of *semantic meaning* of the operations intended by the operation code symbols. Some mathematical operations are clear (e.g., operation codes for addition, multiplication, hash function), but others may introduce some degree of ambiguity across systems.

Similar to the variety of technologies implementing LANs and local routing in the 1980s and 1990s, today there are several technological aspects that differentiate one blockchain system from another:

- *Governance model* The term *governance* in the context of blockchain systems typically is used to refer to the combination of the human-driven policies for the community of participants, the rules of operations that are encoded within the blockchain software and hardware fabric itself, and the intended application of the blockchain, which is often expressed as the "smart contracts" (stored procedures available on nodes), which are application-specific.

- *Speed of confirmation* The speed (or "throughput") of a blockchain system refers to the confirmation speed, based on the population size of the participating nodes and other factors.
- *Strength of consensus* An important consideration is the size of the population of nodes (i.e., entities contributing to the consensus) at any given moment and whether this information is obtainable. Obtaining this information may be challenging in systems where nodes are either anonymous, or perhaps unobtainable by external entities, in the case of permissioned systems.
- *Degrees of permissibility* Currently the permissionless/permissioned distinction refers to the degree to which users can participate in the system.[29] Interoperability across permissioned blockchains poses additional questions with regard to how data recorded on the ledger can be referenced (referred to or "pointed to") by transactions in a foreign domain (i.e., another blockchain system).
- *Degrees of anonymity* There are at least two degrees of anonymity that are relevant to blockchain systems. The first pertains to the anonymity of end users (i.e., identity anonymity[30]), and the second is the anonymity of the nodes participating in processing transactions (e.g., nodes participating in a given consensus instance). Combinations are possible, such as where a permissioned system may require that all consensus nodes be strongly authenticated and identified but allows end users to remain permissionless (and even unidentified or unauthenticated).
- *Cybersecurity and assurance levels of nodes* The robustness of a blockchain system consisting of a peer-to-peer network of nodes

is largely affected by the security of the nodes that make up the network. If nodes are easily compromised directly (e.g., via hacks) or via indirect means (e.g., dormant viruses), the utility of the blockchain system degrades considerably.[31]

12.4 DESIGN PRINCIPLES FOR BLOCKCHAIN GATEWAYS

As mentioned previously, similar to the internet architecture consisting of a network of autonomous systems, in the future the deployments of blockchain technology may evolve to become a network of interconnected blockchain systems—each with different internal consensus protocols, incentive mechanisms, permissions, and security-related constraints. Key to this interconnectivity is the notion of blockchain gateways. In this section, we discuss the potential use of blockchain gateways to provide interoperability and interconnectivity across different blockchain systems and service types.

12.4.1 Blockchain Domains: Intradomain and Interdomain Nodes

Similar to a routing autonomous system composed of one or more routing domains, interoperability requires distinguishing between functions that pertain to the interior of a blockchain system and functions that pertain to the exterior interaction between blockchain systems. In routing terminology, this is akin to interior routing protocols within a subnet and exterior routing protocols that interconnect autonomous systems.

We use the terms *interior nodes* and *gateway nodes* of a blockchain system to distinguish the types of functions that nodes implement in the context of cross-domain (cross-chain) interoperability. Thus, just as routers in a routing domain operate one or more routing protocols to achieve the best routes through that domain, nodes in a blockchain domain contribute to maintaining a shared ledger by running one or more ledger management protocols (e.g., consensus algorithms, membership management) to achieve stability and fast convergence (i.e., confirmation throughput) of the ledger in that domain:

- *Interior nodes*   These are nodes and other entities whose main task is to maintain ledger information and conduct transactions within one blockchain domain. For certain blockchain configurations (e.g., private or permissioned), the interior nodes may be prohibited from engaging external entities without authorization.
- *Gateway nodes*   These are nodes and other entities whose main task is to deal with cross-domain transactions involving different blockchain autonomous systems.

Figure 12.4 provides a high-level illustration of gateway nodes G within two blockchain domains (interior nodes are not shown). Although figure 12.4 shows a small number of nodes G to be designated as interdomain gateway nodes, ideally all nodes in a given blockchain autonomous system should have the capability (i.e., correct software, hardware, trusted computing base) of becoming a gateway node. This allows dynamic groups (subsets) of the population of nodes to become *gateway groups* that act collectively on behalf of the blockchain system as a whole.[32]

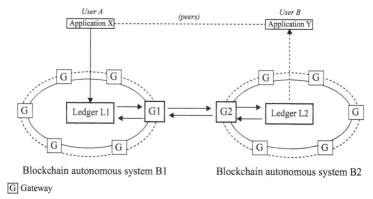

Blockchain autonomous system B1   Blockchain autonomous system B2

G Gateway

Figure 12.4
Overview of gateway-to-gateway transfer of virtual assets.

12.4.2   Design Principles

There are several design principles for blockchain gateway-to-gateway interoperability, with two key principles being the following:[33]

▪ *Opaque blockchain resources* The interior resources of each blockchain system must be assumed to be opaque to (hidden from) external entities. In the context of two gateway nodes performing an asset transfer from one blockchain system to another, any resources to be made accessible to one gateway must be made explicitly accessible by the other gateway node with proper authorization (and vice versa). The opaque resources principle permits the interoperability architecture to be applied in cases where one or both blockchain systems are permissioned (private). It is the analog of the autonomous systems principle in IP networking,[34] where interior routes in local subnets are not visible to other external autonomous systems.

- *Externalization of value*   A gateway-to-gateway protocol must be agnostic (oblivious) to the economic or monetary value of the virtual asset being transferred. The value-externalization principle permits asset transfer protocols to be designed for efficiency, speed, and reliability—independent of the changes in the perceived economic value of the virtual asset. It is the analog of the end-to-end principle in the internet architecture,[35] where contextual information (economic value) is placed at the endpoints of the transaction. In the case of virtual asset transfers, the originator and beneficiary at the respective ends are assumed to have a common agreement regarding the economic value of the asset.

A key aspect of the autonomous system principle in the internet architecture is that routing data (e.g., interior route advertisements) belonging to an ISP is opaque (invisible) to other ISPs and external entities. This provides the freedom for an ISP to innovate within the confines of its own network (e.g., using new routing protocols and routers) while not impacting other ISPs. The ISP-to-ISP interaction occurs through the deployment of an exterior interdomain routing protocol (e.g., BGPv4) that acts as a standardized interface between networks. The role of a gateway node therefore is also to mask (hide) the complexity of the interior constructs of the blockchain system that it represents. Overall, this approach ensures that a given blockchain system operates as a true autonomous system.

Note that the opaque ledgers assumption has implications for smart contract cross-chain conditionals, such as cross-chain hash locks[36] and time locks—which assume that the ledgers on both sides of the cross-chain transfer are readable and writeable (e.g., see Ezhilchelvan, Aldweesh, and van Moorsel,[37] Zakhary, Agrawal, and Abbadi,[38] Herlihy,[39] and Heilman, Lipmann, and Goldberg[40]).

12.5 A GATEWAY INTEROPERABILITY ARCHITECTURE

The goal of a gateway interoperability architecture is to permit two gateway nodes belonging to distinct blockchain systems to conduct a virtual asset transfer between them in a secure and nonrepudiable manner while ensuring that the asset does not exist simultaneously on both blockchains (the double-spend problem).

The architecture must recognize that there are different blockchain systems currently in operation and evolving, and that in many cases the interior technical constructs in these blockchains may be incompatible with one another. The resources within a blockchain system (e.g., ledgers, public keys, consensus protocols) must be assumed to be opaque to external entities in order to permit a resilient and scalable protocol design that is not dependent on the interior constructs of particular blockchain systems. This ensures that the virtual asset transfer protocol between gateways is not conditioned or dependent on these interior technical constructs.

12.5.1 Functional Requirements

There are a number of functional requirements for cross-chain transfers of virtual assets between two blockchain systems or domains:[41]

- *Asset validation before transfer*   There must be some means for the recipient entity (in the destination blockchain) to validate the asset type and legal status prior to engaging with the transfer.

- *Commitment atomicity* Asset transfers across blockchain systems must employ an atomic commitment scheme that prevents or detects the same asset being present simultaneously on both blockchains (e.g., using 2-phase commit protocol (2PC)[42]). There are several efforts today to reuse the atomic commitment protocols from the field of distributed databases and concurrency control (e.g., see Zakhary, Agrawal, and Abbadi[43]). The overall aim of many of these schemes is to interpret (recast) the ACID properties (atomicity, consistency, isolation, durability)[44] of these protocols in the context of asset transfers, at least for unidirectional transfers (database transactions are typically unidirectional). Additional properties (e.g., safety, liveliness) have also been suggested (e.g., cross-chain deals[45]).
- *Transfer nonrepudiability* There must be sufficient evidence regarding the finality and settlement at both blockchain systems to obviate disputes. Evidence of settlement can consist of the combination of confirmed transactions on the blocks of both ledgers, local logs signed by the nodes handling the cross-chain transfer, logs from the commitment layer, and others.
- *Policy federation as part of peering agreements* Blockchain systems need compatible policies along several axes, including: the type of regulated asset being transferred; the legal jurisdiction of operations of the entities (VASPs) owning the nodes; the types of operations permitted (e.g., unidirectional unconditional transfers only, conditional transfer); the agreed commitment protocol and nonrepudiation protocol to be used (or negotiated from a common standard list); and the configurations of the nodes handling the transfers on both sides based on the node-device attestation evidence (see Hardjono and Smith[46] and Hardjono[47] for discussions on node device identities and node attestations).

12.5.2 Identifiers for Blockchain Domains and VASP Numbers

Each autonomous system (AS) on the internet is allocated a globally unique AS number. For example, in the United States, this task is managed by the American Registry for Internet Numbers (ARIN).[48] For the European Union, the organization is RIPE (Réseaux IP Européens) Network Coordination Centre, for Africa it is AFRINIC (African Network Information Centre), for Asia and the Pacific it is APNIC (Asia Pacific Network Information Centre), and so on.[49]

Today, the VASP and virtual asset industry globally have yet to agree on a common VASP numbering scheme and customer identification scheme. The notion of a unique VASP number has been proposed by Riegelnig[50] and InterVASP,[51] while other mechanisms have been contemplated, such as using the VASP's legal entity identifier (LEI)[52] within the VASP KYC certificate.[53]

12.5.3 Asset Locking during Cross-Domain Transfers

A requirement for cross-domain asset transfers between two blockchain domains is preventing double spending of the asset (inadvertently or otherwise) on the part of the customer (originator) who owns it. In this case, a double spend would consist of a customer initiating a cross-domain transfer of their asset while at the same time using the same asset in a different transaction (e.g., locally in the same blockchain domain).

One approach to solving this dilemma is for the gateway node to temporarily *lock* the asset while the transfer process is under way. The notion of "locking" is borrowed from the classic field of database transaction and concurrency control.[54] In transactional database systems, locking techniques are used to "mark" a data item (e.g., database row) as undergoing an update by one process. Other processes are unable to access (write to) the data item until the lock is released.

Given the diversity of blockchain transaction processing models (e.g., UTXO in Bitcoin, externally owned accounts and smart contract accounts in Ethereum), we believe that the ledger is the only reliable shared-state and synchronization method for all the nodes in a blockchain network,[55] and therefore the lock-state information for cross-domain transfers must be recorded on the ledger so that the lock state is visible to all nodes in the same blockchain domain. From an audit and security perspective, the recording of lock/unlock information on the ledger provides the benefit of historical traceability of cross-domain events in the case of disputes.

The specific lock/unlock mechanism is dependent on the cross-domain atomic commitment protocol used by gateway nodes. However, in general they must perform the following tasks:

- *Asset-lock transaction* This transaction marks an asset associated with a customer public key as being in a locked state, and therefore it will not be processed by other nodes. A time duration may be set in the transaction header denoting the duration of validity of the lock, after which the lock automatically expires and the asset is considered unlocked.
- *Asset-unlock transaction* This is an explicit unlock transaction that marks the asset as being "free" (unlocked state) on the ledger. An asset- unlock transaction must match an existing asset-lock transaction on the same ledger, and it is typically issued by the same gateway node that issued the lock. The purpose of an explicit unlock is to terminate a lock before the expiration of its

timer. This feature is useful for cases such as an aborted cross-domain transaction (e.g., abort request from customer).

- *Asset-lock committed transaction* This transaction marks a virtual asset as being henceforth permanently unavailable because of the asset exiting (being transferred out of) the origin blockchain. Typically, this transaction must refer to (include a hash of) a previous asset-locked transaction confirmed on the ledger. It may include an identifier that points to the new home (destination blockchain) of the virtual asset.[56]

Although a discussion of the specific locking mechanism is beyond the scope of this chapter, lock/unlock transactions must generally include at least the following parameters: the identifier of the asset being locked, the address (public key) of the current holder (customer), the identity of the gateway node issuing the lock, the time stamp value (or timer), and the hash of the confirmed transaction on the ledger where the asset was last used. Similarly, an asset-unlocked transaction must include a hash of the earlier confirmed asset-locked transaction.

12.5.4 Example of Flows in a Cross-Domain Transfer

An example of the flows that occur in a cross-domain transfer between two blockchain domains is shown in figure 12.5. The gateway nodes are shown as G1 in domain BD1 and G2 in domain BD2, respectively. Alice is the originator (customer C1), while Bob is the beneficiary (customer C2). Gateway G1 is assumed to be legally owned by a VASP, making it the originator VASP. Similarly, gateway G2 is assumed to be legally owned and operated by a beneficiary VASP.[57]

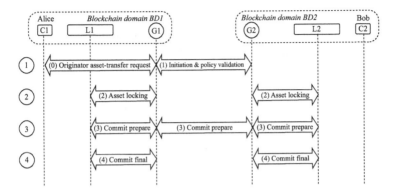

Figure 12.5
Summary of flows in a cross-domain transfer.

The transfer consists of four general phases, including the commitment protocol embedded in the flows:

Phase 1: Initiation of transaction and policy validation There are a number of pretransfer tasks that need to occur in this phase:

- The processing node (gateway G1) must locate the correct destination domain BD2 where the beneficiary (Bob) is thought to reside.
- Gateway G1 must validate that gateway G2 is owned by a registered VASP, and vice versa (see Jevans et al.[58] and Hardjono[59] for discussions of VASP status validation).
- Gateway G1 must request that gateway G2 seek consent from the beneficiary (Bob) to receive the asset to be transferred. This protects the beneficiary and the owner of G2 by giving them exculpatory evidence. An explicit consent from a beneficiary is a requirement in some jurisdictions (e.g., see FINMA[60]).

- Gateway G2 must validate that the virtual asset to be transferred from G1 is compatible with the core operating policies of the blockchain domain BD2.
- Gateway G1 and G2 may optionally perform attestations of their respective node hardware, firmware, and software.
- If all is well, gateway G2 transmits an acknowledgment to G1 that the transfer can proceed.

Phase 2: Local locking of asset In this phase, gateway G1 issues a local asset-locked transaction on ledger L1 to the asset in question. This prevents double spending on the part of the originator.

Optionally, gateway G2 may indicate an incoming asset by issuing a candidate lock on its ledger L2. The candidate lock is not binding but serves as an audit trail in case of later disputes.

Phase 3: Preparation to commit In this phase, gateway G1, acting as the coordinator (in the context of the embedded 2PC protocol[61]), signals readiness to commit to gateway G2.

Phase 4: Finalization of commit In this phase, gateway G1 as coordinator signals to gateway G2 to perform the global commitment on ledger L2. Gateway G1 then issues an asset-lock committed transaction on ledger L1 to close its previous asset-locked transaction in phase 2.

Gateway G2 records the new asset on its local ledger L2, assigning it to the public key of the beneficiary, Bob. If G2 employed a candidate-lock transaction on L2 previously in phase 2, then G2 can also close that transaction with its own asset-locked transaction on ledger L2.

12.5.5 Interdomain Trust Establishment: Node Attestations

Another potential use of gateways in the context of blockchain interoperability is to support the establishment of trust (i.e., technical trust) across blockchain autonomous systems. We believe there is a promising role for trusted hardware to implement many functions of the gateways. As mentioned previously, ideally all nodes in a given blockchain autonomous system should possess the relevant trusted hardware and software to allow them to take on the role of gateways as required. Trusted hardware in nodes provides the basis for nodes to perform attestation of each other as part of phase 1 of the asset transfer. Similarly, trusted hardware can be used to secure keys in end-user wallets and provide a means for the wallet to attest to its current configuration. This may be useful from an asset insurance perspective.[62]

Examples of trusted hardware include the TPM,[63] with its various roots of trust for measurement, storage, and reporting. The first successful version was TPM v1.2, which supported a one-size-fits-all approach that primarily targeted the PC market. The second-generation TPM v2.0 expanded trusted computing features to better support vertical markets. TPM v2.0 introduced platform-specific profiles that define mandatory, optional, and excluded functionalities for PC client, mobile, and automotive thin-platform categories. Platform-specific profiles allow TPM vendors flexibility in implementing TPM features that accommodate a specific market. Additionally, TPM v2.0 supports three key hierarchies, for storage, platform, and endorsement. Each hierarchy can support multiple keys and cryptographic algorithms. We believe that TPM v2.0 profiles for trusted gateways could be developed for the blockchain infrastructure market.

Another example of trusted hardware is the *software guard extensions* (SGX) from Intel Corporation.[64] The SGX offers another perspective on a trusted computing base where a trusted environment exists within a user process called an enclave. The SGX trusted computing base (TCB) consists of hardware-isolated memory pages; CPU instructions for creating, extending, initializing, entering, exiting, and attesting the enclave; and privileged CPU modes for controlling access to enclave memory. A second-generation SGX (see McKeen et al.[65]) added support for dynamic memory management, where enclave runtimes could dynamically increase or decrease the number of enclave pages.

There are multiple steps to establish measurable technical trust that can be input into legal frameworks in the context of peering. Some of these are:

- *Mutual verification of gateway device identities*   Prior to interacting, two gateways belonging to separate blockchain autonomous systems must mutually verify their device identities (e.g., AIK certificates in TPM).[66]
- *Mutual attestation of gateway device status*   As part of trust establishment, each gateway may be required to attest to its hardware and software stack[67] as well as the current state of some of its hardware registers (e.g., quote protocol[68]).
- *Mutual session key establishment*   For use cases involving session keys, the gateways have the additional task of negotiating the keying parameters and establish the relevant session keys.
- *Mutual reporting of transaction settlement*   In use cases involving one or both private blockchains, an additional requirement could be the signing of assertions using a gateway's device keys.

12.5.6   Peering Points for Peering Business Agreements

Gateways in the context of blockchain interoperability can be used to serve as the peering points identified within peering agreements or contracts. Historically, in the case of the various ISPs that constitute the internet, the peering agreements are legally binding contracts that define the various interconnection aspects (e.g., traffic bandwidth, protocols) as well as fees ("settlements") and possible penalties. For the interoperability of autonomous blockchain systems, a notion similar to peering agreements must be developed that possesses features specifically for blockchain technology and the governance model used by the systems.

Peering agreements for blockchain systems should include, among other features, the following:

- *Identification of gateways chosen as peering points*   A blockchain peering agreement should require the clear identification of gateways that are permitted to peer with other gateways. This agreement may specify the device certificates, hardware and software manifest (e.g., hash of the manifest), root certificates, device status attestations, and other things.
- *Specify the minimum trust establishment mechanisms and parameters*   A peering agreement should specify the trust negotiation and establishment protocols, the respective known parameters (e.g., size of key parameters), the key management protocols, standards compliance required, minimum assurance level required, and other things.
- *Specify warranties and liabilities*   Similar to peering agreements for ISPs and the certificate practices statement for certificate authorities (CAs), blockchain peering agreements should clearly identify the liabilities of parties (e.g., in monetary terms) in negative or catastrophic scenarios (e.g., when a gateway is compromised).

12.6   CONCLUSIONS

The fundamental goals underlying the internet architecture have played a key role in determining the interoperability of the various networks and service types, which together comprise the internet as we know it today. Interoperability is key to survivability. A number of design principles emerged from the evolution of internet routing in the 1970s and 1980sthat have ensured the scalable operation of the internet over the last three decades.

We believe that a similar design philosophy is needed for interoperable blockchain systems. The recognition that a blockchain system is an autonomous system is an important starting point that allows notions such as reachability, referencing of transaction data in ledgers, scalability, and other aspects to be understood more meaningfully—beyond the current notion of throughput ("scale"), which is often the sole measure of performance used with regard to many blockchain systems today.

Furthermore, interoperability forces a deeper rethinking of how permissioned and permissionless blockchain systems can interoperate without a third party (such as an exchange). A key aspect is the semantic interoperability at the value level and at the mechanical level. Interoperability at the mechanical level is necessary for interoperability at the value level but does not guarantee it. The mechanical level plays a crucial role in providing technological solutions that can help humans quantify risk by using a more measurable notion of technical trust. Human agreements (i.e., legal contracts) must be used at the value level to provide semantically compatible meanings to the constructs (e.g., coins, tokens) that circulate in the blockchain system.

NOTES

1. J. Martin, "Vitalik Proposes Solution to Embarrassing Lack of Bitcoin–Ethereum Bridge," *Cointelegraph*, March 2020, https://cointelegraph.com/news/vitalik-proposes-solution-to-embarrassing-lack-of-bitcoinethereum-bridge.

2. S. Haber and W. Stornetta, "How to Time-Stamp a Digital Document," in *Advances in Cryptology—CRYPTO'90*, ed. A. J. Menezes and S. Vanstone, Lecture Notes in Computer Science 537 (Berlin: Springer, 1991), 437–455; D. Bayer, S. Haber, and W. Stornetta, "Improving the Efficiency and Reliability of Digital Time-Stamping," in *Sequences II: Methods in Communication, Security and Computer Science*, ed. R. Capocelli, A. DeSantis, and U. Vaccaro (New York: Springer, 1993), 329–334.

3. T. Hardjono, A. Lipton, and A. Pentland, "Towards an Interoperability Architecture: Blockchain Autonomous Systems," *IEEE Transactions on Engineering Management* 67, no. 4 (November 2020): 1298–1309, https://doi.org/10.1109/TEM.2019.2920154.

4. D. Clark, "The Design Philosophy of the DARPA Internet Protocols," *ACM Computer Communication Review—Proceedings of SIGCOMM 88* 18, no. 4 (August 1988): 106–114; V. G. Cerf and R. E. Khan, "A Protocol for Packet Network Intercommunication," *IEEE Transactions on Communications* 22 (1974): 637–648.

5. J. Abbate, *Inventing the Internet* (Cambridge, MA: MIT Press, 1999).

6. Clark, "The Design Philosophy of the DARPA Internet Protocols"; Cerf and Khan, "A Protocol for Packet Network Intercommunication."

7. J. Saltzer, D. Reed, and D. Clark, "End-to-End Arguments in System Design," *ACM Transactions on Computer Systems* 2, no. 4 (November 1984): 277–288.

8. S. Kent and R. Atkinson, "Security Architecture for the Internet Protocol," IETF Standard RFC2401, November 1998, http://tools.ietf.org/rfc/rfc2401.txt.

9. D. Harkins and D. Carrel, "The Internet Key Exchange (IKE)," IETF Standard RFC2409, November 1998, http://tools.ietf.org/rfc/rfc2409.txt.

10. T. Dierks and C. Allen, "The TLS Protocol Version 1.0," IETF Standard RFC2246, January 1999, http://tools.ietf.org/rfc/rfc2246.txt.

11. J. Hawkinson and T. Bates, "Guidelines for Creation, Selection, and Registration of an Autonomous System (AS)," IETF Standard RFC1930, March 1996, http://tools.ietf.org/rfc/rfc1930.txt.

12. G. Malkin, "RIP Version 2," IETF Standard RFC2453, November 1998, http://tools.ietf.org/rfc/rfc2453.txt.

13. J. Moy, "OSPF Version 2," IETF Standard RFC2328, April 1998, http://tools.ietf.org/rfc/rfc2328.txt.

14. K. Lougheed and Y. Rekhter, "Border Gateway Protocol (BGP)," IETF Standard RFC1105, June 1989, http://tools.ietf.org/rfc/rfc1105.txt.

15. ARIN, "American Registry for Internet Numbers—Autonomous System Numbers (asn.txt)," 2018, https://www.arin.net.

16. J. H. McFadyen, "Systems Network Architecture: An Overview," *IBM Systems Journal* 15, no. 1 (1976): 4–23.

17. S. Wecker, "DNA: The Digital Network Architecture," *IEEE Transactions on Communications* 28, no. 4 (1980): 510–526.

18. Abbate, *Inventing the Internet.*

19. S. Nakamoto, "Bitcoin: A Peer-to-Peer Electronic Cash System," Bitcoin, 2008, https://bitcoin.org/bitcoin.pdf.

20. V. Buterin, "Ethereum: A Next-Generation Cryptocurrency and Decentralized Application Platform," Ethereum Foundation white paper, January 2014, https://github.com/ethereum/wiki/wiki/White-Paper.

21. E. Androulaki, A. Barger, V. Bortnikov, C. Cachin, K. Christidis, A. De Caro, D. Enyeart, et al., "Hyperledger Fabric: A Distributed Operating System for Permissioned Blockchains," in *Proceedings of the Thirteenth*

EuroSys Conference (Eurosys'18), ed. R. Oliveira, P. Felber, and C. Hu (New York: ACM, 2018), 30:1–30:15, https://doi.org/10.1145/3190508.3190538.

22. R3CEV, "R3," R3, 2018, https://www.r3.com.

23. A. Lipton and A. Pentland, "Breaking the Bank," *Scientific American* 318, no. 1 (2018): 26–31; A. Lipton, T. Hardjono, and A. Pentland, "Digital Trade Coin (DTC): Towards a More Stable Digital Currency," *Journal of the Royal Society Open Science (RSOS)* 5, no. 7 (July 2018): 1–15, https://doi.org/10.1098/rsos.180155.

24. D. Yaga, P. Mell, N. Roby, and K. Scarfone, "Blockchain Technology Overview," NIST Draft Internal Report 8202, January 2018, https://csrc.nist.gov. Quotation is at p. 50.

25. Clark, "The Design Philosophy of the DARPA Internet Protocols"; Cerf and Khan, "A Protocol for Packet Network Intercommunication."

26. I. Eyal and E. G. Sirer, "Majority Is Not Enough: Bitcoin Mining Is Vulnerable," in *Financial Cryptography and Data Security—18th International Conference, FC2014*, March 2014, ed. N. Christin and R. Safavi-Naini (Berlin: Springer, 2014), 436–454, https://doi.org/10.1007/978-3-662-45472-5; A. Gervais, G. O. Karame, V. Capkun, and S. Capkun, "Is Bitcoin a Decentralized Currency?," *IEEE Security and Privacy* 12, no. 3 (2014): 54–60; B. Schneier, "There's No Good Reason to Trust Blockchain Technology," *Wired*, February 2019, https://www.wired.com/story/theres-no-good-reason-to-trust-blockchain-technology/.

27. J. Postel, "User Datagram Protocol," IETF Standard RFC0768, August 1980, http://tools.ietf.org/rfc/rfc0768.txt.

28. Cerf and Khan, "A Protocol for Packet Network Intercommunication."

29. Yaga et al., "Blockchain Technology Overview."

30. D. L. Chaum, "Untraceable Electronic Mail, Return Addresses, and Digital Pseudonyms," *Communications of the ACM* 24, no. 2 (February 1981): 84–88; J. Camenisch and E. Van Herreweghen, "Design and

Implementation of the Idemix Anonymous Credential System," in *Proceedings of the 9th ACM Conference on Computer and Communications Security*, ed. V. Atluri (New York: ACM, 2002), 21–30; T. Hardjono and N. Smith, "Cloud-Based Commissioning of Constrained Devices Using Permissioned Blockchains," in *Proceedings of the Second ACM International Workshop on IoT Privacy, Trust, and Security (IoTPTS 2016)*, ed. R. Chow and G. Saldamli (New York: ACM, 2016), 29–36, https://doi.org/10.1145/2899007.2899012.

31. Schneier, "There's No Good Reason to Trust Blockchain Technology."

32. T. Hardjono and N. Smith, "Decentralized Trusted Computing Base for Blockchain Infrastructure Security," *Frontiers Journal—Special Issue on Finance, Money and Blockchains* 2 (December 2019): 1–15, https://doi.org/10.3389/fbloc.2019.00024.

33. T. Hardjono, A. Lipton, and A. Pentland, "Towards a Contract Service Provider Model for Virtual Assets and VASPs," September 2020, https://arxiv.org/abs/2009.07413.

34. Clark, "The Design Philosophy of the DARPA Internet Protocols."

35. Saltzer, Reed, and Clark, "End-to-End Arguments in System Design."

36. T. Nolan, "Alt Chains and Atomic Transfers," Bitcoin Talk, May 2013, https://bitcointalk.org/index.php?topic=193281.msg2224949#msg2224949.

37. P. Ezhilchelvan, A. Aldweesh, and A. van Moorsel, "Non-blocking Two Phase Commit Using Blockchain," in *Proceedings of the 1st Workshop on Cryptocurrencies and Blockchains for Distributed Systems (CryBlock18)* (New York: ACM, 2018), 36–41, https://doi.org/10.1145/3211933.3211940.

38. V. Zakhary, D. Agrawal, and A. E. Abbadi, "Atomic Commitment across Blockchains," June 2019, https://arxiv.org/pdf/1905.02847.pdf.

39. M. Herlihy, "Atomic Cross-Chain Swaps," in *Proceedings of the ACM Symposium on Principles of Distributed Computing PODC'18*, ed. C. Newport and I. Keidar (New York: ACM, 2018), 245–254, https://doi.org/10.1145/3212734.3212736.

40. E. Heilman, S. Lipmann, and S. Goldberg, "The Arwen Trading Protocols (Full Version)," 2020, https://eprint.iacr.org/2020/024.pdf.

41. T. Hardjono, "Blockchain Gateways, Bridges and Delegated Hash-Locks," February 2021, https://arxiv.org/pdf/2102.03933.

42. I. L. Traiger, J. Gray, C. A. Galtieri, and B. G. Lindsay, *Transactions and Consistency in Distributed Database Systems,* IBM Research Report RJ2555, 1979; J. Gray, "The Transaction Concept: Virtues and Limitations," in *Very Large Data Bases—Proceedings of the 7th International Conference,* Cannes, France, September 1981 (New York: IEEE, 1981), 144–154.

43. Zakhary, Agrawal, and Abbadi, "Atomic Commitment across Blockchains."

44. T. Haerder and A. Reuter, "Principles of Transaction-Oriented Database Recovery," *ACM Computing Surveys* 15, no. 4 (December 1983): 287–317, https://doi.org/10.1145/289-291.

45. M. Herlihy, B. Liskov, and L. Shrira, "Cross-Chain Deals and Adversarial Commerce," *Proceedings of Very Large Data Bases 2019* 13, no. 2 (October 2019), https://doi.org/10.14778/3364324.3364326.

46. T. Hardjono and N. Smith, "Towards an Attestation Architecture for Blockchain Networks," *World Wide Web* (2021), https://doi.org/10.1007/s11280-021-00869-4.

47. Hardjono, "Trust Infrastructures for Virtual Asset Service Providers," in *Proceedings of ESORICS International Workshops, DETIPS, DeSECSys, MPS, and SPOSE, September 2020,* ed. I. Boureanu, C. Drăgan, M. Manulis, T. Giannetsos, C. Dadoyan, P. Gouvas, R. Hallman, et al. (Berlin: Springer, 2020), 74–91, https://doi.org/10.1007/978-3-030-66504-3.

48. ARIN, "American Registry for Internet Numbers."

49. Wikipedia, "Regional Internet Registry," 2020, https://en.wikipedia.org/wiki/Regional Internet registry.

50. D. Riegelnig, "OpenVASP: An Open Protocol to Implement FATF's Travel Rule for Virtual Assets," OpenVASP white paper, November 2019, https://www.openvasp.org/wpcontent/uploads/2019/11/OpenVasp_Whitepaper.pdf.

51. InterVASP, "InterVASP Messaging Standards IVMS101," Joint Working Group on InterVASP Messaging Standards, Working Draft—Issue 1—Draft G, March 2020.

52. Global Legal Entity Identifier Foundation (GLEIF), *LEI in KYC: A New Future for Legal Entity Identification*, GLEIF Research Report, May 2018, https://www.gleif.org/en/lei-solutions/lei-in-kyc-a-new-future-for-legal-entity-identification.

53. D. Jevans, T. Hardjono, J. Vink, F. Steegmans, J. Jefferies, and A. Malhotra, "Travel Rule Information Sharing Architecture for Virtual Asset Service Providers, TRISA, Version 7," white paper, June 2020, https://trisa.io/wp-content/uploads/2020/06/TRISAEnablingFATFTravelRuleWhitePaperV7.pdf.

54. P. Bernstein, V. Hadzilacos, and N. Goodman, *Concurrency Control and Recovery in Database Systems* (New York: Addison-Wesley, 1987); Traiger et al., *Transactions and Consistency in Distributed Database Systems*; Gray, "The Transaction Concept."

55. T. Dickerson, P. Gazzillo, M. Herlihy, and E. Koskinen, "Adding Concurrency to Smart Contracts," in *Proceedings of the ACM Symposium on Principles of Distributed Computing (PODC'17)*, ed. E. Schiller (New York: Association for Computing Machinery, 2017), 303–312, https://doi.org/10.1145/3087801.3087835; M. Herlihy, "Blockchains from a Distributed Computing Perspective," *Communications of the ACM* 62, no. 2 (February 2019): 78–85, https://doi.org/10.1145/3209623.

56. Hardjono, Lipton, and Pentland, "Towards an Interoperability Architecture"; Hardjono and Smith, "Decentralized Trusted Computing Base for Blockchain Infrastructure Security."

57. Financial Action Task Force (FATF), "International Standards on Combating Money Laundering and the Financing of Terrorism and Proliferation," FATF Revision of Recommendation 15, October 2018, http://www.fatf-gafi.org/publications/fatfrecommendations/documents/fatf-recommendations.html.

58. Jevans et al., "Travel Rule Information Sharing Architecture for Virtual Asset Service Providers, TRISA, Version 7."

59. Hardjono, "Trust Infrastructures for Virtual Asset Service Providers."

60. Swiss Financial Market Supervisory Authority (FINMA), *FINMA Guidance: Payments on the Blockchain*, FINMA Guidance Report, August 2019, https://www.finma.ch/en/~/media/finma/dokumente/dokumentencenter/myfinma/4dokumentation/finma-aufsichtsmitteilungen/20190826-finma-aufsichtsmitteilung-02-2019.pdf.

61. Traiger et al., *Transactions and Consistency in Distributed Database Systems*; Gray, "The Transaction Concept."

62. T. Hardjono, A. Lipton, and A. Pentland, "Wallet Attestations for Virtual Asset Service Providers and Crypto-Assets Insurance," June 2020, https://arxiv.org/pdf/2005.14689.pdf.

63. Trusted Computing Group, "TPM Main—Specification Version 1.2," Trusted Computing Group Published Specification, October 2003, http://www.trustedcomputinggroup.org/resources/tpmmainspecification.

64. F. Mckeen, I. Alexandrovich, A. Berenzon, C. Rozas, H. Shafi, V. Shanbhogue, and U. Savagaonkar, "Innovative Instructions and Software Model for Isolated Execution," in *Proceedings of the Second Workshop on Hardware and Architectural Support for Security and Privacy (HASP) 2013*, Tel-Aviv, June 2013, https://sites.google.com/site/haspworkshop2013/workshop-program.

65. F. McKeen, I. Alexandrovich, I. Anati, D. Caspi, S. Johnson, R. Leslie-Hurd, and C. Rozas, "Intel Software Guard Extensions (Intel SGX) Support for Dynamic Memory Management Inside an Enclave," in *Proceedings of the Workshop on Hardware and Architectural Support for Security and Privacy*

(HASP) 2016, Seoul, June 2016, http://caslab.csl.yale.edu/workshops /hasp2016/program.html.

66. T. Hardjono and G. Kazmierczak, "Overview of the TPM Key Management Standard," Trusted Computing Group (TCG), May 2008, https:// trustedcomputinggroup.org/wp-content/uploads/Kazmierczak20Greg20 -20TPM_Key_Management_KMS2008_v003.pdf.

67. Hardjono and Smith, "Towards an Attestation Architecture for Blockchain Networks."

68. Trusted Computing Group, "TPM Main—Specification Version 1.2"; Mckeen et al., "Innovative Instructions and Software Model for Isolated Execution."

EXCHANGE NETWORKS FOR VIRTUAL ASSETS

Thomas Hardjono, Alexander Lipton,
and Alex Pentland

13.1 INTRODUCTION

In the nascent area of cryptocurrency and transactions of virtual assets, a new type of entity is slowly emerging, called the
virtual asset service provider (VASP). The most common example
of a VASP today is the cryptocurrency exchanges, which support
end users in delivering cryptocurrencies (e.g., bitcoins) from one
blockchain address (public key) to another. There are a number
of growing pains for VASPs, especially in light of the long history
of interbank wire payments (e.g., correspondent banking) and the
body of regulations that govern these kinds of banking activities.

Currently, many VASP businesses face various technical, operational, and legal challenges that need to be addressed before the
cryptocurrencies and virtual assets sector can begin to grow and
mature. Some examples of these challenges include:

• *The Travel Rule for virtual assets* FATF Recommendation 15[1]
requires VASPs to retain information regarding the originator and
beneficiaries of virtual asset transfers. This includes the originator's

name; the originator's account number (e.g., at the originating VASP); the originator's geographical address, national identity number, or customer identification number (or date and place of birth); the beneficiary's name; and the beneficiary's account number (e.g., at the beneficiary VASP).

- *FinCEN compliance requirements* The FinCEN anti-money-laundering (AML) rules of 2014[2] require that customer due diligence (CDD) be performed for convertible virtual currencies.[3]
- *Decreasing trust of consumers in institutions* Over the last decade, there has been a continuing decline in trust on the part of individuals with regard to the handling and fair use of personal data.[4] This situation has been compounded by the various recent reports of attacks and theft of data (e.g., Anthem,[5] Equifax[6]).
- *Emergence of data privacy regulations* The enactment of the General Data Protection Regulation (GDPR)[7] in Europe has influenced the discourse regarding data privacy in other nations (e.g., the state of California followed with the California Consumer Privacy Act[8]). Given the prominent role of data in the new digital economy, the emergence of a US federal privacy act cannot be ruled out.[9]

Today, many users possessing virtual assets (e.g., cryptocurrencies) expect asset transfers through VASPs to be confirmed or settled in a matter of seconds. However, the need for VASPs to exchange and validate customer information prior to asset transfers may impose delays on the settlement of transfers. Furthermore, VASPs do not yet have an agreed mechanism to exchange their respective customer information in a secure and reliable manner.

We believe that this lack of an information exchange mechanism points to a more fundamental challenge facing the VASP community worldwide—the lack of a *trust infrastructure* that is highly scalable and interoperable, which permits business trust and legal trust to be established for peer-to-peer transactions of virtual assets across different jurisdictions as part of global exchange networks. There are several forms of trust infrastructure needed for VASPs, and in this chapter we discuss three forms or types of such infrastructure. The first is an *information-sharing infrastructure* specifically for VASPs. The main purpose of a VASP information-sharing infrastructure is to securely and confidentially share customer information related to transfers of virtual assets. Related to this network is the VASP *identity infrastructure*, which permits VASPs and other entities to quickly ascertain the legal business status of other VASPs. Next is an *attestation infrastructure* that can support VASPs and asset insurers in obtaining better visibility into the state of customer wallets based on trusted hardware. Finally, there is a need for a *claims infrastructure* for customer data sources that integrates seamlessly into the existing digital identity infrastructure for users.

13.2   VIRTUAL ASSETS AND VASPS

The Financial Action Task Force (FATF) is an intergovernmental body established in 1989 by the ministers of its member countries or jurisdictions. The objectives of the FATF are to set standards and promote effective implementation of legal, regulatory, and operational measures for combating money laundering, terrorist financing, and other related threats to the integrity of the international financial system. The FATF is a "policy-making body" that works to generate the necessary political will to bring about national legislative and regulatory reforms in these areas.

With the emergence of blockchain technologies, virtual assets, and cryptocurrencies, the FATF recognized the need to adequately mitigate the money laundering and terrorist financing risks associated with virtual asset activities. In its most recent recommendation, Recommendation 15,[10] the FATF defines the following:

- *Virtual asset* A virtual asset is a digital representation of value that can be digitally traded, or transferred, and can be used for payment or investment purposes. Virtual assets do not include digital representations of fiat currencies, securities, and other financial assets that are already covered elsewhere in the FATF recommendations.
- *Virtual asset service provider* (VASP) Virtual asset service provider means any natural or legal person who is not covered elsewhere under the recommendations and as a business conducts one or more of the following activities or operations for or on behalf of another natural or legal person: exchange between virtual assets and fiat currencies; exchange between one or more forms of virtual assets; transfer of virtual assets; safekeeping and/or administration of virtual assets or instruments enabling control over virtual assets; and participation in and provision of financial services related to an issuer's offer and/or sale of a virtual asset.

In this context of virtual assets, transfer means to conduct a transaction on behalf of another natural or legal person that moves a virtual asset from one virtual asset address or account to another. Furthermore, to manage and mitigate the risks emerging from virtual assets, the recommendations state that countries should ensure that VASPs are regulated for purposes of AML and countering financing of terrorism and be licensed or registered and subject to effective systems for monitoring and ensuring compliance with the relevant measures called for in the FATF recommendations.

13.3 THE TRAVEL RULE AND CUSTOMER DUE DILIGENCE

One of the key aspects of FATF Recommendation 15 is the need for VASPs to retain information regarding the originator and beneficiaries of virtual asset transfers. The implication of the 2019 FATF Guidance[11] is that cryptocurrency exchanges and related VASPs must be able to share originator and beneficiary information for virtual asset transactions. This process—also known as the *Travel Rule*—originates from the US Bank Secrecy Act (BSA) (31 U.S.C. 5311–5330), which mandates that financial institutions deliver certain types of information to the next financial institution when a transmittal of funds involves more than one financial institution. This rule became effective in May 1996 and was issued by the Treasury Department's Financial Crimes Enforcement Network (FinCEN) concurrently with the new BSA record-keeping rules for fund transfers and transmittals.

Given that today a virtual asset on blockchain is controlled through the public and private keys bound to that asset, we believe there is other information (in addition to the customer and account information) that a VASP needs to retain in order to satisfy the Travel Rule:[12]

• *Key ownership information* This is information pertaining to the legal ownership of cryptographic public and private keys. When a customer (e.g., originator) presents their public key to the VASP for the first time, there must be "chain of provenance" evidence regarding the customer's public and private keys that assures that the customer is the true owner. Proof of possession of the private key (e.g., using a challenge-response protocol such as CHAP (RFC1994)) does not prove legal ownership of the public and private keys.

- *Key operator information* This is information or evidence pertaining to the legal custody by a VASP of a customer's public and private keys. This information is relevant for a VASP that adopts a key-custody business model in which the VASP holds and operates the customer's public and private keys to perform transactions on behalf of the customer.

In the 2014 FinCEN know your customer (KYC) requirements under the BSA,[13] the proposed rules contained explicit customer due diligence (CDD) requirements and included a new regulatory requirement to identify "beneficial owners" of customers who are legal entities. It is worth noting that the CDD requirements include *conducting ongoing monitoring to maintain and update customer information* and to identify and report suspicious transactions. Collectively, these elements comprise the minimum standard of CDD, which FinCEN believes is fundamental to an effective AML program.

The FATF definition of virtual assets means that VASPs—like traditional financial institutions—need to establish an effective AML and CDD program in the sense of FinCEN.[14] We believe that VASPs must additionally obtain and retain the originator and beneficiary cryptographic key ownership information as a central part of monitoring the movement of virtual assets.

It is important to emphasize that a VASP as a business entity must be able to respond comprehensively to legitimate inquiries from law enforcement regarding one or more of its customers owning virtual assets (e.g., legal SAR inquiries and warrants). More specifically, both the originator VASP and beneficiary VASP must possess complete and accurate *actual* personal information (i.e., data) regarding their account holders (i.e., customers). This need for actual data therefore precludes the use of advanced cryptographic techniques that aim to prevent disclosure while yielding implied knowledge, such as those based on zero-knowledge proof (ZKP) schemes.[15]

One of the key challenging issues related to the Travel Rule is the privacy of customer information once it has been delivered between VASPs. This problem can be acute when one VASP is located within a jurisdiction with strong privacy regulations (e.g., EU with GDPR[16]) while the other is located in a jurisdiction with incompatible privacy regulations.[17] More specifically, if a beneficiary VASP is located under a different legal jurisdiction (e.g., foreign country) observing weaker privacy regulations than the originator's jurisdiction, there are no means for the originator to ensure their customer information is not leaked or stolen from that beneficiary VASP.

13.4 INFORMATION-SHARING INFRASTRUCTURE FOR VASPS

A central part of an information-sharing infrastructure is a network shared among VASPs to exchange information about themselves and their customers. The notion of an *out-of-band* (off-chain) network for VASPs to share information about themselves and their customers was first proposed by Hardjono[18] as part of the broader discussion within the FATF Private Sector Consultative Forum leading up to the finalization of Recommendation 15 in mid-2019.

The idea of an information-sharing network is not new, and the banking community established a similar network (the SWIFT network[19]) over two decades ago. Today, this network is the backbone for global correspondent banking.

Therefore, similar to banking data networks, a "network" is needed for VASPs to securely exchange information about themselves and about their customers for Travel Rule compliance and other requirements. This information-sharing network should be layered atop the proven TCP/IP internet in order to provide the best connection resilience and speed.

There are several fundamental requirements for an information-sharing network for VASPs (figure 13.1):

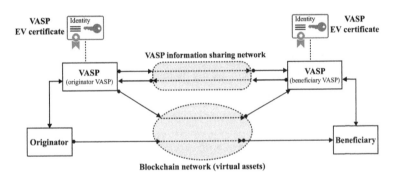

Figure 13.1

Overview of VASP information sharing network (after T. Hardjono, "Compliant Solutions for VASPs," presentation to the FATF Private Sector Consultative Forum (PSCF) 2019, Vienna, May 6, 2019; D. Jevans, T. Hardjono, J. Vink, F. Steegmans, J. Jefferies, and A. Malhotra, "Travel Rule Information Sharing Architecture for Virtual Asset Service Providers, TRISA, Version 7," June 2020).

- *Security, reliability, and confidentiality of transport* The VASP information-sharing network must provide security, reliability, and confidentiality of communications between an originator VASP and beneficiary VASP. Several standards exist to fulfill this requirement (e.g., IPsec virtual private networks,[20] TLS secure channels[21]).

- *Strong endpoint identification and authentication* VASPs must use strong endpoint identification and authentication mechanisms to ensure source and destination authenticity and to prevent or reduce man-in-the-middle types of attacks. Mechanisms such as X.509 certificates[22] have been used for over two decades across various industries, government, and defense as a practical means of achieving this goal.[23]

- *Correlation of customer information with on-chain transactions* There must be a mechanism to permit a VASP to accurately correlate (match) between customer information (exchanged within the VASP information-sharing network) and the blockchain transactions belonging to the respective customers. This must be true also in the case of *batch transactions* performed by a VASP (e.g., in the commingled accounts business model).

- *Consent from originator and beneficiary for customer information exchange* Unambiguous consent[24] must be obtained by VASPs from their customers with regard to the transmittal of customer personal information to another VASP. Explicit consent must also be obtained from the beneficiary for receiving asset transfers from an originator. That is, a beneficiary VASP must obtain consent from its customer to receive asset transfers into the customer's account.

Efforts are currently under way to begin addressing the need for a VASP information-sharing network to support VASPs in complying with the various aspects of the Travel Rule (see Jevans et al.[25] and Riegelnig[26]). A standard customer information model has recently been developed[27] that would allow VASPs to interoperate with each other with semantic consistency.

We use the term *VASP information sharing* broadly to denote the interaction between VASPs in the context of the delivery of subject (originators, beneficiaries, and VASPs) information related to a virtual asset transfer. The VASP information-sharing network must address the various aspects of communications between VASPs: the definition of the data being transferred; reliable delivery at the VASP application layer; interoperability of the delivery layer (e.g., TCP/IP, intrachain P2P delivery mechanism); and external representation of identifiers and keys, and the legal identity of entities who own or control those identifiers and keys.

Figure 13.2 illustrates one possible logical *layered architecture* of the VASP information-sharing network. These are described in the following subsections. Similar to the layered architecture of the internet,[28] one of the main goals of a given layer is to *support the function of an upper layer* by abstracting functions (hiding details of this layer) to the higher layer.

13.4.1 Terminology

We adopt the terminology for blockchain technology from NIST.[29] For the definitions of virtual assets, we adopt those defined by the FATF recommendations[30] and FinCen.[31] Additionally, we may introduce qualifications to the terms as a means of increasing the clarity of the discussion.

- *Virtual asset service provider (VASP)* This means any natural or legal person who is not covered elsewhere under FATF Recommendation 15.[32]

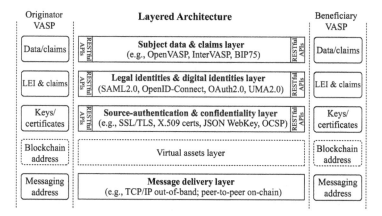

Figure 13.2
Logical layers of the VASP information-sharing network.

- *Messaging protocol* The mechanism used within the VASP information-sharing network to deliver a message (e.g., bytes of any length) from one VASP to another. A standard for the precise information to be communicated using the protocol has been defined by InterVASP.[33]

- *Subject* The person or organization (legal entity) involved in a virtual asset transfer.[34] The subject (whose information is being delivered) can be the originator, beneficiary, originator VASP, or beneficiary VASP.

- *Claim (assertion)* A digitally signed statement from an authoritative entity that is attesting to the accuracy and truthfulness of the information contained regarding a subject. In this case, the signer is the VASP and the subject can be the VASP itself or one of its customers. Several formats for claims or assertions have been standardized (e.g., OASIS,[35] Farrell, Housley, and Turner,[36] and Sporny, Longley, and Chadwick[37]).

- *Claims provider* An authoritative entity that issues signed assertions or statements regarding a subject (person or organization). By digitally signing a claim, the claims provider is attesting to the truthfulness of the assertion. The assertion itself may be embellished by additional information (e.g., context indicator, trustworthiness score, date of issuance, expiration date, data-source indicators, algorithm identifiers).

- *Address (blockchain address)* A short, alphanumeric string derived from a user's public key using a hash function, with additional data to detect errors. Addresses are used to send and receive virtual assets.[38]

- *Virtual asset blockchain* The blockchain system within which the transfer of virtual assets between two entities occurs (e.g., originator to beneficiary, originator VASP to beneficiary VASP).

- *VASP network address* The network address used by VASPs to deliver information regarding a subject in a virtual asset transfer, as well as other parameters related to a VASP system.

- *Transport address* The ephemeral address used at the delivery layer (e.g., IP address).

- *Legal entity identifier (LEI)* A 20-character alphanumeric code to uniquely identify legally distinct entities that engage in financial transactions.[39]

13.4.2 Subject Data and Claims Layer

The topmost layer of figure 13.2 pertains to the information or data regarding subjects (originators, beneficiaries, VASPs) involved in a given virtual asset transfer. The goal of this layer is simply to communicate data and information from one VASP to another in a reliable and accurate manner following a standardized syntax, such as OpenVASP.[40] Thus, for example, issues such as an asset transfer request and response and transfer confirmations[41] or invoice requests and payment requests[42] must be handled by constructs at this layer.

The syntactic definition of the data and information being communicated must be defined using a separate information lexicon and data model such as the InterVASP proposal.[43] Data or information obtained by a VASP from another source entity must be delivered in a standard assertion or claim format that is signed by that source. This allows the receiving VASP (e.g., beneficiary VASP) to know its origin or provenance and assess the veracity of the signed claims or assertions.

13.4.3 Digital Identity and Legal Identity Layer

At the endpoint of the transfer of subject data and claims are VASPs, which as legal entities are bound by certain legal regimes. For VASPs, two key questions (among others) that need to be addressed in this layer are (1) the identity and authenticity of the VASP entity at the opposite end of the interaction and (2) the legal status of that VASP (assuming it has been correctly identified and authenticated).

At this layer, identity management protocols may play a crucial role in identifying and authenticating entities with whom a VASP interacts. Several identity management protocols have been standardized and are in wide deployment today (e.g., SAML2.0,[44] OpenID Connect[45]). The association or *binding* between a digital identity and the owner of that identity in the legal context also occurs at this layer. Legal constructs such as the LEI[46] are captured and represented at this layer.

13.4.4 Source Authentication and Confidentiality Layer

The digital identity layer relies on cryptographic keys and protocols that allow entities to prove their digital identity. Thus, at this layer the management of private and public keys is crucial (e.g., see Kuhn et al.,[47] Barker,[48] and National Institute of Science and Technology[49]). The protocols to negotiate mutual session keys and establish secure end-to-end encrypted channels also occur at this layer (e.g., ECDH, TLS/SSL).

Mechanisms and protocols to prove legal ownership of public and private keys correspondingly occur in this layer. These can be via certification performed by third parties (e.g., certification authorities) who issue public-key certificates (e.g., X.509 standard[50]).

13.4.5 Message Delivery Layer

The bottommost layer of the layer architecture is the actual message delivery mechanism and protocols that underlie VASP-to-VASP interaction. There are a number of design principles that should be observed in the delivery of claims.

Independence of the VASP information-sharing network from the virtual asset transfer mechanism The messaging mechanism (protocol) used between VASPs must not be dependent on any specific virtual asset blockchain. VASPs must be able to communicate directly (out of band) with other VASPs (pairwise direct) without depending on the asset blockchain system that they employ to transmit virtual assets. This ensures that as new blockchain technologies emerge or evolve, the VASP information-sharing infrastructure can support new blockchain systems.

- *Default messaging channel* There must be a default mechanism by which two VASPs who wish to interact directly can establish a pairwise secure channel. VASPs must have the freedom to initiate and negotiate a pairwise secure channel with another VASP in an unmediated fashion. However, there are circumstances in which a common method cannot be found (e.g., both parties suggest incompatible protocols). To address such cases, a default mechanism must be defined to which both parties must resort (e.g., plain TCP/IP using TLS1.3).

- *Default channel-protection negotiation mechanism* There must be a default mechanism by which two VASPs who wish to interact directly can establish security parameters to secure their shared messaging channel. We suggest using the standard key establishment protocols (e.g., ECDH protocol) regardless of the ensuing messaging protocol being used (e.g., Whisper in OpenVASP,[51] SSL).

13.5 A TRUSTED IDENTITY INFRASTRUCTURE FOR VASPS

A central part of the VASP information-sharing infrastructure is a VASP *trusted identity infrastructure* that permits VASPs to prove their identity, public key(s), and legal business information. A trusted identity infrastructure must address the various challenges around VASP identities and provide the following types of mechanisms:

- *Discovery of VASP identity and verification of business status* Mechanisms are needed to permit any entity on the internet from ascertaining whether a virtual asset service provider is a regulated VASP within a given jurisdiction. An originator VASP must be able to easily locate the identity information for a beneficiary VASP and to rapidly determine the business and legal status of that beneficiary VASP (and vice versa).

- *Discovery and verification of VASP public keys*   Mechanisms are needed to permit any entity on the internet from ascertaining whether a given public key legally belongs to (is operated by) a given VASP.

- *Discovery and verification of VASP service endpoints*   Mechanisms are needed to permit a VASP to ascertain whether it is connecting to the legitimate service endpoints (e.g., URI) of another VASP (and not a rogue endpoint belonging to an attacker).

- *Discovery of VASPs using customer identifiers*   Mechanisms are needed to permit a VASP to search and discover a binding (association) between a customer's user-friendly identifier (e.g., email address) and the VASP (one or more) that may hold an account for that customer.

13.5.1   Extended Validation Certificates
for VASP Business Identity

The problem of discovering and verifying service provider public keys and service endpoints was faced by numerous online merchants nearly two decades ago. For the end user (i.e., home consumer), it was increasingly difficult to distinguish between a legitimate service provider (e.g., online merchant) and rogue web servers that mimic the look and feel of legitimate merchants' websites. In response to a growing trend of man-in-the-middle attacks, a number of browser vendors established an alliance about a decade ago—called the *CA Browser Forum* (CAB forum)—that brought together browser vendors and X.509 certification authorities (CAs). The CAB forum, as an organization defining industry standards, published a number of industry technical specifications referred to as *extended validation* (EV) identity certificates.[52] The overall goal was to enhance the basic X.509 certificate[53] with additional business-related information regarding the subject (i.e., the online merchant). The CA that issues EV certificates must perform the various checks on background information regarding the subject to ensure that the subject is a legitimate business. Correspondingly, the browser vendors supported EV certificates by preinstalling in their browser software a copy of the root CA certificate of all compliant CAs.

We believe a similar approach is suitable for fulfilling a number of the VASP requirements discussed. Some of the subject (VASP) business information to be included in the EV certificate to identify a VASP could be as follows:[54]

- *Organization name* The organization field must contain the full legal name of the VASP legal entity controlling the VASP service endpoint, as listed in the official records in the VASP's jurisdiction.
- *VASP alternative name extension* The domain name(s) owned or controlled by the VASP and to be associated with the VASP's server as the endpoint associated with the certificate.
- *VASP incorporation number or LEI* (if available) This field must contain the unique incorporation number assigned by the incorporating agency in the jurisdiction of incorporation. If an LEI number is available, then that number should be used instead.

- *VASP address of place of business*   This is the address of the physical location of the VASP's place of business.
- *VASP jurisdiction of incorporation or registration*   This field contains information regarding the incorporating agency or registration agency.
- *VASP number*   This is the globally unique VASP number, if used (see OpenVASP[55]).
- *VASP regulated business activity*   Currently, no formal definition of business activity specific to VASPs has been defined. Note that in reality VASPs may operate different functions in the virtual asset ecosystem (e.g., cryptoexchanges, fund managers dealing in virtual assets, stablecoin issuers).
- *EV certificate policy object identifier*   This is the identifier for the policies that determine the certificate processing rules. Such policies could be created by the organization using the certificate, such as a consortium of VASPs (see subsection 13.5.3).

13.5.2   VASP Transaction-Signing and Claim-Signing Certificates

For assets in commingled accounts managed by a VASP, the asset transfer on the blockchain is performed by the VASP using its own private-public key pair on behalf of the customer. The customer holds no keys in the commingled cases. We refer to these private and public keys as the VASP *transaction-signing keys,* and we refer to the corresponding certificates as the *transaction-signing key certificates.* The purpose of signing key certificates is to certify the ownership of the private and public keys as belonging to the VASP. A given VASP may own multiple transaction-signing keys and therefore multiple signing key certificates.

Because a VASP must stand behind the customer information it provides to other VASPs, any *claims*[56] or *assertions*[57] that a VASP produces about its customers must be digitally signed by the VASP. We refer to these private and public keys as *claim-signing keys*, and we refer to the corresponding certificates as the *claim-signing key certificates*.

It is crucial for a VASP that these three key pairs be distinct. This is because the purposes of the keys are different, and each key may have a different lifetime. Depending on the profile of a transaction-signing key certificate and the claim-signing key certificate, they may include the serial number (or hash) of the identity EV certificate of the VASP. This provides a mechanism for a recipient to validate that the owner of these two certificates is the same legal entity as the owner of the VASP identity EV certificate.

13.5.3 Consortium-Based VASP Certificate Hierarchy

In order for VASPs to have a high degree of interoperability—at both the technical and legal levels—a *consortium* arrangement provides a number of advantages for the information-sharing network. Members in a consortium are free to collectively define the common *operating rules* that members must abide by. The operating rules become input matter into the definition of the *legal trust framework* that expresses the contractual obligations of the members.

A well-crafted set of operating rules for a VASP information-sharing network provides its members with several benefits. First, it provides a means for the members to *improve risk management* because the operating rules will allow members to quantify and manage risks inherent in participating in the network.

Second, the operating rules provide members with *legal certainty and predictability* by addressing the legal rights, responsibilities, and liabilities of participating in the network. Third, the operating rules provide *transparency* to the members of the network by having all members agree to the same terms of membership (i.e., contract). Since the operating rules are a legal contract, they are legally enforceable on all members. Finally, a set of operating rules that define common technical specifications (e.g., APIs, cryptographic functions, certificates) for all the members provides the highest chance of technical interoperability of services. In turn, this reduces overall system-development costs by allowing entities to reuse implementations of those standardized technical specifications. Several examples of consortium-based operating rules exist today (e.g., NACHA,[58] OIX[59]).

Using as an example the identity EV certificates mentioned , the common operating rules would define the technical specifications (profile) of the EV certificate (e.g., cryptographic algorithms, key lengths, duration of validity, issuance protocols, revocation protocols) as well as the legal information that must be included in the EV fields of the certificate (e.g., legal incorporation number, LEI number, place of business).

Business interoperability can only be achieved if all members of the information-sharing network observe and implement these common operating rules and if there is legal and monetary liability for not doing so. This approach is not new and is used for group peering agreements among IP routing service providers (i.e., access ISPs and backbone ISPs). Technological interoperability of identity EV certificates dictates that members of the information-sharing network participate under a common *certificate hierarchy*, which is rooted at the consortium organization. This is shown in figure 13.3, where the consortium becomes the root CA for the certificates issued to all VASPs in the consortium organization.

Certificate hierarchies have been successfully deployed in numerous organizations, ranging from government organizations,[60] to financial networks,[61] to mobile devices and networks,[62] to consortia of cable device manufacturers.[63] An example of a consortium that brings together device manufacturers (e.g., cable modem and set top box vendors) and service operators (e.g., regional cable access providers) is Cable Laboratories (CableLabs). The combined type of membership in CableLabs permits cable operators to detect and isolate counterfeit devices and provide end-to-end protection for valuable content (e.g., movies). This combined approach may be relevant for VASPs dealing with customer wallet devices.

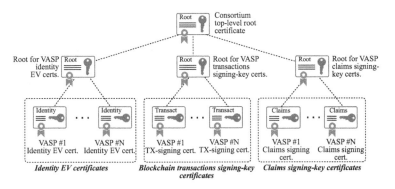

Figure 13.3
Overview of a certificate hierarchy for a VASP consortium.

13.6   VASP INTEGRATION INTO CONSUMER
IDENTITY INFRASTRUCTURE

Today's cryptoasset management systems need to be integrated seamlessly with existing identity management infrastructure functions, including identity authentication services, authorization services, and consent management services.

13.6.1   Customer Identities and Digital Identifiers

Currently, most users employ their email address as a form of user *identifier* when obtaining services on the internet. Many of these identifiers do not represent the user's full personal (core) identity[64] and have ephemeral value (i.e., the identifier can be replaced with a new one). Typically, the entities who issue the identifiers are email providers and social media platforms. The industry jargon used to describe them (rather inaccurately) is *identity provider* (IdP). Besides providing email-routable identifiers to users, the identity provider's role in the identity ecosystem is to provide mediated authentication services and credential management on behalf of the user.[65]

Mediated authentication—such as single sign-on—provides convenience for the user by obviating the need for them to authenticate multiple times for each online service provider (e.g., online merchant) they visit. The online merchant redirects the user temporarily to the IdP for user authentication, and upon success the user is returned back to the merchant.

The predominance of email identifiers for users is a matter of consideration for VASPs because some users may wish to use their email address as the main identifier for account creation at the VASP. They may also seek to use the email identifier of a beneficiary in the context of asset transfers. Furthermore, a user may have multiple accounts, each at a different VASP and each employing a different email identifier obtained from different IdPs.

An interesting approach is used in the PayID scheme,[66] where the user is identified using a string similar to the *addr-spec* identifier (RFC5322) but with the "at" (@) symbol replaced by the dollar sign ($) while retaining the local part and the domain part. For example, if Alice has an account at a PayID provider (e.g., ACMEpay.com), then her PayID identifier would be alice$acmepay.com.

13.6.2 Identifier Resolvers

The matter of user identifiers is important not only from the customer usability perspective but also from the need for interoperability of services across VASPs within the information-sharing network. When an originator VASP employs a user-identifier scheme to identify an originator and beneficiary, the beneficiary VASP must have the same syntactic and semantic understanding of the identifier scheme. That is, both VASPs must be identifying the same pair of originator and beneficiary customers. Thus, another use of the VASP information-sharing infrastructure discussed previously is for VASPs to exchange the list of identifiers of their respective customers. This can be achieved by each VASP in the network by employing an *identifier resolver service* (server) that is accessible to other VASPs in the network (see figure 13.4).

A (nonexhaustive) list of some of the general requirements for a VASP resolver service would include:

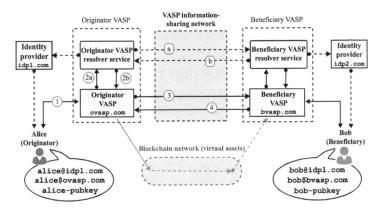

Figure 13.4
Alice and Bob with multiple identifiers.

- *Support for multiple user identifiers*   The resolver service must permit multiple types of user identifiers to be associated with the customer of the VASP.

- *Fast lookup for VASP determination*   The resolver service must support fast lookups or searches based on an identifier string by other VASPs in the network. Such lookups may be part of an asset transfer request from a VASP's customer, and any delays in identifying the beneficiary VASP may add to the overall transfer settlement time as perceived by the customer.

- *Protected service APIs*   The service endpoint APIs (e.g., RESTful, PubSub) of the resolver service must be protected. A caller VASP must be authenticated and authorized to use the APIs.

- *Validation of user identifier to IdP*   Optionally, for every user-identifier string submitted (added to) by a customer to their account at the VASP, the resolver service of the VASP should validate the string to its original issuer (if it was not the VASP). Thus, if customer Alice wishes to employ her email address alice@idp1.com, then the resolver service should seek to validate that Alice is known to the provider IdP1.

Figure 13.4 illustrates that both Alice and Bob can be recognized using three different means: (1) their email address issued by an IdP (e.g., alice@idp1.com); (2) their PayID address managed by a VASP (e.g., alice$ovasp.com); or (3) their bare public keys (e.g., alice-pubkey).

Using figure 13.4, consider the example of Alice, who wishes to transfer virtual assets to Bob but only knows Bob's email address (e.g., bob@idp2.com). Alice does not know Bob's public key or his VASP. This means that Alice's originator VASP must query its resolver service—as shown in steps 2(a) and 2(b) of figure 13.4—to discover which other VASPs in the network may know of the string bob@idp2.com (i.e., uses the string in an account). Assuming the resolver service returns a positive response (i.e., VASP identifier or VASP number found), the originator VASP can begin inquiring to that VASP about Bob per the Travel Rule, as summarized in steps 3 and 4 of figure 13.4.

Note that the resolver service of the originator VASP may return more than one possible beneficiary VASP identifier or VASP number. This could mean that Bob has an active account at each of these VASPs (each possibly using a different private-public key pair). In such cases, the originator VASP may need to request further information (regarding Bob) from Alice.

It is worth noting that identifier resolvers are not new, and several resolver protocols have been standardized and have been in wide deployment for over two decades (e.g., Domain Name

System (RFC1035), Handlesystem (RFC3650)). Therefore, the nascent VASP industry should consider using and extending these well-deployed systems instead of designing something from scratch.

13.6.3 Customer Privacy and Resolving to Public Keys

In general, we believe that a VASP resolver service should not return customer public keys in the first instance in order to preserve customer privacy. The purpose of the VASP resolver service is to aid other VASPs in determining whether an entity (person or organization) is a customer of one (or more) of the VASPs in the network. That is, the resolver service is aimed at solving the VASP *discoverability* problem by looking up VASP identifiers (VASP numbers) in order to engage that VASP.

Second, the information (metadata) about the association between a user identifier and a VASP is less revealing than the association between a user identifier and a public key. As we mentioned earlier, user identifiers (e.g., email addresses) associated with a customer account at a VASP can be changed by the customer at any time without impacting the virtual assets bound to the customer's public key. In contrast, a change to the customer's public key is visible on the blockchain system.

Finally, different VASPs may employ different business models (e.g., key custodian, commingled funds (accounts only), regulated customer wallets). Therefore, in some cases (commingled funds) there is in fact no unique public key associated with a given customer.

13.6.4 Federation of Resolvers:
VASP Information-Sharing Network

In order for VASP resolver services to scale up, the VASPs must *federate* their resolver services under a common legal framework (i.e., the consortium model discussed earlier). A federation agreement allows VASPs to share customer identifier information (as known to the VASP) over the information-sharing network. Indeed, this is one of the main purposes of the network.

For example, using the information-sharing network, VASPs can regularly (e.g., overnight) exchange knowledge about each other's customer identifiers. This is shown in figure 13.4 in steps (a) and (b), which run between the VASP resolver services.

Although a discussion of the precise protocol is beyond the scope of this chapter, in its simplest form the exchange of customer identifier information between VASP resolver services can consist of pairs of VASP-identifier values and customer-identifier values (i.e., the list of customer identifiers as known to the VASP):

VASP identifier, customer id-1, customer id-2, . . . customer id-N

This approach is akin to IP routed link-state advertisements (LSAs) used within some link-state routing protocols (e.g., OSPF (RFC2328)). In this case, a VASP is "advertising" its knowledge of customers bearing the stated identifiers. The exchange of customer-identifier information between two VASP resolver services must be conducted through an SSL/TLS secure channel established using the VASP X.509 EV certificates to ensure traffic confidentiality and source authenticity.

13.6.5 Customer-Managed Access to Claims

In some cases, static attributes regarding a customer (e.g., age, state of residence, driver's license) can be obtained from authorized entities (e.g., government departments) in the form of asserted claims in one format or another[67] with a fixed validity period. Within the identity industry, entities that issue signed assertions or claims are referred to as the *claims providers* (CPs). A given customer of a VASP may already possess a signed claim (e.g., driver's license number) from an authoritative CP (e.g., Department of Motor Vehicles) where the claim signature is still valid. The customer may keep a copy of the signed claim in their personal *claims store* (e.g., mobile device, home server, cloud storage). The customer could provide its VASP with a copy of the claims or may provide its VASP with access to their claims store.

There are several requirements and challenges for VASP access to the claims store managed by the customer:

- *Customer-managed authorization to access the claims store* Access to the customer's claims store must be customer driven, where access policies (rules) are determined by the customer as the claim owner.
- *Notice and consent from customer to use specific claims* The customer as the claim owner must determine via access policies which claims are accessible (readable) to the VASP, the usage-purpose limitations of the claims, and the right for the customer to retract the consent.[68] The customer's claims store must provide notice to the VASP, and the VASP must agree to the terms of use.
- *Consent-receipt issuance to VASP* The customer's claims store must issue a *consent receipt*[69] to the VASP, which acts as exculpatory evidence covering the VASP.

An extension to the OAuth2.0 framework,[70] called the *user-managed access* (UMA) protocol,[71] can be the basis for customer-managed access to the claims store. In the example in figure 13.5, the originator VASP is seeking to obtain signed claims regarding the originator customer (Alice) located in her claims store. Access policies have been set by Alice in step (a). In step 1, Alice provides her VASP with the location of this service provider. When the VASP reaches the UMA service provider (step 2)—which acts as the authorization server in the OAuth2.0 and UMA context—the VASP is provided with an authorization token that identifies the specific claims the VASP is authorized to fetch (step 3). The VASP wields the authorization token to the claims store (step 4). The VASP obtains access to the relevant claims and is provided with a consent receipt by the claims store (step 5).

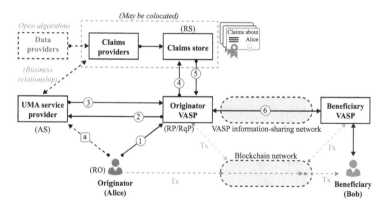

Figure 13.5

Overview of originator authorization for VASP to retrieve claims.

A claims store can be implemented in several ways. For example, it can be a resource server under the control of the CP, it can reside on Alice's own mobile device, it can be placed in a cloud-based trusted execution environment,[72] or it may be implemented in a decentralized file system, such as IPFS/Filecoin,[73] based on a decentralized identifier (DID) scheme.[74]

13.6.6 Linking Claims to Decentralized Identifiers on Blockchains

Although not directly relevant to the problem of deriving insights (claims) from data in a privacy-preserving manner, more recently there have been efforts to use blockchain technology to enable the user to better control access to endpoints on the internet, where signed claims may reside.

Referred to as *decentralized identifiers* (DIDs),[75] the basic idea is that the user would "register" to the blockchain a DID record containing specific endpoint configuration information (e.g., URLs and APIs) on the internet, where a requesting party can obtain information about the user (e.g., location of a store of signed claims). The record on the blockchain is digitally signed by the user, indicating that it is the user who self-declares that the information about the service endpoint is true. Since the user holds the matching private key, if later the user seeks to update the DID record, the user can simply replace it with a newer record (with a newer time stamp).

The idea of a DID as a persistent identifier follows from a long history of efforts on persistent and resolvable digital identifiers on the internet. The most prominent of these identifier schemes is the *digital object identifier* (DOI),[76] with its accompanying *Handle* resolver system.[77] Similar in protocol behavior to the DNS infrastructure, the DOI and Handle provide an efficient lookup of copies of files (e.g., library catalog entries) stored at repositories all over the internet. The DOI and Handle system have been successfully deployed at a wide scale for over a decade (e.g., for publications and library records).

The use of a DID is illustrated in figure 13.6. Here, in step 1, in addition to the request to the VASP to transfer assets, the subject (customer originator) provides the VASP with a DID structure (either a public DID or pairwise DID). The VASP resolves the

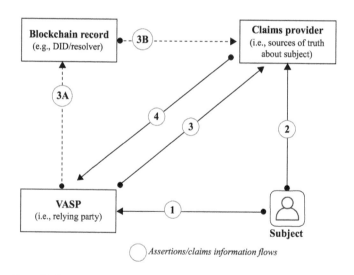

Figure 13.6
The claims provider flow with originator VASP seeking claims about the customer (subject).

DID value (via the blockchain or DID resolver) in step 3A, which brings the VASP to the correct claims provider—who holds the subject's claims in step 3B. The claims provider responds by delivering the signed claims in step 4.

Although the DID/blockchain approach is useful for certain use cases (e.g., users self-managing their public keys), in the context of providing relying parties (i.e., VASPs) with truthful and accurate information about a subject in a privacy-preserving manner, the role of DIDs remains unclear.[78]

13.6.7 Recent VASP Standardization Efforts

Since the issuance of FATF Recommendation 15,[79] there have been efforts to develop standards to support VASPs in complying with the FATF and Travel Rule in the context of virtual asset transfers.

The OpenVASP[80] effort borrows from existing modern payment standards, recast for the context of cross-VASP exchanges of information. The goal of OpenVASP is to establish a shared communications protocol for VASPs to exchange virtual asset transfer information as required by the FATF recommendations. A related approach is the Travel Rule information-sharing architecture (TRISA),[81] which seeks to develop a peer-to-peer mechanism for complying with these regulations. Finally, several organizations in the nascent virtual assets industry are collaborating to create an InterVASP data model for use in the submission of required originator and beneficiary information by originator VASPs to beneficiary VASPs.[82]

13.7   VASP CUSTOMER DATA PRIVACY IN THE CONTEXT OF KYC

As mentioned previously, the Travel Rule requires an originator VASP to transmit the originator customer's information to the beneficiary VASP (and vice versa). In general, this means VASPs sharing *verified information* about customers, which typically consists of static attributes about the customer (e.g., age, address, citizenship).

However, in the broader context of the FinCEN know your customer (KYC) requirements,[83] VASPs may be required to know more about their customers than the verified attributes demanded by the Travel Rule. VASPs therefore may need to conduct ongoing monitoring to maintain and update customer information and to identify and report suspicious transactions. This introduces another dimension of the customer relationship of a VASP: the need for a VASP to preserve the privacy of its customers when performing its KYC and CDD processes.

Today, in order to fulfill the need for ongoing monitoring of a given subject (person or organization), data analytics can be performed to identify certain trends or to pinpoint certain anomalies. Extensive data analytics can be performed only if data is readily accessible. In reality, however, today data regarding a subject is typically stored (siloed) within different institutions across different sectors of industry (e.g., financial data, health data, social platform behavior data). Furthermore, each of these data repositories may be operating under different regulatory jurisdictions, which makes it difficult to combine this data in order to derive better insights.[84] Thus, today we live in a kind of paradox in that huge amounts of digital data are increasingly being accumulated, but using it for the betterment of individuals and communities is increasingly being hampered by various constraints.

13.7.1 Open Algorithms for KYC Processes

With this backdrop, we believe that the MIT *open algorithms* (OPAL)[85] paradigm (discussed in previous chapters) may provide a path forward for VASPs and their data providers to work together to fulfill the CDD requirements while preserving customers' data privacy in the following ways:

- *KYC data sources of known provenance*   Instead of a VASP collecting (hoarding) data about customers—often data obtained from third-party data aggregators and therefore having weak or unknown origins—the VASP could establish a business relationship with the various data providers that specialize in certain types of *strongly provenanced* data. For example, a mobile telecom network operator will possess mobility data of known provenance because the data was generated by the operator's own network elements (e.g., mobile cell phone towers).
- *Data providers executing vetted algorithms for insights*   Many data providers may be regulated in their domains and thus may be prohibited from providing data directly to external entities (i.e., VASPs). However, the data provider is able to execute algorithms internally in its back-end infrastructure to yield insights that are relevant to VASPs. For example, private blockchain networks may possess data about a customer. This customer (a person or organization) may be a customer of a VASP who is not a member of the private blockchain. The private blockchain's governance may be prohibited from exporting this data to an external VASP, but it may be able to run analytics on the private ledger and share the resulting insights with an external VASP.
- *Customer consent for algorithm execution*   A key aspect of the OPAL approach is that subject (customer) consent by default

means *permission to execute an algorithm*, which is different from the current industry interpretation of consent (typically meaning permission to export or copy data out of the repository).

The OPAL approach was piloted in Colombia and Senegal in 2017–2018 in the context of preserving privacy related to research using mobility data in those countries.[86] A commercial implementation of OPAL for sharing insights among financial industry entities is currently under way. An extensive discussion of OPAL is beyond the scope of this chapter and has been treated elsewhere (e.g., see Hardjono and Pentland[87]).

13.7.2 Data Provider Network

For many data providers (data holders), the open algorithms approach provides the most practical solution that does not require data providers to give up data—which is central to their business. In many circumstances, the requesting party (i.e., a VASP) simply needs attributes and insights about a subject, not raw data about the subject. Therefore, for many data holders, the open algorithms paradigm may offer them new sources of revenue through the creation of algorithms to match the data in their possession and by making these resulting insights available (e.g., as claims) to fee-paying customers (i.e., VASPs).

A greater effect is created when data providers from distinct industries (e.g., banking and finance, health, telecom) collaborate to achieve deeper insights about subjects. These deeper insights are what KYC and CDD programs require in the context of virtual assets and VASPs. We refer to a coalition or consortium of cross-industry data providers as *data provider trust networks* (see figure 13.7). For the nascent VASP industry, collaboration with these

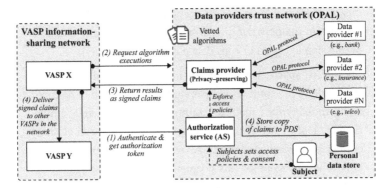

Figure 13.7
The data provider trust network based on open algorithms (after T. Hardjono and A. Pentland, "Open Algorithms for Identity Federation," in *Proceedings of the 2018 Future of Information and Communication Conference (FICC), Vol. 2*, ed. K. Arai, S. Kapoor, and R. Bhatia (New York: Springer-Verlag, 2018), 24–43).

data provider trust networks may be crucial in order to obtain access to these insights based on the open algorithms approach. In this way, VASPs can obtain insights and attributes based on data of high provenance, without needing to resort to third-party data brokers or aggregators.[88]

Figure 13.7 illustrates the notion of a data provider trust network supplying insights and attributes in a privacy-preserving manner using the open algorithms approach. The interface to the VASP (as the requesting party) is the claims provider service. In figure 13.7, before the VASP is permitted to engage the claims provider service, the VASP as a relying party must first be authenticated and be authorized by the *authentication service* (AS). This is shown in step 1 of figure 13.7. The VASP is permitted to choose only from a published list of vetted algorithms. In step 2, the VASP submits a request to the claims provider. Responses coming back from the data providers are collated by the claims provider and packaged in the form of a claim or assertion using the relevant format (e.g., see OASIS[89] and Sporny, Longley, and Chadwick[90]). The claims or assertions are digitally signed by the claims provider and then transmitted to the VASP in step 3. A copy of all issued claims or assertions is also placed in the *claims store* of the subject, located, for example, within the *personal data store* (PDS)[91] of the subject. The copies of signed claims in the subject's PDS claims store allow the subject to independently make use of the claims for other purposes—which is consistent with the recommendation of the World Economic Forum's 2014 report on personal data.[92]

13.8 AREAS FOR INNOVATION

With the increasing number of individuals and organizations holding private and public keys bound to virtual assets on a blockchain, there is increased risk of the loss and/or theft of private keys. VASPs who are custodians of a customer's private and public keys and VASPs who employ their own keys to transact on behalf of customers face the problem of key management. Therefore, the use of *electronic wallets* based on *trusted hardware*—such as the trusted platform module chip,[93] which offers key protection, may increasingly become a necessity for VASPs' own business survival. Fund insurance providers[94] may seek to obtain evidence of the use of trusted hardware by VASPs and their customers. This brings to the foreground the challenge of establishing an *attestation infrastructure* for VASPs that assists them in obtaining greater visibility into the state of wallets implemented using trusted hardware.

In what follows, we use the term *regulated wallet* to denote a wallet system (hardware and software) that is in the possession of a customer of a supervised (regulated) VASP.[95] We use the term *private wallet* to denote a wallet system belonging to an *unverified entity*.[96] In some cases, a VASP may decline to perform an asset transfer to a public key thought to be controlled by a wallet simply because the wallet holder's information is unattainable by a VASP despite the VASP querying other VASPs in the information-sharing network.

13.8.1 Wallet Attestation Evidence Types for VASPs and Asset Insurers

We use the term *attestation* to mean the capability of some trusted hardware to provide *evidence* (proof) that a device (platform) using the trusted hardware can be trusted to correctly and truthfully report the internal state of the device.[97] The information reported is signed by the trusted hardware using an internal private key that is nonreadable by external entities and *nonmigrateable* (i.e., cannot be extracted) from the trusted hardware. Thus, the recipient (e.g., a verifier) of the evidence obtains assurance that the signed report came from a particular device with the specific trusted hardware.[98] These features provide interesting capabilities for VASPs in addressing some of their key management challenges as well as AML/FT compliance needs.

For VASPs and asset insurance providers, there are several types of *attestation evidence* information that can be obtained from a wallet regarding keys used to sign asset-related transactions on the blockchain. The type of attestation evidence is dependent on the specific type of trusted hardware but generally consists of the following:[99]

- *Key creation evidence* The trusted hardware used in a wallet must have the capability of providing evidence regarding the origins of cryptographic keys held by the hardware. More specifically, it must be able to attest to whether it generated a private-public key pair internally or whether the key pair was imported from outside.
- *Key movability evidence* The trusted hardware used in a wallet must have the capability to provide evidence as to whether a private key is migrateable or nonmigrateable.[100] This evidence permits the VASP to perform risk evaluation regarding the possibility that the wallet holder (i.e., its customer) has dishonestly exported a copy of a private key to another wallet (and then used the key pair in an unregulated manner).
- *Wallet system stack composition evidence* The trusted hardware used in a wallet should be capable of providing evidence of the software stack present in the wallet.[101]

A given VASP may demand that customers use only approved wallets based on suitable trusted hardware. The VASP may also demand that customers create and use new key pairs in the trusted hardware for all transactions (i.e., from the time the user becomes a legal customer of the VASP). This strategy provides the VASP with a clear line of responsibility and accountability under the Travel Rule with regard to customer-originated transactions. The VASP has exculpatory evidence regarding the onboarding of the new customer and the start of use of the new key pair.

Figure 13.8 provides an overview of wallet attestation, where the beneficiary (Bob) is the holder of a regulated wallet employing trusted hardware. In step 1, the originator (Alice) requests that her originator VASP transfer virtual assets to Bob's public key. The originator VASP interacts with the beneficiary VASP to exchange customer Travel Rule information (step 2), including requesting that the beneficiary VASP obtain attestation evidence from Bob's wallet (step 3). In step 4, the beneficiary VASP delivers the customer account information and wallet attestation evidence to the originator VASP.

If the originator VASP is satisfied with the customer account information and wallet attestation evidence, the originator VASP performs the asset transfer to Bob's public key on the blockchain in step 5. Bob is able to validate that the asset transfer was successful in step 6, and the beneficiary VASP is able to correlate the transaction on the blockchain with Bob's account at the beneficiary VASP.

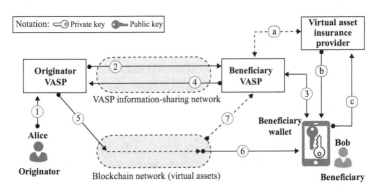

Figure 13.8

Overview of wallet device attestation and asset insurance providers.

13.8.2 Onboarding and Offboarding Customers

There are a number of challenges related to the onboarding of a customer already possessing a wallet. In the case where the customer wallet is regulated and previously known to another regulated VASP, there are some practical considerations that the *acquiring* VASP needs to address. These include, among other tasks, validating whether prior to onboarding the wallet was regulated or private; validating that the keys present within the wallet correspond to the customer's historical transactions (confirmed on the blockchain); verifying whether a backup or migration of the wallet has occurred in the past; and determining whether the customer's assets should be moved to new keys and, if so, how the old keys will be treated.

The case of a customer leaving a VASP (i.e., offboarding) also introduces a number of questions that may be relevant under the Travel Rule. The *releasing* VASP may need to address, among other issues, the following: preparing evidence that the wallet was in a regulated state while the owner of the wallet was a customer of the VASP; determining whether the customer's assets should be moved to a temporary set of keys, denoting the end of the VASP's responsibilities for the customer under the Travel Rule; and obtaining evidence from the wallet that the old keys (nonmigrateable keys) have been erased from the wallet device, thereby rendering the keys unusable by the customer in the future.

13.8.3 Regulated Wallets and Virtual Asset
Insurance Providers

Virtual asset insurance providers (e.g., cryptofund insurers) need evidence regarding the physical location of private keys as well as the degree of technological protection afforded to those private keys.[102] This is because a private key is the control point for virtual assets on a blockchain. Furthermore, a dishonest user could claim loss or theft of a private key very soon after the user moved the asset to a new anonymous private key on the blockchain. Therefore, for an insurance provider, the attestation evidence information—key-creation evidence, key-movability evidence, and wallet-system composition —obtainable from a wallet using trusted hardware is crucial to its risk-management assessment.

There are a number of classic protocols that permit the holder to sign a challenge message, providing the challenger with proof of possession (POP) of the private key.[103] However, although proof of possession is useful for general applications, most classic POP protocols do not permit the key holder to provide proof that there is only one copy of a private key and that it resides in a given trusted hardware.

Returning to figure 13.8, the beneficiary VASP is assumed to have a business relationship (i.e., purchased insurance) with the virtual asset insurance provider (step a). At any time, the insurance provider must have the ability to directly query the beneficiary's wallet (step b) in order to obtain attestation evidence regarding the wallet (step c).

13.9 CONCLUSIONS

VASPs face a data problem—they need accurate information regarding subjects, such as originators, beneficiaries, and other VASPs involved in a virtual asset transfer—as required by FATF Recommendation 15 and the Travel Rule.

The VASP information-sharing network is a central component of the trust infrastructure needed if blockchain systems and virtual assets are to be the foundation of the future global digital economy. VASPs need to view this information-sharing network as a foundational building block for other infrastructure to be developed.

VASPs also require a trusted identity infrastructure that allows VASPs to authenticate each other and rapidly ascertain the legal business status of other VASPs. The use of extended-validation digital certificates offers a promising solution to this problem, based on well-understood and widely deployed public-key certificate management technologies.

Finally, other trust infrastructure will be needed in order to address use cases related to customer wallets and device attestations from wallets. In particular, VASPs may need evidence that the customer's private key truly resides within the wallet device. This provides a means for VASPs to prove that they are not the legal operator of the customer's private and public keys.

NOTES

1. Financial Action Task Force (FATF), "International Standards on Combating Money Laundering and the Financing of Terrorism and Proliferation," FATF Revision of Recommendation 15, October 2018, http://www.fatf-gafi.org/publications/fatfrecommendations/documents/fatf-recommendations.html.

2. Financial Crimes Enforcement Network (FinCEN), US Department of the Treasury, Customer Due Diligence Requirements for Financial Institutions (31 C.F.R. 1010, 1020, 1023, 1024, and 1026; RIN 1506AB25),

Federal Register 79, no. 149 (August 2014), https://www.fincen.gov/sites /default/files/shared/CDD-NPRM-Final.pdf.

3. Financial Crimes Enforcement Network (FinCEN), "Application of Fin-CEN's Regulations to Certain Business Models Involving Convertible Virtual Currencies," FinCEN Guidance, May 2019, https://www.fincen.gov/sites /default/files/2019-05/FinCEN\%20CVC\%20Guidance\%20FINAL.pdf.

4. World Economic Forum, *Personal Data: The Emergence of a New Asset Class*, report, 2011, http://www.weforum.org/reports/personal-data-emergence -new-asset-class; World Economic Forum, *Rethinking Personal Data: A New Lens for Strengthening Trust*, report, May 2014, http://reports.weforum.org /rethinking-personal-data.

5. R. Abelson and M. Goldstein, "Millions of Anthem Customers Targeted in Cyberattack," *New York Times*, February 5, 2015, https://www .nytimes.com/2015/02/05/business/hackers-breached-data-of-millions -insurer-says.html.

6. T. S. Bernard, T. Hsu, N. Perlroth, and R. Lieber, "Equifax Says Cyber-attack May Have Affected 143 Million in the U.S." *New York Times*, September 7, 2017, https://www.nytimes.com/2017/09/07/business/equifax -cyberattack.html.

7. European Commission, "Regulation (EU) 2016/679 of the European Parliament and of the Council of 27 April 2016 on the Protection of Natural Persons with Regard to the Processing of Personal Data and on the Free Movement of Such Data (General Data Protection Regulation)," *Official Journal of the European Union* L119 (2016): 1–88.

8. California State Legislature, "California Consumer Privacy Act (CCPA)—AB 375," California Civil Code—Section 1798.100, September 2018.

9. C. F. Kerry, *A Federal Privacy Law Could Do Better Than California's*, report, Brookings Institution, Center for Technology Innovation, April

2019, https://www.brookings.edu/blog/techtank/2019/04/29/a-federal
-privacy-law-could-do-better-than-californias/.

10. Financial Action Task Force (FATF), "International Standards on Combating Money Laundering and the Financing of Terrorism and Proliferation."

11. Financial Action Task Force (FATF), "Guidance for a Risk-Based Approach to Virtual Assets and Virtual Asset Service Providers," FATF Guidance, June 2019, www.fatf-gafi.org/publications/fatfrecommendations /documents/Guidance-RBA-virtual-assets.html.

12. T. Hardjono, "Compliant Solutions for VASPs" (presentation to the FATF Private Sector Consultative Forum (PSCF) 2019, Vienna, May 6, 2019); T. Hardjono, A. Lipton, and A. Pentland, "Towards a Public Key Management Framework for Virtual Assets and Virtual Asset Service Providers," *Journal of FinTech* 1, no. 1 (2020), https://doi.org/10.1142/S27051099 20500017.

13. Financial Crimes Enforcement Network (FinCEN), US Department of the Treasury, Customer Due Diligence Requirements for Financial Institutions.

14. Financial Crimes Enforcement Network (FinCEN), US Department of the Treasury, Customer Due Diligence Requirements for Financial Institutions; Financial Crimes Enforcement Network (FinCEN), "Application of FinCEN's Regulations to Certain Business Models Involving Convertible Virtual Currencies."

15. S. Goldwasser, S. Micali, and C. Rackoff, "The Knowledge Complexity of Interactive Proof Systems," *SIAM Journal on Computing* 18, no. 1 (April 1988): 186–208, https://doi.org/10.1137/0218012.

16. European Commission, "Regulation (EU) 2016/679 of the European Parliament and of the Council of 27 April 2016 on the Protection of Natural Persons with Regard to the Processing of Personal Data and on the Free Movement of Such Data (General Data Protection Regulation)."

17. Financial Action Task Force (FATF), *12-Month Review of Revised FATF Standards on Virtual Assets and Virtual Asset Service Providers,*, FATF Report, July 2020, http://www.fatf-gafi.org/publications/fatfrecommendations /documents/12-month-review-virtual-assets-vasps.html.

18. Hardjono, "Compliant Solutions for VASPs."

19. Finextra, "Swift to Introduce PKI Security for FIN," *Finextra News*, October 2004, https://www.finextra.com/newsarticle/12620/swift-to-introduce -pki-security-for-fin.

20. S. Kent and R. Atkinson, "Security Architecture for the Internet Protocol," IETF Standard RFC2401, November 1998, http://tools.ietf.org/rfc /rfc2401.txt.

21. D. Rescorla, "The Transport Layer Security (TLS) Protocol Version 1.3," IETF Standard RFC8446, August 2018, https://tools.ietf.org/html/rfc8446.

22. D. Cooper, S. Santesson, S. Farrell, S. Boeyen, R. Housley, and W. Polk, "Internet X.509 Public Key Infrastructure Certificate and Certificate Revocation List (CRL) Profile," RFC5280, May 2008, http://tools.ietf.org/rfc /rfc5280.txt; International Organization for Standardization, "Information Technology—Open Systems Interconnection—the Directory—Part 8: Public-Key and Attribute Certificate Frameworks," ISO/IEC 9594–8:2017, February 2017.

23. Hardjono, "Compliant Solutions for VASPs."

24. European Commission, "Regulation (EU) 2016/679 of the European Parliament and of the Council of 27 April 2016 on the Protection of Natural Persons with Regard to the Processing of Personal Data and on the Free Movement of Such Data (General Data Protection Regulation)."

25. D. Jevans, T. Hardjono, J. Vink, F. Steegmans, J. Jefferies, and A. Malhotra, "Travel Rule Information Sharing Architecture for Virtual Asset Service Providers, TRISA, Version 7," white paper, TRISA, June 2020, https://trisa.io/wp-content/uploads/2020/06/TRISAEnablingFATFTrave lRuleWhitePaperV7.pdf.

26. D. Riegelnig, "OpenVASP: An Open Protocol to Implement FATF's Travel Rule for Virtual Assets," white paper, OpenVASP, November 2019, https://www.openvasp.org/wp-content/uploads/2019/11/OpenVasp_Whitepaper.pdf.

27. InterVASP, "InterVASP Messaging Standards IVMS101," Joint Working Group on InterVASP Messaging Standards, InterVASP Data Model Standard—Issue 1—Final, May 2020.

28. D. Clark, "The Design Philosophy of the DARPA Internet Protocols," *ACM Computer Communication Review—Proceedings of SIGCOMM 88* 18, no. 4 (August 1988): 106–114; J. Saltzer, D. Reed, and D. Clark, "End-to-End Arguments in System Design," *ACM Transactions on Computer Systems* 2, no. 4 (November 1984): 277–288.

29. D. Yaga, P. Mell, N. Roby, and K. Scarfone, *Blockchain Technology Overview*, National Institute of Standards and Technology Internal Report 8202, October 2018, https://doi.org/10.6028/NIST.IR.8202.

30. Financial Action Task Force (FATF), "International Standards on Combating Money Laundering and the Financing of Terrorism and Proliferation"; Financial Action Task Force (FATF), "Guidance for a Risk-Based Approach to Virtual Assets and Virtual Asset Service Providers."

31. Financial Crimes Enforcement Network (FinCEN), "Application of FinCEN's Regulations to Certain Business Models Involving Convertible Virtual Currencies."

32. Financial Action Task Force (FATF), "International Standards on Combating Money Laundering and the Financing of Terrorism and Proliferation."

33. InterVASP, "InterVASP Messaging Standards IVMS101."

34. Financial Crimes Enforcement Network (FinCEN), "Application of FinCEN's Regulations to Certain Business Models Involving Convertible Virtual Currencies."

35. OASIS, "Assertions and Protocols for the OASIS Security Assertion Markup Language (SAML) V2.0," March 2005, http://docs.oasisopen.org/security/saml/v2.0/saml-core-2.0-os.pdf.

36. S. Farrell, R. Housley, and S. Turner, "An Internet Attribute Certificate Profile for Authorization," RFC5755, January 2010, http://tools.ietf.org/rfc/rfc5755.txt.

37. M. Sporny, D. Longley, and D. Chadwick, "Verifiable Credentials Data Model 1.0," W3C, W3C Recommendation, November 2019, https://www.w3.org/TR/verifiable-claims-data-model.

38. Yaga et al., *Blockchain Technology Overview*.

39. Global Legal Entity Identifier Foundation (GLEIF), *LEI in KYC: A New Future for Legal Entity Identification*, GLEIF research report, May 2018, https://www.gleif.org/en/lei-solutions/lei-in-kyc-a-new-future-for-legal-entity-identification.

40. Riegelnig, "OpenVASP."

41. Riegelnig, "OpenVASP."

42. J. Newton, M. David, A. Voisine, and J. MacWhyte, "BIP75: Out of Band Address Exchange Using Payment Protocol Encryption," Bitcoin Improvement Proposal (BIP) 75, July 2019, https://github.com/bitcoin/bips/blob/master/bip-0075.mediawiki.

43. InterVASP, "InterVASP Messaging Standards IVMS101."

44. OASIS, "Assertions and Protocols for the OASIS Security Assertion Markup Language (SAML) V2.0."

45. N. Sakimura, J. Bradley, M. Jones, B. de Medeiros, and C. Mortimore, "OpenID Connect Core 1.0," OpenID Foundation, Technical Specification v1.0—Errata Set 1, November 2014, http://openid.net/specs/openid-connect-core-10.html.

46. Global Legal Entity Identifier Foundation (GLEIF), *LEI in KYC*.

47. D. R. Kuhn, V. C. Hu, W. T. Polk, and S.-J. Chang, "Introduction to Public Key Technology and the Federal PKI Infrastructure," National Institute of Standards and Technology Special Publication 800–32, February 2001, https://nvlpubs.nist.gov/nistpubs/Legacy/SP/nistspecialpublication800-32 .pdf.

48. E. Barker, "Recommendation for Key Management (Part 1)," National Institute of Standards and Technology Special Publication 800–57, Part 1, Rev. 4, January 2016, http://dx.doi.org/10.6028/NIST.SP.800-57pt1r4.

49. National Institute of Standards and Technology, "Electronic Authentication Guideline," NIST Draft Special Publication 800–63-1, December 2008, http://csrc.nist.gov/publications/PubsDrafts.html.

50. R. Housley, W. Ford, W. Polk, and D. Solo, "Internet X.509 Public Key Infrastructure Certificate and CRL Profile," RFC2459, IETF, January 1999, http://tools.ietf.org/rfc/rfc2459.txt; Cooper et al., "Internet X.509 Public Key Infrastructure Certificate and Certificate Revocation List (CRL) Profile"; International Organization for Standardization, "Information Technology—Open Systems Interconnection—the Directory—Part 8."

51. Riegelnig, "OpenVASP."

52. CA Browser Forum, "Guidelines for the Issuance and Management of Extended Validation Certificates," Specification Version 1.7.2, March 2020.

53. Cooper et al., "Internet X.509 Public Key Infrastructure Certificate and Certificate Revocation List (CRL) Profile"; International Organization for Standardization, "Information Technology—Open Systems Interconnection—the Directory—Part 8."

54. Jevans et al., "Travel Rule Information Sharing Architecture for Virtual Asset Service ProvidersTRISA, Version 7."

55. Riegelnig, "OpenVASP."

56. Sporny, Longley, and Chadwick, "Verifiable Credentials Data Model 1.0."

57. OASIS, "Assertions and Protocols for the OASIS Security Assertion Markup Language (SAML) V2.0."

58. National Automated Clearing House Association (NACHA), "Operating Rules and Guidelines," Specification, 2019, https://www.nacha.org.

59. E. Makaay, T. Smedinghoff, and D. Thibeau, "OpenID Exchange: Trust Frameworks for Identity Systems," June 2017, http://www.openidentityexchange.org.

60. Kuhn et al., "Introduction to Public Key Technology and the Federal PKI Infrastructure."

61. Finextra, "Swift to Introduce PKI Security for FIN."

62. Apple Inc., "Apple Public CA Certification Practice Statement," June 2019, https://images.apple.com/certificateauthority/pdf/ApplePublicCACPSv4.2.pdf.

63. Cable Laboratories, "Cablelabs New PKI Certificate Policy Version 2.1," Technical Specifications, January 2019, https://www.cablelabs.com/resources/digital-certificate-issuance-service.

64. T. Hardjono and A. Pentland, "Core Identities for Future Transaction Systems," in *Trusted Data—a New Framework for Identity and Data Sharing*, ed. T. Hardjono, A. Pentland, and D. Shrier (Cambridge, MA: MIT Press, 2019), 41–81.

65. T. Hardjono, "Federated Authorization over Access to Personal Data for Decentralized Identity Management," *IEEE Communications Standards Magazine—the Dawn of the Internet Identity Layer and the Role of Decentralized Identity* 3, no. 4 (December 2019): 32–38, https://doi.org/10.1109/MCOMSTD.001.1900019.

66. A. Malhotra, A. King, D. Schwartz, and M. Zochowski, "PayID Protocol," PayID.org Technical Whitepaper v1.0, June 2020, https://payid.org/whitepaper.pdf.

67. OASIS, "Assertions and Protocols for the OASIS Security Assertion Markup Language (SAML) V2.0"; Sporny, Longley, and Chadwick, "Verifiable Credentials Data Model 1.0."

68. European Commission, "Regulation (EU) 2016/679 of the European Parliament and of the Council of 27 April 2016 on the Protection of Natural Persons with Regard to the Processing of Personal Data and on the Free Movement of Such Data (General Data Protection Regulation)."

69. M. Lizar and D. Turner, "Consent Receipt Specification Version 1.0," Kantara Initiative, March 2017, https://kantarainitiative.org/confluence /display/infosharing/Home.

70. D. Hardt, "The OAuth 2.0 Authorization Framework," RFC6749, IETF, October 2012, http://tools.ietf.org/rfc/rfc6749.txt.

71. T. Hardjono, E. Maler, M. Machulak, and D. Catalano, "User-Managed Access (UMA) Profile of OAuth2.0—Specification Version 1.0," Kantara Initiative, Kantara Published Specification, April 2015, https://docs .kantarainitiative.org/uma/rec-uma-core.html; E. Maler, M. Machulak, and J. Richer, "User-Managed Access (UMA) 2.0," Kantara Initiative, Kantara Published Specification, January 2017, https://docs.kantarainitiative .org/uma/ed/uma-core-2.0-10.html.

72. Enterprise Ethereum Alliance, "Off-Chain Trusted Compute Specification," Technical Specification v1.1, March 2020, https://entethalliance .github.io/trusted-computing/spec.html.

73. Protocol Labs, "Inter Planetary File System (IPFS)," 2019, https://docs .ipfs.io.

74. D. Reed and M. Sporny, "Decentralized Identifiers (DIDs) v0.11," W3C, Draft Community Group Report, July 9, 2018, https://w3c-ccg.github.io/did -spec/.

75. Reed and Sporny, "Decentralized Identifiers (DIDs) v0.11."

76. International Organization for Standardization, "Digital Object Identifier System—Information and Documentation," ISO 26324:2012, June 2012, http://www.iso.org/iso/cataloguedetail?csnumber=43506.

77. S. Sun, L. Lannom, and B. Boesch, "Handle System Overview," RFC3650, IETF, November 2003, http://tools.ietf.org/rfc/rfc3650.txt.

78. T. Hardjono and E. Maler, *Blockchain and Smart Contracts Report*, Kantara Initiative Report, June 2017, https://kantarainitiative.org/confluence/display/BSC/Home.

79. Financial Action Task Force (FATF), "International Standards on Combating Money Laundering and the Financing of Terrorism and Proliferation."

80. Riegelnig, "OpenVASP."

81. TRISA, "Travel Rule Information Sharing Architecture for Virtual Asset Service Providers (TRISA)—Version 5," white paper, December 2019, https://trisacrypto.github.io/white-papers/white-paper-trisa-v5.pdf.

82. InterVASP, "InterVASP Messaging Standards IVMS101."

83. Financial Crimes Enforcement Network (FinCEN)—US Department of the Treasury, Customer Due Diligence Requirements for Financial Institutions.

84. A. Pentland, *Social Physics: How Social Networks Can Make Us Smarter* (New York: Penguin Books, 2015).

85. A. Pentland, "Saving Big Data from Itself," *Scientific American* 311, no. 2 (August 2014): 65–68, https://www.jstor.org/stable/26040214.

86. OPAL Project, *OPAL: Status and Plans 2018–19*, OPAL Project Status Report, May 2018, https://www.opalproject.org/general-overview.

87. T. Hardjono and A. Pentland, "Open Algorithms for Identity Federation," in *Proceedings of the 2018 Future of Information and Communication Conference (FICC), Vol. 2*, ed. K. Arai, S. Kapoor, and R. Bhatia (New York: Springer, 2018), 24–43; T. Hardjono and A. Pentland, "MIT Open Algorithms," in

Trusted Data—a New Framework for Identity and Data Sharing, ed. T. Hardjono, A. Pentland, and D. Shrier (Cambridge, MA: MIT Press, 2019), 83–107.

88. T. Cook, "You Deserve Privacy Online. Here's How You Could Actually Get It," *Time,* January 2019, https://time.com/collection-post/5502591/tim-cook-data-privacy/.

89. OASIS, "Assertions and Protocols for the OASIS Security Assertion Markup Language (SAML) V2.0."

90. Sporny, Longley, and Chadwick, "Verifiable Credentials Data Model 1.0."

91. T. Hardjono and J. Seberry, "Strongboxes for Electronic Commerce," in *Proceedings of the Second USENIX Workshop on Electronic Commerce* (Berkeley, CA: USENIX Association, 1996); Y. A. de Montjoye, E. Shmueli, S. Wang, and A. Pentland, "OpenPDS: Protecting the Privacy of Metadata through SafeAnswers," *PLoS One* 9, no. 7 (July 2014): 13–18, https://doi.org/10.1371/journal.pone.0098790.

92. World Economic Forum, *Rethinking Personal Data.*

93. Trusted Computing Group, "TPM Main—Specification Version 1.2," Trusted Computing Group Published Specification, October 2003, http://www.trustedcomputinggroup.org/resources/tpmmainspecification.

94. O. Kharif, B. Louis, J. Edde, and K. Chiglinsky, "Interest in Crypto Insurance Grows, Despite High Premiums, Broad Exclusions," *Insurance Journal,* July 23, 2018, https://www.insurancejournal.com/news/national/2018/07/23/495680.htm.

95. Swiss Financial Market Supervisory Authority (FINMA), *FINMA Guidance: Payments on the Blockchain,* FINMA Guidance Report, August 2019, https://www.finma.ch/en/~/media/finma/dokumente/dokumentencenter/myfinma/4dokumentation/finma-aufsichtsmitteilungen/20190826-finma-aufsichtsmitteilung-02-2019.pdf; Swiss Financial Market Supervisory Authority (FINMA), "FINMA Anti-Money Laundering Ordinance (AMLO)," Verordnung der Eidgenssischen Finanzmarktaufsicht ber die Bekmpfung von Geldwscherei und Terrorismusfinanzierung im Finanzsektor, June

2015, https://www.admin.ch/opc/de/classified-compilation/20143112/index .html.

96. Financial Action Task Force (FATF), *12-Month Review of Revised FATF Standards on Virtual Assets and Virtual Asset Service Providers.*

97. Trusted Computing Group, "TCG Glossary," Trusted Computing Group Published Specification—Version 1.1, Revision 1.0, May 2017, https:// trustedcomputinggroup.org/wp-content/uploads/TCG-Glossary-V1.1-Rev-1 .0.pdf.

98. T. Hardjono and N. Smith, "TCG Core Integrity Schema," Trusted Computing Group Specification—Version 1.0.1, Revision 1.0, November 2006, https://trustedcomputinggroup.org/wp-content/uploads/IWG-Core -Integrity\Schema\Specification\v1.pdf; N. Smith, ed., "TCG Attestation Framework," Trusted Computing Group Draft Specification—Version 1.0, February 2020.

99. T. Hardjono, A. Lipton, and A. Pentland, "Wallet Attestations for Virtual Asset Service Providers and Crypto-Assets Insurance," June 2020, https:// arxiv.org/pdf/2005.14689.pdf.

100. T. Hardjono and G. Kazmierczak, "Overview of the TPM Key Management Standard," Trusted Computing Group, 2008, http://www.trustedcom putinggroup.org/files/resourcefiles/.

101. T. Hardjono and N. Smith, "TCG Core Integrity Schema"; Smith, "TCG Attestation Framework."

102. A. John, "Cryptocurrency Industry Faces Insurance Hurdle to Mainstream Ambitions," Reuters, December 2018, https://www.reuters.com /article/us-crypto-currency-insurance/cryptocurrency-industry-faces -insurance-hurdle-to-mainstream-ambitions-idUSKCN1OJ0BU; Kharif et al., "Interest in Crypto Insurance Grows, Despite High Premiums, Broad Exclusions."

103. T. Hardjono, "Future Directions for Regulated Private Wallets," in *Proceedings of the IEEE International Conference on Blockchain and Cryptocurrency*, May 2021 (forthcoming).

IV

CONCLUSIONS

14

CONCLUSION: LEGAL ALGORITHMS

Alex Pentland

14.1 INTRODUCTION

Code is law, and law is increasingly becoming code. This change
is being driven by the growing need for access to justice and the
ambition for greater efficiency and predictability in modern business. Most laws and regulations are just algorithms that human
organizations execute, but now legal algorithms are beginning to
be executed by computers as an extension of human bureaucracies. Computer tools are already commonly used to help humans
make legal determinations in areas such as finance, aviation, and
the energy sector, and most of the logic is computerized and only
later subject to human oversight.

Even court proceedings are becoming increasingly reliant on
computerized fact discovery and precedent, which will likely lead
to more and more cases being settled out of court. Moreover, the
execution of legal algorithms by computers is likely to expand
dramatically as digital systems become more ubiquitous.

As evidenced by the interest and engagement that young lawyers and visionary legal scholars have shown, the legal profession

is quietly seizing the opportunities provided by the transition to computer-aided human legal practice. It may surprise readers to learn that several law schools have established entrepreneurship programs and incubators focused on legal technology, including Suffolk University Law School and Brooklyn Law School. Faculty of both law schools are among the founders of our *MIT Computational Law Report*, which can be found at http://law.mit.edu.

Young lawyers in training are similarly engaged. I was pleasantly surprised to see that the recent "Blockchain for Open Music" hackathon,[1] organized by the founders of our report, was hosted by nine law schools on four continents. The legal profession is beginning to go fully digital! Nevertheless, as legal algorithms transition to being executed by computers, we must be careful not to lose the guardrails of human judgment and interpretation to ensure that the legal algorithms improve justice in our society. We must continue to safeguard, and even substantially increase, human oversight of our legal algorithms.

We must also recognize that current legal and regulatory systems are often poorly designed or out-of-date. As we transition to computer execution of legal algorithms, we have a unique opportunity to make laws more responsive and precise. Related to this, we should recognize that many legal algorithms fail to achieve their intended aims or have unintended consequences, and we must ask whether there is a better method of ensuring the performance and accountability of each legal algorithm.

14.2 COMPUTATIONAL LAW

How can we achieve greater oversight and accountability of legal algorithms while harvesting their potential to provide greater efficiency, ease of access, and fairness? The obvious answer is to learn from the *human-machine systems framework*,[2] which has evolved over the last century to become the standard practice in designing and fielding human-machine systems across the world. Leading examples of this framework include Amazon's fulfillment and delivery systems and internet connectivity systems.

The stunning efficiency and reach of these systems comes, perhaps surprisingly, from modesty: the idea that you can never build human-machine systems that "just work." Instead, you will have to continually tweak, reiterate, and redesign them. Once you accept the limitations of the human intellect, you realize that the system must be modular so you can revise the algorithms easily; that the system must be densely instrumented so you can tell how well each algorithm is working; and, less obviously, that the design of the system and each of its modules has to be clearly and directly connected to the goals of the system so that you know what modules to redesign when things go wrong and how to redesign them.

To be clear, some "modules" are software but others are people or groups of people, all working to execute the algorithms that make up the human-machine system. "Redesigning" human "modules" means reorganizing and perhaps retraining the people, a process familiar as Kaizen[3] in manufacturing and as quality circles[4] in business generally. Note that for the quality circle process to work, the people in the system must clearly understand their connection to the overall goals of the system.

A key element of this design paradigm is testing. We simply cannot design a complex human-machine system that works without extensive testing, field piloting, and evaluation. Testing always begins with a simulation of key components and then the entire system and concludes with pilot deployments with representative communities as an experiment in which participants give informed consent. Moreover, this testing and evaluation is not just as part of creating the system; it must also happen continuously after large-scale deployment of the system. Things change and, in order to adapt, we must continue to tweak and reengineer the system.

The ability for workers (or regulatory staff members) to critique and revise their jobs (e.g., the quality circle process) is key to the success of the overall system. In traditional legal systems, the task of auditing and revising modules based on performance feedback is the role of senior regulators and the courts. The task of auditing and revising the overall system architecture is traditionally the role of legislators.

When the legal system process is compared to more successful human-machine systems, it becomes clear that our current legal processes give insufficient thought to instrumenting modules (e.g., why did it take a decade to evaluate broken windows policing?) and to designing systems that are modular and easy to update (e.g., the healthcare system or tax code). A subtler problem is that current legal algorithms are insufficiently clear about the goals they are intended to achieve and what evidence can be used to evaluate their performance.

14.3 SIMPLE EXAMPLES OF COMPUTATIONAL LAW SYSTEMS

Some simple examples of using this design framework to build successful legal algorithms may help illustrate these ideas. The first example is a government setting up an automatic, algorithmic legal system—specifically a traffic congestion taxation system.

This system, implemented in Sweden, reads car license plates and charges drivers for use of roads within Stockholm. We can see each of the components of proper legal algorithm design in the Wikipedia description of the system.[5]

- The motivation for the congestion tax was stated as the reduction of traffic congestion and the improvement of certain air-quality metrics in central Stockholm. Consequently, the *goals* of the system were clear, and the *measurement criteria* for system performance were well understood.
- Following seven months of *testing* during a trial period, the tax was implemented permanently.
- After initial deployment, the system design was *adopted and revised* to obtain better performance by charging higher prices for the most central part of Stockholm.
- The system was *audited* for the first five years of operation and demonstrated a decrease in congestion, with some motorists turning to public transport.

While the elements of algorithmic design may seem quite obvious in this example, such considerations often are not present in the creation and operation of algorithmic legal systems. Sweden's congestion tax system has since been used as a model by city governments and urban planners around the world.

The second example is commercial and is drawn from my personal experience helping guide Nissan in creating an autonomous driving system for its cars. This system design is now the largest deployed autonomous driving system in the world (at level 2). The development of the system began with specifying the design objective:

- The *goal* of the car's navigation system should be to achieve safer driving without distracting the driver. It should feel like you are just driving the car as usual, but the car just naturally does "the right thing." The human is always fully engaged and in charge.
- Laboratory *testing* of the system revealed that the car's idea of "what to do" must match the judgment of human drivers so that the car never does anything the driver does not expect or understand.
- The system was *adapted and revised* through pilot deployments that determined when the car could usefully help the driver and when it should not try to help. The system was also improved iteratively as new sensing technologies became available.
- Following commercial deployment, the system has been continuously *audited* for safety and customer satisfaction and is continuously updated.

The consequence is that driving has become much safer, and people love the system, although sometimes they fail to appreciate just how much the system is doing. For instance, drivers often fail to appreciate how the system subtly teaches them to be better drivers. Instead of functioning merely as a tool that replaces humans or human reasoning, these types of systems are more akin to training wheels or guardrails. In fact, the original name for the system was "magic bumper."

14.4 MISSING COMPONENTS OF SUCCESSFUL COMPUTATIONAL LAW

Unfortunately, several of the elements just highlighted are underdeveloped or even missing from current legal and regulatory system processes. These include specification of system performance goals, measurement and evaluation criteria, testing, robust and adaptive system design, and continuous auditing.

Specification of system performance goals The creation of a new system of legal algorithms (e.g., a law and associated regulation) requires a debate among citizens and legislators concerning objectives and values that results in a clear specification of the overarching goals of the system's objectives. The failure to specify objectives increases the likelihood that the resulting legal system will fail to provide good governance and may produce negative unintended consequences.

Measurement and evaluation criteria To have any chance of determining whether something is a success, we need to have an appropriate point of comparison. For example, how do we know when the system is performing well? How do we know when each module (individual algorithm) within the system is performing well? The connection between the measurements and objectives must be clear and be very broadly understood by citizens. Without this understanding, the informed debate demanded by our governance system, and the informed consent of the governed, is unlikely.

Testing Currently, laws proposed by the US Congress undergo simulation testing by the Office of Management and Budget, and often regulations are subject to simple cost-benefit and environmental evaluation. Helpful as this testing may be, it is inadequate if we are to build responsive and adaptive algorithmic legal systems. More seriously, there is almost no tradition of testing new legal algorithms (whether executed by human bureaucracies or by computers) on a representative (and consenting) sample of communities. This failure to test is hubris, tantamount to believing that we can build systems that are perfect ab initio. It is a recipe for creating low-quality legal systems.

Robust adaptive system design The system of legal algorithms (e.g., a law and associated regulations) must be modular and continuously auditable, with a clear connection between measurement criteria and system goals, so that it is easy to revise or update modules (legal algorithms) and their organization. A failure to implement modern system design tools makes it likelier that the resulting legal system will be opaque, unresponsive to harms, and difficult to update.

Continuous auditing Systems of legal algorithms (e.g., a law and associated regulations) must have an operational mechanism for continuous auditing of all modules and overall system performance. Such auditing requires involvement and oversight by all human stakeholders and must include, by default, the capacity for those stakeholders to modify algorithms or system architecture so that the system meets specified performance goals. The failure to audit ensures that we will have serious failures of our legal system as society and our environment evolve. I suggest that the ability to modify algorithms be accomplished by requiring regulators, legislators, and courts (as appropriate) to respond promptly to stakeholder concerns.

14.5 MISSING IMPLICATIONS FOR THE PRACTICE OF LAW

What does this mean for lawyers and legislators? Historically, legal careers have begun with the drudgery of wordsmithing and searching through legal documents. As happened with spell-checks and web searches, this work is now being streamlined by AI-driven document software that searches large document stores to find relevant clauses and suggests common wordings.

These trends are often seen as reducing the demand for legal services, but there are also new opportunities for developing legal agreements using tools originally intended for creating large software systems. These tools are beginning to allow lawyers and legislators to design much more agile, interpretable, and robust legal agreements.

As a consequence, the legal profession has the opportunity to transition from being a cost center and a source of friction to a center for new business and opportunity creation. The goal of the *MIT Computational Law Report* is to help seize this opportunity, to support new legal scholars in their enthusiasm for using new digital technologies, and to improve our systems of contracts and governance.

14.6 VALUES AND PRINCIPLES

What are the underlying values and principles—the social contract—that can guide creation of this new phenomenon of computational law and governance? One concept for how to guide computational technology to support the values and principles embodied in our social contract is summarized by the phrase "stakeholder capitalism"; that is, capitalism that benefits all stakeholders in the community. This idea has recently surged in popularity because it is envisioned as preserving the dynamism of capitalism but harnessing it to better benefit all society rather than just the few. Unfortunately, it is not yet clear how to implement stakeholder capitalism so that it leads to a vibrant, inclusive, fair society.

Capitalism that benefits everyone cannot be measured by money alone, because money is not the only way to measure value. Various groups have developed ad hoc ESG (environment, social, governance) metrics to measure corporate impact, but these have proven unreliable, rendering claims of corporate social responsibility largely meaningless. However, there is an alternative to the ESG metrics currently at hand: all around the world, scientists, national statistics offices, and multilateral organizations are beginning to use computational methods to measure many aspects of human life instead of just measuring money. These science-based metrics[6] have been developed to quantify the UN's Sustainable Development Goals (SDGs), including poverty, inequality, and many aspects of access to justice and sustainability. Indeed, it may be that the greatest achievement of the UN's SDGs will be that they forced development of statistical tools using digital data and AI in order to quantitatively measure social conditions quite broadly. The capability to measure social conditions enables us to make the promise of stakeholder capitalism real, concrete, and auditable. (I should note that I am on the board of directors for the UN Foundation's Global Partnership for Sustainable Development Data.)

Using a toolkit of quantitative social metrics similar to those developed for measuring the SDGs, it is now possible to measure social properties such as all-inclusive productivity, rate of innovation, sustainability, access to opportunity, justice, education, and health in a reliable, quantitative manner that is comparable across different societies and nations. The importance of these metrics is that they allow us to identify the policies that best promote a more vibrant, sustainable, inclusive, fair, and lower-risk future. We have seen clear metrics and data sharing work wonders in some medical areas—pediatric health and AIDS treatment come to mind—so why not more broadly? And why just for physical health when they can be used for economic and social health as well?

This new vision of stakeholder capitalism, where capitalist performance, measured by methods originally developed to quantify the Sustainable Development Goals (SDGs), is enabled by the fact that technologies such as AI, cryptotechnology, and the Internet of Things are lowering the cost of measurement and coordination[7] to the point where traditional centralized, hierarchical organizations are no longer required for large-scale projects or production. As a consequence, people around the world are beginning to create organizations that are far more distributed, flexible, and resilient, and can operate adjacent to existing capital markets, labor pools, and legal frameworks. Please join us in making this new vision a reality!

NOTES

1. https://github.com/mitmedialab/OpenMediaLegalHack/tree/master/docs.

2. K. Stowers, J. Oglesby, S. Sonesh, K. Leyva, C. Iwig, and E. Salas, "A Framework to Guide the Assessment of Human–Machine Systems," *Human Factors* 59, no. 2 (March 2017): 172–188, https://doi.org/10.1177/0018720817695077.

3. M. Imai, *Kaizen (Ky'zen), The Key to Japan's Competitive Success* (New York: McGraw Hill, 1986).

4. D. C. Hutchins, *Quality Circles Handbook* (New York: Pitman, 1985).

5. https://en.wikipedia.org/wiki/Stockholm_congestion_tax.

6. http://www.data4sdgs.org.

7. https://connection.mit.edu/whitepapers.

CONTRIBUTORS

Alex "Sandy" Pentland holds triple professorial appointments at the Massachusetts Institute of Technology in the Media Lab (SA+P), School of Engineering, and School of Management. He also directs MIT's Connect Science initiative, the Human Dynamics Laboratory, and the MIT Media Lab Entrepreneurship Program, and has been a member of the Advisory Boards for the UN, American Bar Association, Google, Nissan, Telefonica, and a variety of start-up firms. For several years he co-led the World Economic Forum Big Data and Personal Data initiatives. He has pioneered the fields of computational social science and wearable computing, generating several successful start-ups and technology spinoffs. He previously helped create and direct MIT's Media Laboratory, the Media Lab Asia laboratories at the Indian Institutes of Technology, and Strong Hospital's Center for Future Health. In 2012, *Forbes* named Sandy one of the "seven most powerful data scientists in the world," along with the founders of Google and the chief technology officer of the United States, and in 2013 he won the McKinsey Award from Harvard Business Review. Prof. Pentland's books include *Honest Signals*, *Social Physics*, *Trusted Data*, and *Frontiers of Financial*

Technology. He was named to the National Academy of Engineering in 2014. Sandy holds a BGS from the University of Michigan and a PhD from MIT.

Alexander Lipton is cofounder and chief information officer at Sila, visiting professor and dean's fellow at the Hebrew University of Jerusalem, and connection science fellow at MIT. He is an advisory board member at numerous fintech companies worldwide. In 2016 he left Bank of America for Merrill Lynch, where he served for ten years in various senior managerial roles, including quantitative solutions executive and cohead of the Global Quantitative Group. His current professional interests include fintech, mainly distributed ledger technology applications to payments and banking; digital currencies, including stablecoins and asset-backed cryptocurrencies; and robust large-scale asset allocation. In 2000 Alex was awarded the Inaugural Quant of the Year Award, and in 2021 the Buy-side Quant of the Year Award, by *Risk Magazine.* Alex has published eight books and more than a hundred scientific papers.

Thomas Hardjono is the CTO of Connection Science and technical director of the MIT Trust-Data Consortium, located in Cambridge, MA. For several years prior to this he was the executive director of the MIT Kerberos Consortium, helping make the Kerberos protocol to become the most ubiquitously deployed authentication protocol in the world today. Over the past two decades Thomas he has held various industry technical leadership roles, including distinguished engineer at Bay Networks, principal scientist at VeriSign PKI, and chief technology officer roles at several start-ups. He has been at the forefront of several industry initiatives concerning identity, data privacy, trust, applied cryptography, blockchain technology, and cybersecurity.

Yaniv Altshuler is CEO of Endor.com, a leading AI for cybersecurity company, and former postdoctoctoral fellow and current fellow at MIT Connection Science.

Charles Chang is deputy dean of academics, professor of finance, and director of the Fintech Research Center, Fanhai International School of Finance.

Goren Gordon is head of the Curiosity Lab at Tel-Aviv University.

Anne Kim is the CEO and cofounder of Secure AI Labs and a graduate of MIT Connection Science.

José Parra-Moyano is an assistant professor for blockchain and digitalization at the Copenhagen Business School.

Aetienne Sardon is innovation manager in Swisscom's FinTech team, with a focus on digital assets and confidential computing.

Fabian Schär is a professor of fintech and DLT and managing director of the Center for Innovative Finance at the University of Basel.

Karl Schmedders is professor of finance at IMD, and was formerly a professor at the Kellogg School of Management at Northwestern University and at the University of Zurich.

Christian Schüpbach is head of digital assets at Swisscom Digital Business.

Erez Shmueli is a senior lecturer and the head of the Big Data Lab in the Department of Industrial Engineering at Tel-Aviv University and a research affiliate at the MIT Media Lab.

Shahar Somin is a research affiliate at MIT Connection Science and machine learning and network expert at Endor.com.

National Institute of Standards
and Technology (NIST), 164,
172, 374
National Institutes of Health,
4–5
National Rural Electric Coopera-
tive Association, 20
Neighborhood attractiveness
measure, 23–27
Netto, S., 28
Network addresses, 376
Newman, M. E., 250
"New oil," data as, 19, 35, 42, 44
Nissan autonomous driving
system, 425–426
Nodes
attestations, 351–353
types of, 341–343
Nonces, 117
Nonrepudiability, transfer,
346
Notaries
for central bank digital cur-
rency (CBDC), 121
for Ripple, 110–111, 125
Notarization of metadata, 66, 68

OAuth2.0 framework, 63,
175–176, 274–277, 393
Obama, Barack, 162–166
Offboarding of VASP custom-
ers, 405
Office of Management and
Budget, 427

Office of the National Coordinator for Health Information
Technology, 164
OIX, 384
Omni, 289
Onboarding of VASP customers, 405
OPAL. *See* Open algorithms
(OPAL)
Opaque blockchain resources,
343–344
Open access philosophy, 63–64
Open algorithms (OPAL), 161,
166–171, 196
consent for algorithm execution, 272–277
data privacy with, 270–272
extensions and implications,
195
hospital records use case,
184–189
key concepts and principles
behind, 266, 270–271
for know your customer (KYC)
processes, 398–399
molecular libraries use case,
192, 195
multiparty computation and,
178–179
objectives of, 41–42
secure enclaves and, 182–184
OpenID Connect, 63, 377
Open index protocol, 78
OpenVASP, 377, 396